# DEMOCRATIC MANAGEMENT

---

## *The Path to Total Quality with Total Liberty and Equality*

---

**Asim Sen**

University Press of America,® Inc.
Lanham · Boulder · New York · Toronto · Oxford

Copyright © 2003 by
University Press of America,® Inc.
4501 Forbes Boulevard
Suite 200
Lanham, Maryland 20706
UPA Acquisitions Department (301) 459-3366

PO Box 317
Oxford
OX2 9RU, UK

ISBN 0-7618-2612-2 (paperback : alk. ppr.)

# TOTAL QUALITY IS A GOOD LIFE

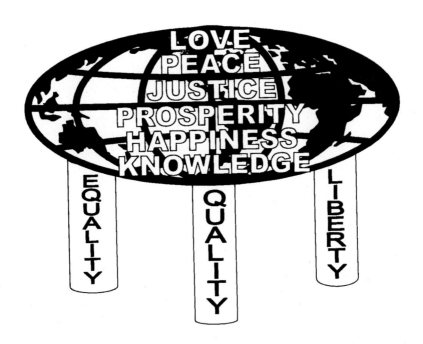

*This book is dedicated to people who utilize democratic management.*

# CONTENTS

PREFACE                                                                                          xi

ACKNOWLEDGEMENTS                                                                        xv

INTRODUCTION                                                                                xvii

### PART ONE:
### UNDERSTANDING OF THE MANAGEMENT
### PRACTICES OF THE PAST AND PRESENT

I. DESIRABLE TOTAL QUALITY AND COMPETITIVENESS                           3

What is Quality?                                                                             4

Multiple Dimension Qualities                                                           4

Productivity as a Quality                                                                 7

Desirable Total Quality and Competitiveness                                    8

Why Total Quality?                                                                          13

Relationships of Total Quality, Competitiveness and

    Management                                                                           19

II. UNDERSTANDING MANAGEMENT                                                  21

Management Concepts                                                                     21

Objectives of Management                                                               22

Styles of Management                                                                      24

Determinants of Management Success                                              25

Management Education                                                                     27

III. HISTORY OF MANAGEMENT DEVELOPMENT AND TOTAL
    QUALITY                                                       29
    Pre-Scientific Management                         30
    Scientific Management                             32
    The Behavioral Management                     36
    Integrative Management Approaches           40
    Contemporary Management Practices          42

IV. SUCCESS AND FAILURE OF THE CONTEMPORARY
    MANAGEMENT PRACTICES                          51
    The Success of Contemporary Management Practices    51
    The Failure of Contemporary Management Practices    54
    Authoritarian Management Practices Are the Main
      Source of Inequality of Income and Wealth        56
    Why Contemporary Management Practices Have to Be
      Changed                                       58
    Where and How to Change?                     62


PART TWO:
TRUE DEMOCRATIC MANAGEMENT PRACTICES
FOR DESIRABLE TOTAL QUALITY


V. TRUE DEMOCRATIC MANAGEMENT PRACTICES       69
    The Nature and Objectives of True Democratic
      Management                                    70
    Major Practices of True Democratic Management      72
    Stakeholders' Authority                         73
    Horizontal Circular Network Organizational Structure   74
    Employee Ownership                          77
    Group Decision Making                        79
    Long-Term Employment                        82

VI. TRUE DEMOCRATIC MANAGEMENT GENERATES
    DESIRABLE TOTAL QUALITY                        85
    Characteristics of Real Team Relations             86
    True Democratic Management and Real Team
      Organization                                90

PART THREE:
DEMOCRATIZATION OF MANAGEMENT
AND ITS CORE FACTORS

VII. DEMOCRATIZATION OF MANAGEMENT                              97
Democratization Process                                        98
Democratization of Core Factors                                99

VIII. DEMOCRATIZATION OF MANAGEMENT EDUCATION                  105
Nature of Management Knowledge                                 105
The Importance of Knowledge for Management                     108
Values Knowledge is Crucial for Management Practices           112
Developing and Utilizing Values Knowledge For
    Management Education                                       115

IX. POLITICAL DEMOCRATIZATION                                  121
Recent Democratization Activities                              121
Authoritarian Political Practices and the Problems             126
Representative Democratic Management Practices
    and the Problems                                           127
Democratization of Political Activities                        129

X. ECONOMICAL DEMOCRATIZATION                                  135
Contemporary Economical Activities Generate Inequality         136
Free Market Economics Is Not Free                              137
The Role of Government in Economics                            139
Democratization of Economical Activities                       141

XI. DEMOCRATIZATION THROUGH TECHNOLOGICAL DEVELOPMENT          145
The Concept of Technology                                      147
The Process of Technological Development                       148
The Impacts of Technological Development                       154
Democratization Through Technological Development              160

XII. UTILIZATION OF INFORMATION TECHNOLOGY FOR
    DEMOCRATIZATION                                            165
Evolution and Revolution of Information Technology             166

XII. UTILIZATION OF INFORMATION TECHNOLOGY FOR
     DEMOCRATIZATION (*cont.*)
    Information Technology, Total Quality and Competitiveness     168
    How Does Information Technology Increase Total
       Quality?     170
    Utilization of Information Technology for Democratization     173

XIII. DEMOCRATIZATION THROUGH GLOBALIZATION     179
    Globalization Increases Political Democratization     180
    Globalization Increases Economical Democratization     182
    Globalization Increases Social Democratization     184
    Globalization Increases Technological Democratization     185
    Globalization Increases Educational Democratization     187

XIV. WHAT CAN BE DONE NOW FOR DEMOCRATIZATION     189
    Educate Public for Democratization     190
    Educate Yourself and Others for Democratization     190
    Educate Managers for Democratization     192
    Educate Parents for Democratization     194
    Educate Educators for Democratization     194

REFERENCES     197
ABOUT THE AUTHOR     223
INDEX     225

# PREFACE

*What authoritarian management was to the 20th century, democratic management will be to the 21st.*

People throughout the world have been trying to live a quality life with liberty and equality. They utilize a variety of management practices and techniques to achieve a good life as their main mission. During the 20th century, management has become one of the most important driving force for achieving the missions of individuals as well as organizations and nations. Contemporary management became the main measure of success and greatness for every aspect of human life. It helped to create enormous wealth for some people and enabled man to walk on the moon. However, management has also caused very serious problems such as poverty, hunger, inequality, revolts, terrorism, environmental destruction, unemployment, bankruptcy, lack of quality, competitiveness and many other problems that threaten many people's lives throughout the world. The results indicate that contemporary management practices are failing to solve these problems and are not able to achieve total quality, with total liberty and equality. Most of the customers, employees and people in general in many industrialized countries are not satisfied with the contemporary management practices. The situation is worse and unhappy voices are louder in many newly industrialized countries. The need for new management practices is clear and widespread throughout the world.

Many management scholars and experts argued that contemporary management practices are too old, rigid and authoritarian. They were designed for the conditions of the past. The current conditions with the new information technology (IT), increasing knowledge especially for employees and customers, emerging global economy, ecological interdependence, new customer demand and increasing competition require new management practices.

Numerous new management practices are developed to solve the current problems and raise the total quality and competitiveness of many organizations and nations. Unfortunately, none of these new techniques such as reengineering, downsizing, restructuring, continuous improvement, lean production, total quality management (TQM) and others were able to solve the contemporary problems and achieve the desirable total quality and competitiveness.

The main cause of the current problems, and lack of total quality and competitiveness is the command and control nature of the contemporary management practices. Some of the new management practices such as employee involvement, participative management, self-managed organizations, and small team approaches have tried to integrate some ideas and principles of democracy in contemporary management practices. But none of these practices were able to utilize democratic ideas and principles in contemporary management practices fully. Command and control principles still dominate the major managerial decisions and actions of contemporary management practices.

This book utilizes the values and principles of democracy into management practices more fully. It develops the understanding of the value of true democratic management and designs its major practices as a comprehensive and unified whole. These practices include sharing the authority, ownership and the outcomes (costs and benefits) of the organization, providing open and close human relations, long term employment and allowing stakeholders especially the employees, to participate in major managerial decisions directly. Democratic principles of equality (equal opportunities) and liberty (economic and political freedom) provide rights and responsibilities for all stakeholders to utilize their resources and capabilities effectively, efficiently and ethically for achieving the desirable total quality and competitiveness in an organization. True democratic management practices provide the main building blocks of real team relations in an organization. The people's authority erases the command and control hierarchy in relations and establishes open and full communication in an organization regardless of rank and profession. The ownership and group decision-making practices eliminate the superiority and inferiority among stakeholders and make everyone feel important to the organization. Finally, the long-term employment opportunities provide security and incentive for all the employees to develop the best knowledge, skills, and values for desirable total quality and competitiveness of the organization.

The book also provides the process of democratization of current educational, economical, political, social, technological and global activities interdependently and wholly, in the short and long term, which is required for the development of true democratic management practices. This process provides some guidelines for executives, managers, educators, professional consultants, development and training specialists, quality directors, technicians, parents and the public in general, for the democratization process. They may find it extremely useful in their efforts to understand, design, and implement true democratic management practices for achieving the sustainable total quality with total liberty and equality to become competitive. The book may also serve as a textbook for undergraduate and graduate management courses and programs.

I have reviewed the scholarly and popular management studies and practices, which have occurred during the last hundred years in the U.S.A., Japan, Germany, and in some newly industrialized countries. I have also consulted many scholars, executives, managers, employees, stakeholders, customers and students in many industrial organizations, military and academic institutions in writing this book. I relied extensively on these sources and my unique and wide real world knowledge, skills, values and research that I conducted and observed with working in many organizations including Boeing Company, Grumman Corporation, Princeton Economic Policy and Research Associates and Aeronautical Research Associates of Princeton; University of Michigan, Polytechnic University of New York, Rutgers University, St. John Fisher College, Middle East Technical University, Bosphorus University, Yeditepe University, NATO, United Nations, Military Academy (Kara Harp Okulu), Air Force Academy (Hava Harp Okulu) and Turkish Air Force. My interdisciplinary knowledge, teaching and experience in a variety of national and international organizations made it possible for me to develop some ideas, insights and perspectives for this book.

My deep devotion to studying and researching in the areas of total quality, liberty and equality and democratic management advanced my ideas, thoughts, skills and values that served as corner stones for this book. The overwhelming interest in my published book, titled *Science, Technology and Development: Lessons from Japan* and more than fifty articles and presentations about total quality, democratic management, and competitiveness lead to developing this book. Most importantly, the urgent need for democratic management for the industrial world motivated and inspired me to write this book. I hope it will be helpful.

Asim Sen, Ph.D.

# Acknowledgements

*It can't be said enough.*

Many people and organizations helped directly or indirectly in developing this book. It is impossible to include all of the people and institutions here because of space limitations. I therefore, would like to acknowledge some of the names of these sources and will always remember others with great appreciation.

Firstly, there are those academic institutions that provided very valuable opportunities for me to study, learn and teach some of the knowledge, skills and values that influenced the ideas and thoughts in this book. I am greatly indebted to these institutions for their opportunities and the support that they provided. Among these, St. John Fisher College, which provided crucial support that made this effort possible. Other institutions include the University of Michigan, Rutgers University, Princeton University, Polytechnic University of New York, Georgetown University, Middle East Technical University, Bosphorus University, Air Force Academy (Hava Harp Okulu), Military Academy (Kara Harp Okulu) and Kuleli High School (Kuleli Lisesi), which provided various opportunities for me to develop the main part of knowledge skills, and values that helped me to develop some of the ideas and thoughts in this book.

Secondly, I am grateful to those professional institutions for letting me work with them in a variety of managerial positions that enabled me to learn, research, observe, and practice many management styles, techniques and practices. The experiences that I gained in these institutions helped me to develop some of the ideas, insights, thoughts and perspectives presented in the book. These institutions include the Turkish Air Force, NATO, United Nations, Boeing Company, Grumman Corporation, Princeton Economic Policy and Research Associates, and Aeronautical Research Associates of Princeton.

Thirdly, I would like to acknowledge indebtedness to the members of Global Awareness Society International, International Management Development Association, American Economic Association, The Association for Evolutionary Economics, International Institute of Forecasting, Global Business and Technology Association, Society of Management Technology, Eastern Academy of Management, The Institute of Management Science and Latin American Studies Council for discussing and sharing their views, perspectives, ideas, principles and practices of management that constituted part of this book.

Fourthly, I am grateful to many people including Fathers Charles Lavery, Patrick Braden and Drs. Donald Bain, Wendell Howard, William Pickett, Thomas McFadden and my colleagues at St. John Fisher College, Middle East Technical University, Rutgers University, Yeditepe University and Bosphorus University who provided me a variety of opportunities to work with them. I would like to extend my most sincere debt and gratitude to Professors Robert J. Alexander, James H. Street, and Peter Ash of Rutgers University and my early teachers Mustafa Cinalioglu and Mehmet Yucesan and many other teachers for helping me to develop ideas, thoughts, and perspectives that constitute the foundation of this book. I would also like to express my deep appreciation to Professors John Roach, Craig Hovey, Jonathan Rich and Ms. Ayseli Sen for reviewing the manuscript and providing some valuable comments and suggestions. I would like to extend my special thanks and gratitude to my colleagues, many managers and scholars for providing an intellectual home that supported this work in many ways. I would also like to acknowledge the valuable help of my assistants, including Ann Lomax, Mine Karahan, and Sevinc Turgut. I owe gratitude and appreciation for the ideas, and perspectives of many authors. The names of these authors are mentioned throughout the book and their publications are listed as reference at the end of the book.

Finally my deepest affection is reserved for my parents Kadir and Ayse Sen and in-laws Ismail and Jale Ariman for their support and patience. I would like to thank my wife Ayse and children Ayseli, Taylan, Tolga and Kerem for their valuable help and understanding during this work.

# PART ONE

## UNDERSTANDING THE MANAGEMENT PRACTICES OF THE PAST AND PRESENT

P art One reviews the current total quality, and productivity concepts and redefines total quality and competitiveness as a good life for people's lifelong mission. Many industrial organizations and nations have been using a variety of management activities to achieve the mission. This part examines the nature of these practices and evaluates their success, failures and impact on many institutions during the last hundred years. In light of these analyses it is concluded that the contemporary authoritarian management practices have to be changed.

# CHAPTER I

# Desirable Total Quality and Competitiveness

*A problem adequately defined is a problem
well on its way to being solved.*
—Buckminster Fuller

People as individuals, families, institutions and nations like to live happy lives throughout the world. Happy life, generally satisfies people's needs and wants through providing quality of goods and services. Goods commonly include material things such as food, shelter, clothes, car television, radio and other material things. Services include health care, transportation, communication, education, entertainment, recreation, medical, childcare, and others. Quality and plenty of these kinds of goods and services make most people happy. People also like to live healthy and long life in clean, beautiful and peaceful environment. They like to have equality (equal opportunities) and liberty (freedom for doing things) for a happy life without harming others and the environment. These often constitute the humanistic needs and wants for the human life.

All the materialistic and humanistic things that satisfy people's needs and wants is called total quality. It includes the quality, equality and liberty aspects of life that make most people happy. The following sections cover these concepts in more detail.

# *What is Quality?*

Quality has been defined in many forms in Western literature. These definitions can be combined into two groups: (a) customer based and (b) multiple dimension qualities.

## Customer Based Qualities

These definitions are solely based on customers' needs and their satisfaction. Some of these definitions are given below.

Quality is:
- Satisfaction of customer needs (Walton, 1991)
- Meeting and/or exceeding customers' expectations (Gronroos, 1983 Parasuraman, Zeithaml, and Berry, 1985)
- The total composite product and service characteristics of marketing, engineering, manufacturing and maintenance through which the product and service in use will meet the expectations of the customer (Feigenbaum, 1991)
- The degree to which a specific product satisfies the wants of a specific consumer (Juran, 1962)
- Conformance to customer requirements (Crosby, 1979)
- Judged by the customer (Malcolm Baldridge National Quality Award, 1994)

These and other customer driven definitions have probably captured the most important characteristics of quality. They all point to the customer coming first. Although this view reflects most real world situations, many practitioners and researchers argue that other stakeholders of an organization such as suppliers, employees, producers, community and government are also important for quality concerns (Rosenbluth, 1992).

The following definitions include some of the stakeholders and quality characteristics that are not covered by the quality definitions based on customer needs and satisfaction.

# *Multiple Dimension Qualities*

These definitions have multiple dimensions and have been used to describe a wide variety of quality characteristics. Some of these definitions are given below.

Quality is:

- The totality of features and characteristics of a product or service that bears on its ability to satisfy stated or implied needs (International Organization for Standardization-ISO-9000, 1994; American National Standards Institute-ANSI, 1994; and American Society for Quality Control-ASQC, 1994);
- Based on transcendent-innate excellence; product attribute; manufacturing characteristics-conformance to requirements or specifications; user ability to satisfy the customer's requirements, expectations and wants; value which gives the customers the most for their money (Garvin, 1988);
- That which makes something what it is characteristic element; basic nature, kind. The degree of excellence, of a thing; superiority; a distinguishing attribute (Webster's New World Dictionary, 1994); and
- A basic business strategy that provides goods and services that completely satisfy both internal and external customers by meeting their explicit and implicit expectations. Furthermore, this strategy utilizes the talents of all employees, to the benefit of the organization in particular and society in general, and provides a positive financial return to the shareholders (Tenner and DeToro, 1992).

These multi-dimensional definitions include not only the customers, but also the suppliers, producers, shareholders, organizations and the society in general that is involved in quality. Furthermore, quality characteristics expanded to include some technological (conformance, specifications), economical (value-worth, return) and social (transcendent) aspects. Every user may select one or more of these characteristics to represent quality for their needs. It is not possible to select a quality for all users universally. These characteristics vary according to the users, place and the time. It may be useful to identify these variations for the individuals, organizations, and nations.

## Quality for Individuals

Every person perceives quality differently. There is probably no one or more quality characteristics that can satisfy everyone. Quality varies with people. However, some quality characteristics may satisfy some segments of population. These segments can be formed based on age, profession and cultural origins. For example, a group of young people like speed, and a group of older people may like safety characteristics for their cars. Most of the higher income professionals may prefer luxury cars, like Cadillacs. Some professionals may prefer less expensive cars. For example, most American drivers prefer medium and large size-cars. Most European drivers prefer smaller cars. Some of the drivers in underdeveloped countries may not have any choice at all, because of the poor economical and technological conditions. They would like to have a car regardless of its characteristics; the quantity is the quality for these people.

The quality characteristics change also over time. For example, the present quality characteristics of an airplane like speed, size and safety are different than original airplane designs. Furthermore, quality characteristics change based on the availability of alternatives for comparison and selection. If the users do not have an alternative, the existent characteristics determine the quality for them.

## Quality for Organizations

Organizations that provide goods and services may prefer different quality characteristics depending on the nature of their objectives. Private organizations often select one or more of the quality characteristics like price, cost, productivity, return, profit, growth and market share as a quality. The non-profit organizations may select contribution, cost and output characteristics as a quality.

The selection of quality characteristics may also depend on the organization's life cycle and industry structure. Some organizations select high growth rate in their early stage of the life cycle. Some others may select price or technological quality characteristics in their stability stage. Some other organizations, which have monopolistic industry structure and close to global competition, may select quantity as a major quality characteristic. Organizations, which have oligopolistic industry structure and are open to global competition, may use market share characteristics as a quality.

The quality characteristics may also change by the stakeholders including owners, top managers, workers, and consumers. Owners and top managers often seek high personal gains for their organizations. They prefer high profit rates as a quality. The workers seek high wages and prefer high wage rate as a quality. Customers on the other hand may prefer low prices as a quality.

## Quality for a Nation

The quality characteristics of a nation are often represented by the productivity, per capita income, per capita gross national product, employment rate, and life expectancy at birth, through aggregating many other quality characteristics. This way, aggregating quality characteristics at the national level overlooks many other characteristics of quality. One or more of these characteristics may be used to represent the quality for a nation in terms of productivity, which is explained below.

# *Productivity as a Quality*

Productivity is usually the ratio of output to input. The outputs are the total value of goods or services that are produced by institutions. The inputs are the resources including labor, capital, materials and equipment that are used to produce outputs. Both the outputs and inputs are measurable in quantity as a value or unit. If we are concerned with the ratio of total outputs to a single input such as labor or capital, we have a partial productivity measure like labor productivity or capital productivity respectively. If the ratio of total outputs to a group of inputs like labor plus capital is concerned, we have a multi-factor productivity. If the ratio of total outputs to total inputs are concerned we have total productivity. Total productivity is used to describe the productivity of an entire organization or a nation. However, it does not represent the satisfaction of all the stakeholders. For example, high productivity may satisfy the stockholders of an organization, but may hurt the employees through low wages, and low fringe benefits or downsizing. It hurts the customers through low quality and high prices. It even hurts the community through polluting air, land and sea.

In order to assure that productivity measurements capture what the organization is doing such issues as customer satisfaction and quality, some organizations redefine productivity. Productivity is also defined as the ratio of effectiveness to efficiency or values to customers and cost to producer. *Effectiveness* is obtaining desired results by doing the right things. It may reflect output quantities, perceived quality or both. *Efficiency* occurs when a certain output is obtained with a minimum input. Even these definitions of productivity cannot tell about the satisfaction of the important stakeholders such as employees, customers, community and the state in general.

Thus, the contemporary definitions of both the quality and the productivity cannot measure the success or performance of an institution. Although many of these definitions, either customer driven or multi-dimensional, are useful for practitioners and researchers, they are incomplete. They lack many technological, economical, social and political aspects of quality characteristics that are important. Furthermore, the environmental and ethical aspects of quality are not included in these definitions. I will attempt to include these aspects into the definition that will help to reflect quality of life more accurately.

## *Desirable Total Quality and Competitiveness*

Total quality represents many physical and nonphysical characteristics like speed, price, taste, openness, cleanliness and justice. We call these, characteristics of quality or quality characteristics. These characteristics have their roots in the sciences and liberal arts domain (see Figure 1.1). In order to understand these roots better and for real world practices, we divide this

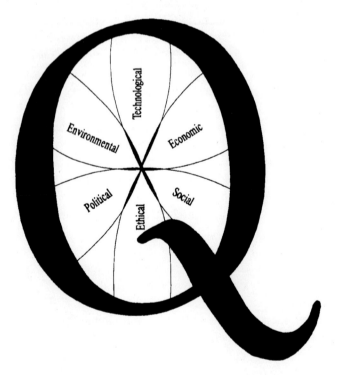

**Figure 1.1. Domain of Quality Characteristics**

domain to technological, economic, social, political, environmental and ethical fields.

Many quality characteristics can be drawn from these fields based on the user's needs. Some of these characteristics may be considered in more than one field.

People, like to have one or more of these characteristics; for products, services, air and water that they consume; for the things that they do; for the places where they work and play; for the land, houses, schools, hospitals and other institutions that they need; and for the people that they work and associate with. In short, the things that people want and do have these characteristics. Thus, quality is the technological, economical, social, political, environmental, and ethical characteristics that satisfy the people's needs and wants. (See Table 1.1).

These characteristics are generalized as the quality, equality and liberty for a good life. The quality, represents many economical, and technological, characteristics that people like to have for their goods and services. For example, the nation's gross national product (GNP), the real per capita income, economic growth, and organization's productivity, and return to its stakeholders may be used to measure quality. Quality generates physical values, satisfies people's physical needs and achieves the materialistic success for individuals, people, institutions and nations.

The sum of all these characteristics that satisfy people's needs and wants we call total quality. Some people like to have all of these quality characteristics in large quantities (get as much as you can), some others may be satisfied with a few of them in small quantities (small is beautiful). In theory people's needs and wants may vary between an infinite amount of things (the richest) and minimum amount (the poorest) things to live. However, in reality, rather than having the end of two cases (the richest and the poorest), most people like to have quality, equality, and liberty. Therefore, most commonly, total quality is the quality, equality, and liberty. However, in order to make most people happy, and living in peace, total quality has to be high, balanced, and sustainable.

The equality means, having the equal political, economic and social rights and opportunities for the people. Having equal rights to participate in political, economic, technological, social, and management activities that may satisfy everyone's needs. Most people want equality (equal opportunity) to achieve quality. Equality is necessary for the quality to satisfy all the people, but it is not sufficient enough. Liberty (freedom) is the right of the people to engage and perform any economical, political, and social activity without

### Table 1.1. Some of the Quality Characteristics

| Technological | Economical | Social | Political | Environmental | Ethical |
|---|---|---|---|---|---|
| Adaptability | Advance | Adaptability | Behavior | Cleanliness | Divisiveness |
| Capacity | Consumption | Attractiveness | Character | Destructiveness | Equality |
| Changeable | Cost | Beauty | Charisma | Hazard | Income Distribution |
| Conformance | Death | Behavior | Communicative | Noise | Just And Fair |
| Durability | Deficit | Care | Conservative | Recyclable | Laws |
| Flexible | Destructive | Communication | Convincing | Scarcity Of Resources | Morality |
| Knowledge | Developed | Competitiveness | Democratic | View | Regulation |
| Maintenance | Employment | Complexity | Dynamism | Wasteless | Rules |
| Mobility | G.N.P. | Cooperative | Education | | Social Responsibility |
| Practical | Growth Rate | Education | Equality | | Unbiasedness |
| Production Rate | Housing | Equality | Freedom | | |
| Productivity | Income Distribution | Flexible | Independent | | |
| Safety | Inflation | Freedom | Initiative | | |
| Shape | Investment | Happiness | Knowledge | | |
| Simplicity | Literacy | Health | Liberal | | |
| Size | Mortality | Honesty | Literacy | | |

## Table 1.1. Some of the Quality Characteristics (*cont.*)

| Technological | Economical | Social | Political | Environmental | Ethical |
|---|---|---|---|---|---|
| Skills | Per Capita Income | Innovativeness | Look | | |
| Speed | Price | Integrity | Popularity | | |
| Stability | Productivity | Knowledge | Reliability | | |
| Time | Quantity | Life Expectancy | Respectful | | |
| Weight | Return | Literacy | Skill | | |
| | Sales | Look | Trust | | |
| | Saving | Mortality | Wealth | | |
| | Scarcity | Profession | | | |
| | Standard Of Life | Reliability | | | |
| | Surplus | Respect | | | |
| | Timeliness | Responsive | | | |
| | Underdeveloped | Skills | | | |
| | Value | Taste | | | |
| | Waste | Transportation | | | |
| | Wealth | Trust | | | |

harming others. Employees would like to have freedom to contribute in managerial decisions and actions without any constraints and fear. Employees, everywhere throughout the world would like to have freedom of speech to contribute, discuss and even criticize constructively some of the decisions and actions that are performed by management. They would like to have open communication with their supervisors. Surely, they would like to have the freedom of their supervisors so that they may not feel as a second-class citizen or a slave of management in an organization.

Total quality has to be high, because people as individuals, families, organizations and nations like to have high quality and quantity of goods and services to satisfy their materialistic needs. The degree of quality determines the competitiveness; the higher the quality, the higher the competitiveness. Therefore, the people and institution become competitive through generating high quality. However, people like to have equal opportunities for having high quality. Equal opportunities provide ways and means for achieving high quality. High quality without equal opportunities generates unequal wealth and income among people, which may cause serious inequality problems in a society. The United States, other industrialized countries including Western European countries and Japan are able to develop high quality relative to other countries and became competitive, but they also generated severe inequality problems (see Chapter IV for more detail). It is desirable to have high quality, but, at the same time, it is necessary to provide equality opportunities for reasonable income and wealth distribution to have a harmonies and peaceful life among people.

People also like to have liberty to do things without hurting others. The freedom of opening a shop, establishing a business, selecting and practicing a profession, giving a speech, writing, traveling and freedom for performing other things are essential for a high quality life. If there are constraints on these things, generating high quality and having equality for everyone is not possible. People could not be motivated to develop their full potentials without the necessary freedom. Some countries who are utilizing authoritarian management practices could neither achieve high quality nor generate equality among their people such as the former Soviet Union and some Eastern European countries. Consequently, the governments in these countries collapsed and are trying different ways to satisfy their people.

Total quality can be visualized like a three-legged flat table. If one of the legs is shorter than the others the table cannot stay stable on a flat ground, but falls. Like the three-legged table, total quality has to be balanced among its three parts. Neglecting one part, and focusing on the others generates instability and eventually causes the collapse of a society. In this case total quality is partial quality, which represents the current situations throughout the world. Partial quality may satisfy some people, or some stakeholders like the investors (owners), but it fails to satisfy most of the other stakeholders like employees, customers and the community of an organization or a nation.

Total quality should also be sustainable for environmental and ethical reasons. Many organizations and nations have been polluting air, sea, and land in order to generate high quality (high profit). This may be acceptable for those who share profits, but it harms other stakeholders, including employees, customers, community, and the public in general through destroying the environment. Furthermore, some resources are limited and scarce on earth. Increasing world population and consumption depletes these resources for the high quality objectives of a few people at cost for future generations. High total quality should not be achieved at the expense of others at present and in the future. These kinds of practices are not ethical, and may generate serious problems in the future. Thus, total quality has to be sustainable to satisfy everyone at present and in the future.

In sum, total quality has to be high, balanced, and sustainable to satisfy everyone and become competitive. We call this desirable total quality. It may not be possible to achieve it in a short time, but if we direct and commit our resources toward achieving this kind of total quality, we will be better off and live in a better world. The main objective of this book is to develop ways of establishing desirable total quality.

The new definition of total quality includes most of the aspects and characteristics of quality in general. It specifies the main boundaries of the quality concepts. Any individual, group, organization and nation can define quality within these boundaries and select the quality characteristics that fit into their purpose. However, all of these definitions may still have problems related to their measurement and aggregation. The selection and its usefulness should be left to the users. In this book we use total quality, which include quality, equality and liberty.

## *Why Total Quality?*

Total quality has been very important for the human life throughout history. People, institutions and nations have always wanted to have total quality for their physical and emotional needs. Total quality helps them to develop values, satisfy needs, and succeed in life.

## Total Quality Generates Values

Total quality generates the physical and emotional values of human needs. Total quality of individuals as a quantity, and other characteristics such as knowledge, skills and values has become the most important asset for the organizational and national developments (Reich, 1992; Harbison, 1973; Drucker, 1993; and Garfield, 1992). Every individual contributes to the development of the world, however, quality individuals made possible most of the physical and emotional values. Their individual inventions, innovations, successes provided the main ingredients of the developments of institutions, nations and the globe (Pursell, Jr., 1981 and Bernall, 1954).

Quality of technologies in the form of capital equipment and know how generate the most valuable characteristics of goods and services. The value of newness, use, cost, variety, return and quality of technologies plays a major role for the success of institutions. Institutions as a supplier, producer, and distributor look for quality to generate value in terms of cost, time, sales and return. Quality of capital and other input resources are also very important to generate value of goods and services. The possibility of production and the cost of the products and services depend heavily on the quality characteristics of capital as a quantity and cost. The quantity and other quality characteristics of resources are also important to generate value for goods and services.

Customers look for quality characteristics and make their preferences based on the final value of these quality characteristics. They judge quality with its value as a quantity, price, cost, use, convenience, look, size, service, life expectancy and many other quality characteristics that determine the value of a product or service for them. The quality as a value plays an important role for the preferences of the customers.

Quality generates values for the nations. The quality of human resources, the institutions including schools, hospitals, business corporations, technologies and the resources determine the most important values in terms of per capita income or standard of life. Quality as a job opportunity and security, employment rate, sustainable economic growth, education, health care, transportation, communication, life expectancy and retirement benefits are of great value for the people.

Quality of laws and justice to protect peoples' rights and wealth and provide security and social order and preserve environmental standards concerning air, water, land, national parks, historical arts, buildings and museums are also important values for the people.

Quality of ethics, social responsibility, cultural attitudes, beliefs and values including honesty, integrity, goodwill and many other quality characteristics (see Table 2) play an important role generating physical and emotional values for the people to satisfy them.

## Quality Satisfies

Quality satisfies people's physical and emotional needs. Quality products and services satisfy people. Quality food, clothes, housing, cars and any other goods that people consume and use satisfy people's needs. When people's needs are satisfied, they prefer more of the same thing. This increases demand and generates new incentives for producing more of it. For example, when customers are satisfied by the particular product or service, they will tell it to other customers and may prefer the same thing for their next purchase. Consequently, demand for these products and services will increase. Increasing demand will satisfy suppliers, producers and other stakeholders.

Quality of work as an activity, process, safety and an environment, satisfies people. Satisfied people such as a worker, player, performer and giver will do better to satisfy their customers. Institutions try to satisfy their customers with the quality of goods and services that they provide. Customer satisfaction will increase demand for their goods and services. Consequently, their sales and returns will increase, and most of their objectives will be satisfied.

The citizens of a nation are satisfied mainly by the quality of economic goods and social services that they get from their government. Every government tries to provide quality economic and social policies, adopt quality laws, and establish quality foreign relations and perform many activities to satisfy most of their citizens. These qualities determine the citizens' satisfaction of their government. Consequently, they vote for the public officials who provide the most qualities for them.

Quality of values such as care, honesty, flexibility, openness, cooperation, respect, responsiveness and many others (see Table 1.2) satisfies everyone including workers, managers, customers, students, teachers and the public in general. People prefer to work, play and associate with people who have these qualities. These qualities satisfy everyone. Thus, quality as a quantity and as other characteristics satisfies the people's physical and emotional needs. The people, institutions, and governments try to develop quality to satisfy themselves and their customers.

### Table 1.2. Some Values as a Quality

| | |
|---|---|
| Adaptability | Flexibility |
| Agility | Get Along Well |
| Agreeableness | Global View |
| Appreciation | Goodwill |
| Articulateness | Helpfulness |
| Beauty | Honesty |
| Belief | Initiative |
| Benevolence | Innovative |
| Care | Integrity |
| Carefulness | Just |
| Charisma | Learner |
| Cleverness | Listener |
| Cohesiveness | Morality |
| Collectivity | Motivator |
| Commitment | Multicultural |
| Communicative | Openness |
| Companionship | Organizer |
| Comparison | Participative |
| Competent | Persuasiveness |
| Compromiser | Precise |
| Cooperativeness | Puller |
| Courage | Punctuality |
| Courtesy | Rationality |
| Creativeness | Receptiveness |
| Decisive | Recognition |
| Democratic | Respect |
| Dependable | Responsibility |
| Diligence | Responsiveness |
| Discipline | Team Player |
| Diversity | Tolerant |
| Effectiveness | Trust |
| Efficiency | Understanding |
| Ethics | Unity |
| Fairness | Willpower |

## Quality Succeeds

People, institutions and nations try to develop quality to succeed in their objectives. Quality plays an important role in human success. It is mostly because of personal qualities that people succeed in their work, games and life. Institutions succeed mainly because of their quality products and services. Nations succeed in establishing high levels of advancement through quality of its human resources, institutions and national resources. Quality characteristics such as knowledge and know how play an important role for producing capital goods and services that enable nations to succeed in their economic and militaristic activities.

People try to develop quality of knowledge, skills and values to obtain good jobs, to do better in their work, and to live a successful life. People spend considerable amounts of time, money and make an effort to develop these qualities at home, school, and in the workplaces. They often try to re-educate, retrain, and seek other ways to improve these qualities for their professions. Most of the public and private institutions, military and government look to hire people who have these qualities. Some of these institutions reeducate and retrain their employees to increase these qualities continuously. These qualities are often the bases of obtaining the high paying positions and promotions (Green and Seymour, 1991).

Quality human resources (workers, technologists, engineers, lawyers, doctors, scientists, entrepreneurs, managers and the public) are the main factors of the institutional and national development. They provide the idea, labor, knowledge, skill and values, develop technologies, utilize national resources, accumulate capital and establish social, economic and political institutions to carry out the successful national development (Harbison, 1973). Quality human resources play an important role in institutions' success by producing the quality products and services. Institutions producing quality products and services can sell, grow, and compete successfully in domestic and global markets.

If the institutions are monopolistic, they dominate the market and maximize the return through the large amount of quantity of products and services. If they are not monopolistic, they try to increase quality characteristics of their products and services to stay in the market. Those who are able to develop superior qualities for their products and services win the competition and capture the large share of the market. Consequently, the suppliers and other stakeholders of these institutions will succeed through quality.

Quality plays an important role for the success of institutions at the early stages of its product life cycle (Sen, 1982). Institutions have little or no market pressure to improve or develop new quality characteristics at the introduction and growth stages. However, as the products and services become standardized, new institutions and nations enter the market and the fierce competition starts. Institutions and nations that provide the best quality characteristics win the market competition and become the leader of that industry. Those institutions or nations that cannot provide the best quality products or services find it very difficult to compete and eventually lose the market share and many leave the market completely.

Quality plays an important role in the nations' development. Throughout history, nations rise and fall parallel to the qualities of their human resources, technologies, and quality of their economic, political, social and military institutions (Kennedy, 1989). Nations have been trying to develop quality economies for the welfare of their citizens and quality militaries to protect their national interests and sovereignties. Quality is the major objective for governments. They make plans, laws and provide incentives and take measures to develop quality for their citizens, institutions and nation.

Quality is the most important factor for generating physical and emotional values, satisfying people's needs and desires and achieving success for people, institutions and nations. Quality played an important role, for the success of people, institutions and nations. Quality is the leading factor of any success.

Quality helped the Dutch to lead the world in textile industries during the period of 1700 to 1786 (Grayson, Jr., 1988). Later, England was the leader during 1785–1890. Germany, the United States, and Japan developed better quality characteristics and surpassed the Dutch and England. Presently, some of the Newly Industrialized Countries (NICs) and many developing countries including India, China, South Korea, Brazil, Mexico and Turkey are supplying a large portion of the textile industry, through quality of their products.

As the new producers enter the market, competition becomes more difficult and those that provide higher quality characteristics win the market leadership of the world. Developed countries including United States, Germany, and Japan are competing for many capital incentive industries like automobiles, chemicals, steel, commercial aircraft, consumer electronics, machine tools, computer and copiers. The ones that provide the highest quality characteristics win the competition and gain the leadership in that industry. Many developed and developing countries are also joining this global competition. Some experts indicate that the twenty-first century will be a quality century, and a nation that provides highest quality in many industries will become the industrial leader of the world (Thurow, 1993; Grayson, 1988; and Dertouzes, Lester and Solow, 1989).

## *Relationships of Total Quality, Competitiveness and Management*

Competitiveness of an individual, organization or a nation is the degree of total quality. The high level of competitiveness can be determined by developing a high level of total quality (Porter, 1990 and Grayson, 1988). Competitiveness is about generating values (physical and non physical), and satisfying the needs and wants of people in the highest degree. The highest competitiveness wins the competition. The individual with most points wins in competition based on his speed, skill and knowledge for a task. A firm within a given industry wins the competition based on the quality characteristics such as value, price, and the life expectancy of its product. Also, a nation wins a large market share in global market because of its high total quality products and services. Thus, the total quality characteristics determine the competitiveness of an individual, organization and the nation. The Council on Industrial Competitiveness defined the international competitiveness as follow:

"Competitiveness for a nation is the degree to which it can, under free and fair market conditions, produce goods and services that meet the test of international markets while simultaneously maintaining and expanding the real incomes of its citizens. Total quality is the major contributor to a country's industry or company's competitive position."

Industrialized countries including the U.S.A, Germany, U.K, France, Italy and Japan have established relatively high total quality and became the most competitive nation in certain manufacturing sectors. Many Newly Industrialized Countries (NICs) have also been trying to increase their competitiveness in global market through increasing their total quality. The growth rate, measured by GDP of these countries, is higher than the industrialized countries during the last decade (see Chapter IV).

Management activities have been the key factor of determining total quality, and competitiveness (see Chapter II and III). Management is responsible making all the major decisions and their implementation. Decisions including development of product and technology, selecting and utilizing all the resource, distributing and sharing the costs and outcomes, employment, training and educating the work force, and many others are made and controlled by the management. Much of the low total quality growth and other problems related to competitiveness, such as inadequate quality, insufficient capital investment, and sluggish technological innovation, has been attributed to human behavior—especially American managers' attitudes, capabilities, and strategies (Deming, 1989; Hayes and Abernathy, 1980; and Dertouzaos, Lester and Solow, 1989.)

The advancements in technology especially in information technology and knowledge have had an enormous impact on global competition. The organization that can utilize technology and knowledge in its management practices appropriately is able to provide relatively higher quality products and services at lower prices and hence higher competitiveness in the global market. The recent management practices of some automobile organizations in the U.S. and other countries have almost doubled their productivity and have gained competitive advantages in the global market. During 1982–1985, Japanese automobile organizations including Honda, Nissan, Toyota, Mazda, Mitsubishi and Suzuki opened production facilities in the U.S. either on their own or through partnership with one of the American Automobile Organizations like the New United Motor Manufacturing Inc. (NUMMI). These organizations quickly became the highest productivity plants in the automobile industry and gained considerable competitive advantages in the global market (Womack, Jones and Roos, 1990). These organizations, with the same workforce that other American automobile plants employed, but with very different management practices, were out performing all other plants in the country. Similar results can be seen in other high-tech organizations. Most recently, the productivity of Fuji Film, operating in the U.S., surpassed the productivity of Kodak.

The key factor of high productivity of these organizations has been the utilization of different management practices. The management practices provide the major decisions for selecting and developing the products and services, technology, employment, distribution of gains and pains of an organization. The management practices determine the rights and responsibilities of employees to generate the "real team" organization and provide incentives for a high level of productivity and competitiveness. The recent studies clearly indicate that total quality and competitiveness of an organization depend on its management practices. In order to fully understand this process, the next two chapters provides the basic understanding of management and its development, and analyze relationship to total quality, and competitiveness in a historical perspective.

# CHAPTER II

# Understanding Management

*Under the sun everything is management.*
—Peter Drucker

Management is the most important factor for human life. People as individuals, in families, institutions and nations utilize management activities to establish high total quality. In order to be successful in the mission we have to develop, improve and adopt appropriate management practices. It is therefore necessary to understand management concepts, its objectives, styles and major determinants.

## *Management Concepts*

Management can be defined, broadly, as a process of doing things to satisfy human needs and wants. The process usually includes activities such as developing mission and objectives, designing strategies and operations, determining and utilizing resources and providing controls. All of these activities involve decision-making and taking actions. Sometimes, management is defined as a process of making decisions and taking actions for implementation and decision-making (Koontz, 1961; Drucker, 1954; and Wilson and Alexis, 1962).

Management activities are also divided in different fields such as human resources, production, finance, accounting, marketing, information and others. Each of these represents a management function or called management itself such as human resource management, production or operations management describing the different parts of management activities in a specialized format. A more recent management concept is used to describe more specialized activities such as inventory management, sales management, water management, waste management, etc. (Fayol, 1949; Mintzberg, 1971; Taylor, 1911; Mayo, 1933; and Fallett, 1949). Thus, management can represent all the activities in macro as well as in micro level. Peter Drucker said it best, "under the sun everything is management."

Some management activities are part of our daily lives, like getting up every morning, washing, eating and going to work, etc. These are relatively simple and ordinary things, which can be done with quick decisions and easy actions. Some other activities like building a house, machine, automobile, airplane, or establishing institutions like a family, school, hospital, factory, military unit and government are relatively more complicated and require complex decisions and sophisticated actions. All of these activities and others that generate value (physical and non physical) are generally considered the function of management (Bernard, 1938; Gilbreth, 1917; Geisler and Streger, 1962; and McGregor, 1960).

Management activities also include determining why, where and "how to" aspects of doing things: such as producing goods and services, selecting and utilizing necessary resources for these activities, and distributing the outcomes and related costs and returns.

People want total quality in all activities and in the things they consume. They also want equal opportunities (economic, political, social and technological) and liberty for deciding and doing things without hurting others. The community and the government want management to preserve the healthy environment and enough resources for the future generations. Thus, management includes all the things that are essential for human life (Ways, 1996; Drucker, 1998; Richards and Nielander, 1963; and Crainer, 2000).

## *Objectives of Management*

The main objective of management is to provide desirable total quality for the people who are involved and affected by management. Desirable total quality means quality, equality and liberty. Quality is often characterized by the economical, political, social and technological characteristics of goods and services that satisfy human needs and wants (as described in Chapter I). Equality provides equal opportunities for everyone who is involved and affected by the management activities such as establishing business organizations, joining these institutions with equal ownership and opportunities, providing resources and sharing their production fairly. Equal opportunity means, having equal employment opportunities for any institutions, opportunities to participate in all the management decisions. Liberty is having not only the equal opportunities, but also the freedom to speak, discuss, communicate and contribute ideas, opinions and act humanly without any constraints, prejudices and fear in an institution.

The stakeholders of any institutions would like to have quality, equality and liberty for their management activities. In the family, the stakeholders include all family members such as the parents and children. In organization, the stakeholders include the investors, employees, customers, community and the state. For the government of a nation the stakeholders include all the citizens of that nation. In the United Nations, every nation and every individual is stakeholder of that institution.

The management objective is to satisfy its stakeholders' needs and wants effectively, efficiently and ethically. Effectively, means doing right things for the people, community, organization, nation, environment and the globe. Thus, management seeks to select feasible goods, and services and use appropriate resources including human resources, capital, technology and raw material to provide the highest total quality. Ethically, means covering the moral aspects of doing things. Management has to provide equal opportunities for everyone to do things, distribute its gains and costs fairly without harming others and the future generation and the environment. Thus, management's objective is in summary, "to do the right things right."

In practice total quality is usually measured in terms of gross national product (GNP), per capita income (PCI), productivity and other quantitative measures such as profits and sales. None of these measurements represent total quality, because they do not include the equality and liberty aspects of total quality. People like to have balance between quality, equality and liberty. Achieving the high quality without equality cannot satisfy all the stakeholders, and generate serious conflict among them. For example, management in the United States provides one of the highest quality in terms of GNP, per capita income, wealth and military power. But it fails to provide equality in terms of income and wealth among its stakeholders. Most of the quality went to the stockholders and the top managers. The employees get low income and wages, and high-cost through downsizing and cutting benefits. Income inequality causes many social and political problems (see Chapter IV for more details).

On the other hand, trying to achieve equality without quality and liberty upsets most of the people and causes serious problems. Some of these problems may even generate revolts, and uprising against governments. Dissolving the former Soviet Union was mainly caused by these kinds of problems. The government of the Soviet Union could neither achieve the high quality nor liberty while trying to keep equality among its citizens. Quality, equality and liberty have to be balanced for all the stakeholders. Only the balance and high total quality satisfy most of the stakeholders in an institution. Thus, the objective of management is to make people happy though achieving high and balanced total quality. Without total freedom, and total equality, there can be no total quality.

Institutions and nations also want to become competitive in global market. Competitive institutions and nations will be able to increase their market share in global markets. Consequently, they will be able to provide additional economic benefits for stakeholders through increasing their employment, income and investment opportunities. Therefore, one of the major objectives of management is to achieve the highest total quality which enable institutions and nations to become competitive in global markets.

In sum, the objective of management is to achieve the highest and balanced total quality and become competitive in global market. The question is then what kind of management can achieve this objective successfully. Following sections will attempt to answer this question.

## *Styles of Management*

It has been one of the great challenges for management experts to determine the appropriate management practices to satisfy the needs and wants of institutional stakeholders throughout the world. As stakeholders' needs and wants change over time management studies and practices have also been changed. People demanded quality goods and services at every institution. They also wanted to have equal opportunities and liberty for their economical, political, social, technological, and global activities. Recent technological changes, especially in information technology, help to spread knowledge and information about the quality of goods and services all around the world. These changes increase the global awareness and competition in global market. Consequently, people have opportunities to observe, understand and demand better live through developing better management practices.

There have been plenty of studies about management but still, there is no agreement among the management educators and practitioners about the type of management practices that provide the highest total quality and competitiveness for a specific institution. Most of the existing management practices vary between authoritarian and democratic management practices (see Chapter III for more details). Regardless of the type of these practices, the results of the contemporary management have failed to satisfy most of the stakeholders (see Chapter IV for more details). The main reason of this failure is rooted into the authoritarian (command and control) nature of the contemporary management practices. Authoritarian management practices have been trying to satisfy the top managers and the stockholders at the expense other stakeholders such as employees, customers and community in general. Many organizations in the United States have increased their profits while hurting their employees through cutting wages and other benefits and through downsizing. They hurt their customers by providing low quality, and high price, unsafe goods and services. They also hurt the community and the environment through polluting the air, land and sea. It is clear from the recent results that authoritarian management practices generate severe income and wealth inequalities among stakeholders. This comes from controlling major decisions such as employment, sharing return costs, and ownership (see Chapter IV for more details).

The authoritarian management practices cannot achieve the highest total quality because of their failure to motivate human resources for best results. The authoritarian management practices also failed to balance the total quality among stakeholders. On the other hand less authoritarian and more democratic management practices in some institutions in United States like NUMMI, and many institutions in Germany and Japan have been able to achieve higher quality, and provide better equality and more liberty for their stakeholders. It is mainly because of the more democratic management practices that these institutions became very competitive in global market. All of these, clearly indicate that democratic management practices provide higher total quality and higher competitiveness.

## *Determinants of Management Success*

The success of management mainly depends on the quality of human resources; the higher the quality of human resources the higher the total quality of that institution. Although, other resources, such as land, capital, and raw materials, also play an important role for achieving high total quality. But human resources play the key role of utilizing these resources effectively, efficiently and ethically. Japanese managers achieve high total quality with limited land and with limited raw materials. The quality human resources are key to their great success (Harbison, 1973, and Sen, 1982).

The quality of human resource includes knowledge, skills and values. We often call this, "management knowledge" or "knowledge management." It is multidisciplinary and generally includes political, economical, social and technological sciences. Multidisciplinary knowledge provides a broad and deeper understanding of management activities. It is general knowledge that helps us understand macro aspects of management activities: determining the vision and mission of an organization; analyzing environment which involve economical, political, social, technological and global issues; designing strategies to achieve the objectives; and implementing policies such as employment, ownership, and distributing costs and returns. Managers with a wider knowledge get better management results in general.

Management skills such as writing, communicating, drawing and the ability of doing things are also integral parts of management knowledge. People who have good skills often get good results. Human values such as discipline, care, honesty, integrity, fairness, attitude and others are probably the most important part of the management knowledge that influence managerial decisions and guide the related actions (see Table 1.2). We call this, "values knowledge" or "value-based management."

Every manager, in any organization, has to have general management knowledge, including both the technical and values knowledge for success (see Chapter VIII). The wider management knowledge, the better the management results.

Managers, at every level, working individually and as a team also have to have specific knowledge for specific jobs to achieve better results. Individuals trained in multiple professions might get better results. However, one should get multi-qualifications that are economically and technologically feasible. One can be a manager as an engineer, medical doctor, teacher, policeman, carpenter, custodian and corporate president.

All managers may work alone and with others to provide complex activities. Some work alone, like copier repairmen. Others work with people as a team such as in restaurants, banks, hospitals, factories and governments. In these institutions managers are also responsible for others' work. They select, train, motivate, communicate, coordinate, and integrate individuals and their works as a team for the best results. They help individuals, teams and organizations to achieve high performance through utilizing all the other resources. They must be able to get things done through people. Therefore, people in any organization must have specific, as well as general knowledge, for successful management.

Managers, especially the president and vice president, who are elected by the Board of Directors play an important role in setting management style. They can select authoritarian or democratic management practices, or hybrid styles. The top managers mainly make the major managerial decisions such as employment, stock ownership, distributing gain and costs, personal relations, training, and motivating employees. The success of management, which is gained partly through management style, also depends on the managers who select that style. Therefore, quality human resources play the most important role in management success. People in any institution with a wider knowledge, skills, and values perform well. If people perform well, the institution performs well.

Although the quality of human resources is the main determinant of the management success, the main source of the human qualities is education.

## *Management Education*

Top managers should have an appropriate education to develop general and specific knowledge for management activities. Education provides most of the qualities including knowledge, skills and values that are required for good management. General and specific knowledge can be developed at home, at school and through work. Some families provide the first education for their children at home. Their knowledge increases as they continue to educate themselves through schools including elementary, secondary and universities and colleges.

The nature of the knowledge, mainly, depends on what institutions teach. Although, the students have a choice for selecting their studies according to their abilities, economic conditions and desires, they mostly learn technical fields. Most of the curriculums emphasize the technical sciences, including engineering, medicine, chemistry and others and neglect the liberal arts, which generally teach values. The university and college graduates with technical knowledge and skills get high paying jobs easily. On the other hand, those who study liberal arts have difficulties finding high paying jobs. As a result, liberal arts, which includes general knowledge such as history, politics, social studies and others, have not been in demand as much as technical sciences. Even the liberal arts studies at many universities and colleges do not have courses, which include values knowledge such as peace, democracy, equality, liberty, morality and others (see Table 1.2).

Universities assume that values are soft knowledge, and that people learn them by themselves. Besides, values knowledge is neither required by employees nor promoted by many institutions. As a result, most of the managers in United States do not have formal education in values knowledge and they do not consider values knowledge as an important factor for their decisions and actions. Consequently, most management practices in United States are authoritarian, rather than democratic. The results of the authoritarian management practices in United States, clearly, indicate that this kind of management practices favor the stockholders who elect the top managers and fail to provide total quality for every stakeholder (see Chapter IV).

The balance among quality, equality and liberty, which may satisfy the most stakeholders, can only be achieved through true democratic management. True democratic management is based on the democratic values such as fairness, equality, liberty and other human values (see Table 1.2). The managers at every level have to be educated in values knowledge as much as technical knowledge. Every institution needs to require and promote values knowledge for their employees. Only then can a democratic management be demanded and practiced. Thus, a democratic education is required at home, school, and at the workplace for the true democratic management (see Chapter VIII).

# CHAPTER III

# History of Management Development and Total Quality

*The most reliable way to anticipate the future is
by understanding the past and the present.*
—John Naisbitt

*You shall know the truth, and the truth shall make you mad.*
—Aldous Huxley

M anagement is the process for developing quality characteristics to satisfy people's needs. It involves people, capital, technology and materials. However, the people (managers, owners, workers and customers) play a key role in implementing management practices. They provide required knowledge, skill and values and develop all the other elements of management.

Development of management is a historical process. Its nature, activities, principles and theories are developed, accumulated and improved continuously. Different people made valuable contributions to management at different times and different places throughout the world. It is very difficult to cover all the contributions and developments. This study emphasizes mainly on those contributors who are interested in quality aspects of management. The past studies will help to understand the present and provide prospective to visualize the future aspects of management for quality. The whole study is divided into five periods: pre-scientific management, scientific management, behavioral management, integrative management approaches, and contemporary management.

## *Pre-Scientific Management*

At the early stages of human history, management was provided by people who had the skills, equipment, knowledge and resources to develop quality characteristics. These characteristics were mainly in the form of quantity. During the Medieval period, guilds were dominated in both the production and distribution. They were responsible for training apprentices and controlling the number of craftsmen in their output and the local market. Craftsmen had no social or job mobility. They had little economic gain relative to the guilds.

Business was typically hierarchical in structure and staffs were composed of owners called "master craftsmen" who managed the production, apprentices, and all other aspects of management. The economic conduct, as well as personal conduct, was based on morality and to a large degree on the laws of the church, which housed God's representatives on earth. Business profits were used to glorify God and for good work done in his name (Roth, 1993).

The organizational structure was based on the structure of the church, but the philosophy did not represent values of church and state. Employees participated in decision making social and technical issues of which they had knowledge. Craftsmen were encouraged to cooperate and share their knowledge and innovations with the apprentices. Ethics guided the human relationship and grievances worked out informally within the "family" nature of the business organization. The church provided the family model. The profits were relatively unimportant, and the main quality objective was the well being of the community.

During the Renaissance, these management practices changed. The profit motive of individuals blossomed, and trading groups began gaining power. Craftsmen owned shops, and localism gave way to capitalism. People put money to work to make more money. Trade expanded to the East, North and South American continents. New markets provided opportunities for economic expansion and development of new technologies, as a source of quality.

At a later period craftsmen began losing their job security, and employees no longer had an opportunity to participate in decision making. Their input was limited to their own small technical area. The main goal was profit as a quality. In order to increase profits, workers were exploited. Thus, the conflict between management and workers started to take place, and the emphasis within the work place began to shift from one of cooperation to conflict.

In Europe, small domestic shops replaced guilds operations and dominated the production. Business expanded and developed a network other than families. The owners alone controlled the production, marketing and other aspects of operations. Thus, the individual owners controlled most management activities. Cooperation was replaced with the individual control. The assurance of God's blessing in return for loyalty was lost. Individuality grew as the sense of community and social responsibility suffered. As markets and businesses expanded, a number of individuals began discovering new opportunities to increase their own well-being. Thus, through competition new quality characteristics developed.

When physical needs materialized during the Renaissance, many people that had accepted the emotional security offered by the church and the state now sacrificed their limited amount of emotional security to fight and gain material wealth. During the Renaissance, such men as Galileo, Kepler and Newton had helped to further the understanding of the principles of science and technology. The printing press had been developed and put to use so that the dissemination of knowledge was much broader than during any previous times. Master mechanics and artisans, working in small shops, learned the new methods and materials. Many small inventions and improvements were made possible and, in turn, gave birth to the machine age and the Industrial Revolution, as foundation of new quality (Roth, 1993; Wren, 1972; and George, 1972).

Management practices concentrated on the development of new technologies and new quality characteristics during the Industrial Revolution. The main event was the shift from simple hand tools to machinery, which played an important role for developing new quality characteristics. This made the major change in the agricultural sector. Much common land originally open to all for use was taken over by the rich landlords, and displaced farmers moved to the new industrial centers. They no longer produced goods directly by providing their own power and skill. They now operated machines powered by outside energy resources. Their role and control of their work had diminished.

Adam Smith's (1776) argument, of division of labor, which would increase labor productivity, had been used extensively. The work places were rapidly dehumanized and emphasis was given completely on productivity, no matter what the human cost. "Mechanical authoritarianism" diminished the importance of workers, and they became the feeder of the machines or part of the machine. Their social needs, as well as working conditions, were not considered at all. If one could not perform the specific standard, another person replaced the position. They had no contribution to managerial decision-making and had no power at all in management.

As the revolution progressed, the form of business changed rapidly. Individual proprietors and partnerships were replaced with the corporations. Organizational structure developed into three layers of employees including owners, middle managers and the workers. Capitalists designed the objectives of the organization, middle managers controlled the production, and workers did what they were told.

The workers started exerting some control of their economic destiny and developed labor organizations. By the early 1820s, unions were tolerated in England and gained strength after 1867. Toward the end of the nineteenth century, labor unions were developed in other Western European countries and the United States. The unions represented workers' rights indirectly in some management decisions relating to workers, and their productivity as a quality.

## Scientific Management

The Industrial Revolution of the nineteenth century brought many changes in management and quality. In contrast to the work of craftsmen of prior times, work became centrally located in factories. Beginning in the late nineteenth century and accelerating to the first quarter of the twentieth century, scientific management placed its emphasis on improving productivity in the work place. Researchers studied jobs and the tools used by workers to perform those jobs. They sought the "one best way" to perform each job, and thus, increase productivity.

Frederick W. Taylor in 1947 used scientific methods of logical inquiry idea testing to experiment with work methods in the search for maximum productivity. In 1906, he presented a paper and argued that in order to increase productivity, management would have to perform four duties: (1) develop a science of management for each element of a job to replace the old rule-of-thumb methods, (2) select the best worker for each job and provide workers with training in order to develop their skills, (3) develop hearty cooperation between management and the people who carried out the work, and (4) divide work between management and workers in almost equal shares, each doing what he was best suited to do. Taylor publicized his ideas in a book called *The Principles of Scientific Management* and in other works. Taylor stressed that his concepts were not merely a set of tools but a philosophy of the *sharing of responsibility* and *cooperation between labor* and *management* as a source of productivity (Taylor, 1947).

Taylor is called the father of scientific management, but he was not alone in his pioneering efforts. Among others, Frank and Lillian Gilberth (1917) shared the "one best way" to perform a job and developed the principles of motion study. His scientific studies and analysis of motion increased the worker's productivity significantly. They also were interested in developing man to his fullest capacity through effective training, improving the work environment and tools. They were looking at a healthy psychological environment for productivity (Wren, 1972, George, 1972, and Crainer, 2000).

During the same period, many researchers and followers of Taylor's also contributed to management and efficiency as quality. Among them were Hugo Munsterberg and Walter D. Scott who were interested in psychological aspects of management. Munsterberg (1913) had proposed to use psychology for management problems and its application to industry. His pioneering book of *Psychology and Industrial Efficiency* praised the use of psychology in management and the importance of science for efficiency. He proposed that the role of psychologists in industry should be to determine under what psychological conditions the highest output per man could be achieved. Walter Scott (1913), who was also a psychologist, felt that the human factor of management had been neglected and supervision of employees had not been considered important enough to keep up technological improvements. He was interested in employee attitudes, motivation and productivity in production. Efforts of Scott and Munsterberg in applying psychology to industry provided the important elements of scientific management.

Henry L. Gantt (1916), engineer, and Harrington Emerson (1911), consultant, were also major contributors to scientific management. Gantt developed the bonus system for productivity. According to this system, if an employee accomplished his task for the day, he received a bonus in addition to his regular day rate. If he did not finish the task, he received only the day rate and was not penalized. Application of this system to production increased and then often doubled the productivity. It clearly showed that the bonus system increased the worker's productivity.

Gantt also developed the daily balance chart, known as the "Gantt Chart," showing output time relations and checking real application with the planned one. His charts are still useful for project scheduling; however, his pioneering work helped to develop the Project Evaluation Review Technique (PERT) and Critical Path Method (CPM), which are still very important for project scheduling.

Emerson (1911 and 1913) used the term "efficiency engineering" to describe his brand of consulting. His efficiency concept meant conversation and elimination of waste in government, waste of national resources, and waste in the efficiency of man and machines. His major work, *The Twelve Principles of Efficiency*, was published in 1913. His main principle was that ideas not land, labor and capital, create wealth. Five of his principles of efficiency related to interpersonal relations such as clearly defined ideas, common sense, competent counsel, discipline and fair deal. The remaining seven principles related to methods, which are reliable records, dispatching, schedules, standardized conditions and operations, written rules and efficiency reward. His ideas and principles for efficiency are still useful for management practices.

Henri Fayol (1949), engineer and manager, was probably one of the pioneers of the theory of management. His work, published in France in 1916 and 1949 in the United States thirty-three years later, was *General and Industrial Management*. American pioneers of scientific management did not pay attention to (the French pioneer) Fayol, and believed that scientific management was an American invention. However, Fayol's work was equally important for the development of scientific management.

Fayol thought of management as a universal activity common to all human understanding; including shops, organizations and government. He examined all of the management activities and categorized them into six main groups consisting of production, commercial marketing, financial, security, accounting, and managerial. Managerial activities include planning, organizing, commanding, coordinating and controlling. He emphasized that the managerial activity was most important and should be applied to all activities for productivity. He also developed fourteen principles for effective high productivity management. These principles include division of work, authority and responsibility, discipline, unity of command, unity of direction, centralization, common interest, remuneration, scalar chain (line of authority), order, equity (results from combination of kindness and justice), stability (tenure of personnel), initiative and esprit de corps (union is strength).

Fayol's theory was the most complete and important development for management. His principles, procedures and techniques are applicable to all forms of group activity. His work became known as "organization theory" which has been taught at institutions of higher education. His work constitutes the basis of major activities and functions of contemporary management. His work has been complementary to Taylor's work, which together constitutes the important aspects of management and quality.

During the first half of the twentieth century, scientific management had been practiced extensively and grew rapidly in the following years. During World War II, mathematical and statistical analysis of military data led to new decisions that improved the effectiveness of military activities. Soon after the War, these analytical tools and methods were applied to problems of corporations and government. The objective was the best or optimum result to achieve highest productivity.

In the 1950s, computers were introduced into management. The computer enabled managers to use mathematics and statistics to solve management problems with incredible speed. Computer technology and its rapid improvements and expanded techniques from earlier scientific management is labeled as "management science" or known as "operations research."

Advances in information and communications technology had a major impact on management process. Capabilities such as satellite communication, facsimile transmission, and electronic data interchange have made global operations much easier. The improved ability to record, summarize, analyze, and communicate data has reduced the need for many layers of management. Managers could deal with broader spans of control; organizations become flatter, more flexible and more responsive to the changing environment. Production tasks relied on human effort and energy in the pre-industrial period. With the Industrial Revolution, the machines were used to power the processes, but the processes were still controlled manually. Later, the automation provided automatic control, so that machines could sense the output, compare it to some pre-set target valve and adjust its setting if necessary. Today, information technology, control the machines including instructions, measurements and all other operations and became the main source of quality.

Automated manufacturing continues to become more flexible and versatile. Computers control material handling, inventories, robots, other machines and processes. Combinations of automatic machines and material handling systems coordinated and controlled by the computers. Designers can use computer graphics and simulation programs to develop and test design. The concepts of just-in-time (JIT) production, quality circles and continuous improvement, originally were practiced in Japan, continue to be employed more broadly to increased productivity. Companies operating under this philosophy coordinate their operations so that one work center produces only what is required by subsequent work centers, and the production occurs just when the necessary components are needed (Dilworth B. James, 1992).

## *The Behavioral Management*

The pioneers of scientific management recognized the importance of the human element in management. However, their emphasis was on productivity through, mainly, the technical side of management. During the same period, another group of researchers recognized the need and studied the importance of human relations in management. They argued that in order to make workers more productive, it is necessary to understand their feelings, needs and desires. It follows that productivity depends on worker's satisfaction and managers take measures to satisfy their needs.

In the 1920s and 1930s, Mary Fallett (1924), Elton Mayo (1933), and their friends studied human behavior and conducted the Hawthorne studies at the Western Electric Company. They observed that worker's productivity increased with their experiment because of the more relaxed supervisor worker relationship and friendlier group relationship. It was clear to them that the positive response of workers resulted, mainly, from their feelings that management was paying attention to them as human beings. Their experiments showed that workers were not simply tools but a complex personality, interacting in a group situation that often is different to understand.

Mayo argued that social invention had not kept pace with technical invention to cope with industrial changes. It was this "social lag" that caused the widespread sense of futility and the resultant social disorganization. Rapid economic and technological growth that Americans had experienced had destroyed communal integrity (Mayo, 1933).

He argued that technically advanced society put emphases on the economic logic of efficiency at the expense of social needs of individuals. The individuals were pushed into background, thereby reducing their capacity for collaboration in work. Managerial emphasis on the logic of efficiency stifled the individual's desire for group approval, for social satisfaction, and for social purpose gained through communal life. Mayo postulated that the administrative elite was technically oriented and that "in the important domain of human understanding and control, we are ignorant of the facts and their nature." The administrator must be one who effectively restored opportunities for human collaboration in work and in life by recognizing man's need for social solidarity. The source of efficiency, as Mayo perceived it, was not only in a technical but a social and human one. In his book, *The Social Problems of an Industrial Civilization*, he wrote:

> ...the atomic bomb arrives at this moment to call our attention both to our achievement and our failure. We have learned how to destroy scores of thousands of human beings in a moment of time. We do not know systematically how to set about the task of inducing various groups and nations to collaborate in the tasks of civilization.
>
> It is not the atomic bomb that will destroy civilization. But civilized society can destroy itself...if it fails to understand intelligently and to control the aids and deterrents to cooperation (Mayo, 1945).

Mayo was concerned with the failure of social and political institutions to provide means for effective human collaboration in the huge aggregation of men and materials, which characterized a mass-producing society. Over emphasis on technical progress and material life to the neglect of human and social life would be the downfall of civilization (Wren, 1972).

Wren (1972) stated in his book that Mayo's idea was that the world must rethink its concepts of "authority" by abandoning the notion of unitary authority from a central head, be it the state, the church, or the industrial leader. Mayo concluded that authority should be based on social skills in securing cooperation rather than technical skill or expertise. By building small "groups" to larger ones, and by basing leadership on securing cooperation, social solidarity could be restored and "democracy" preserved.

Mayo also emphasized the new leadership, which would generate collaboration and cooperation in industry, as Taylor pointed out earlier. Following their ideas, Roethlisberger (1977) indicated that the money or economic motivation was secondary importance in stimulating higher productivity. Whether or not a person is going to give his services wholeheartedly to a group depends, in good part, on the way he feels about his job, his fellow workers, and supervisors. The workers wanted social recognition, tangible evidence of social importance, the feeling of security that comes not so much from the amount of money but from being an accepted member of the group.

Thus, Mayo and his friends pointed out that the productivity is not only an economic and technical phenomenon, but a social and human phenomenon as well. The key to this joint multi-factor phenomenon is the management of that group or an organization that must find ways to increase productivity in light of these new realities of human and social aspects of management.

Mayo is recognized as the father of what was then called "human relations" and later became known as "organizational behavior." His work revealed that an organization is a social system and the workers are the most important element in it, and are the key source for productivity.

During the 1940s and 1950s, human relations studies of management continued in the Mayoist tradition, although the focus was on humanism. Earlier among the many contributors to this era was Abraham H. Maslow (1954). His work was mainly in the area of psychology, but it significantly influenced the management. His "hierarchy of human needs" theory related human behavior to need satisfaction. He extended this theory in his book, *Motivation and Personality*. Maslow saw a dynamic interplay of needs in which the summit was the need for "self-actualization." He concluded that the highest productivity could be achieved through motivation.

The 1950s and 1960s mark the emergence of a new philosophy. William G. Scott (1967) called this emerging philosophy of the modern era as "industrial humanism" or "organizational humanism." The main objective of industrial humanism was to offset the authoritarian tendencies of organizations, to provide for democracy and self-determination at work, to integrate individual and organizational goals, and restore man's dignity at work. This new philosophy attempted to replace the softness of the previous human relations philosophies.

Oliver Sheldon (1966) tried to determine the proper balance between the "things of production" and the "humanity of production." He viewed industry as a "body of man" rather than a "mass of machine and technical processes." He argued that workers should be given a more significant role, and their emotional as well as material well being should be increased, to achieve high productivity.

Leon Megginson (1967) claimed that human relation philosophy dominated until the recession of 1957–58, and it failed to meet the economic criteria of productivity and profitability. He argued that the new emphasis was on "human resources" rather than on "human relations." The human resources philosophy views the productivity of employees as being an economic resource of a firm or nation. This philosophy emphasized economic efficiency while recognizing and respecting personal dignity of each human entity. They see management as a way of satisfying human needs while fulfilling the organization's productivity objective. Keith Davis (1957) defined human relations as the integration of people into a work situation in a way that motivates them to work together with economic, psychological, and social satisfaction.

Chris Argyris (1957) has been a proponent of the "personality versus organization" hypothesis or "immaturity-maturity" theory of human behavior. Argyris' organizational "principles" emphasize the hierarchy of authority in which the top controls the bottom of the organization. The workers react to this situation negatively, which may slow productivity.

Argyris attempted to achieve harmony between personality and organization. He argued that participative, employee-centered leadership helps individuals to achieve self-actualization, while helping the organization meet its goals. Argyris advises management to give employees more responsibility and to rely more on employee self-direction and self-control. Argyris requires a "reality-centered" leadership, which has awareness and understanding of self and others. The healthy individuals can be nurtured in a healthy organization and both can achieve their needs and goals. He proposed harmony, which is not sweetness, but the maturation of people in enlightened organizations.

Douglas McGregor (1954 and 1960) taught social psychology and served as the president of a college. He also made significant contributions to behavioral school by moving human relations philosophy to the new "humanism." McGregor examined a set of assumptions of theories X and Y. Theory X can be interpreted as a promoter of authority for productivity, and Theory Y promotes democracy to lead high productivity. McGregor has served as a bridge moving from human relations to the new organizational humanism. He argued that harmony can be achieved by trusting people, and letting people exercise self-motivation, and control.

Frederick Herzberg (1959) developed the "motivation hygiene" theory of motivation based on his extensive empirical investigation. The hygiene factors included supervision, interpersonal relations, physical working conditions, salaries, company policies and practices, benefits, and job security. The factors that led to positive attitudes, satisfaction and motivation are called motivators. He argued that only the motivators led people to superior performance, but this is not enough. The motivation must also come from job enrichment, from more challenging jobs and opportunities for growth, and from the supervisors who were enlightened enough to provide employees the change for self-actualization.

Davis, Herzberg, McGregor and Argyris believed that harmony would not come from a mental revolution nor from social solidarity, but from the use of the behavioral sciences to understand the nature and the needs of people in organizations. Harmony was reciprocity and mutual agreement between people and their organizations, the mutual agreement that requires liberty and equality for productivity.

# Integrative Management Approaches

The classical and behavioral approaches to management produced much theoretical and practical knowledge. Harold D. Koontz (1980) called it "management theory of the jungle" and pointed out that each theory of management was working on its own without collaborating with each other. It was time to bring these two movements together. Many integrative approaches were developed. Among these, the economic development, environmental, contingency planning, and open system approaches are widely used.

### a) Economic Development Approach

This approach developed during the 1950s, and is illustrated best by the work of Harbison and Myers (1959). Management plays a key role in achieving rapid industrial and economic development. It is a macro approach and consists mainly of economic factors. Management plays a significant role in organizing and utilizing resources for the national productivity. Development processes go through four stages and lead society from agrarian-feudalistic conditions to an industrial democratic society. Harbison and Myers conclude that all management approaches tend toward the participative or democratic management philosophy of Theory Y to achieve highest productivity.

### b) Environmental Approach

This is also a macro approach and best exemplified by the work of Farmer and Richman (1965). It assumes that managerial effectiveness and, hence, the productivity is a function of external factors such as social, cultural, technological, economical, political, and educational. This approach expands the economic development approach, which focuses mainly on economic factors to include other external factors more fully.

### c) Open System Approach

The system approach conceptualizes an organization as a set of interrelated parts interacting with each other to accomplish the common objective of the organization. Management plays an important role in achieving the organization's objective. The system approach plays a unifying role among scientific management and behavioral management, which they assume that the whole is equal to the sum of its parts and the whole can be explained in terms of its parts. The system approach, in contrast, assumes that the whole is greater than the sum of its parts. It is argued that the difference is analytic versus synthetic thinking. Analytic thinking is outside in thinking; synthetic thinking is inside-out. Neither downgrades the value of the other, but the synthetic thinking provides information that one cannot obtain through analysis, particularly of collective phenomena (Ackoff, 1973).

The synthetic thinking is often recommended because management practices involve both inward and outward analysis. Managers affect, and in turn are affected by, many other organizational and environmental variables. The system approach provides a basis for understanding organizations and their problems which may one day produce a revolution in organization comparable to the one brought about by Taylor with scientific management (Coleman and Palmer, 1973).

Fayol's (1949) and Bernard's (1938) ideas of system perspectives have encouraged management theorists to study organizations as complex and dynamic wholes instead of piece by piece. Bertalanffey (1972) argued that in order to understand an organized whole, we must know both the parts and the relations between them. His general system theory argues that everything is part of a larger interdependent arrangement. Along the same line, general system theorists argue that all organizations are open systems interacting with their internal and external environment (Johnson, Kast and Rosenzweig, 1973).

The system theorists require a new role for managers to integrate all of the elements of a system to achieve the highest productivity for a system. Managers have to be innovative and creative to adapt all the elements and the system as a whole to the continuously changing external and internal environmental factors. Unlike the traditional specialists, the new systems managers will be super-generalists. As systems managers, they will be concerned with the optimization of overall organizational objectives. They will be a problem-solver instead of a technically-oriented "machinist or specialist." The systems approach is not something like a suit of clothes that can be donned at will; it is rather a way of life itself, a way of thinking, a conceptual frame of reference that must permeate one's every decision and outlook for productivity.

The systems approach provides the basic framework for the integration of relevant management theories, decision making analysis, application and observation of technical and behavioral sciences and for the development of tools that are especially adopted to handle the prevailing and changing situations and complexity environments. It requires the understanding of many complex interrelationships, the design of a sociotechnical system to operate effectively and efficiently, the satisfaction of human participants, and the continuous adaptation of the system in a changing environment.

However, the systems approach does not provide a specific algorithm, the application of which ensures success. It is not a clearly defined bundle of techniques and is not limited in application to particular industries or functional departments. Rather, it is a broad frame of reference, which views the organization as a total system and seeks to achieve the objective of that system by clearly understanding and relating subsystem productivity to the whole.

### d) The Contingency Approach

Contingency management suggests that appropriate managerial behavior in a given situation depends on, or is contingent upon, a wide variety of elements. Appropriate behavior cannot always be generalized (Luthans, 1976; Tosi and Slocum, 1984).

According to the contingency approach, different situation requires different managerial responses. The effectiveness of a given management pattern is contingent upon multitudinous factors and their interrelationship in a particular situation (Shetty, 1974). This suggests that the application of various management tools and techniques must be appropriate to the particular situation, because each situation presents the manager with its own problems. In management practice, the success and the productivity depend upon the situation.

## *Contemporary Management Practices*

In recent decades, there have been new developments in management theory and practice. Most notable among these are participative management and total quality management. The main objective of these approaches is to increase competitiveness through high quality performance.

### a) Participative Management

The participative management approach may be seen as an extension of behavioral management. It focuses on employees and suggests that they should participate in setting goals, making decisions, solving problems, designing and implementing organizational changes (Shashkin 1984). The organization's productivity will be improved by workers' participation in management practices. William Ouchi (1981) attempted to design common elements of participative management practice by integrating the relevant elements of Japanese and American management practices, which is called Theory Z. It suggests that by providing long-term employment, collective decision-making, individual responsibility, and a holistic concern for employees, the organization's productivity will increase.

According to Ouchi, the participative process is one of the mechanisms that provides for the broad dissemination of information and of values within the organization. It also signals the cooperative intent of the organization. Theory Z managers commonly view their organization as a family. Consequently, trust is built that in turn motivates all organization members to do their best to achieve shared objectives.

The participative management is one of the important categories of quality-of-work life (QWL), which also includes flexible work schedules and workplace democracy (Guest, 1979 and Rosow, 1980). These programs give employees a greater than usual degree of control over their work lives which generates greater motivation, hence, higher productivity. Gain sharing plans, share the responsibility and rewards for organizational improvements among all employees (Bullock and Lawler, 1984, and O'Dell, 1981, 1987). Work place democracy generally includes all efforts to provide employee ownership at all levels through either a co-op arrangement or an Employee Stock Ownership Plan (ESOP), (Hoerr, 1985). The amount of employee ownership typically ranges from 15 to 35 percent of the outstanding stock. However, employee ownership does not mean employee control the management. ESOP employees take orders from the managers in the traditional management. As stockholders, they have a direct economic stake in the profitability of their company. The more productive they are, the greater stock dividends will be. The ESOP aims to increase workers' productivity, which will increase stock dividends. However, this does not include workers input into management decisions.

Workers' self-management is also a new attempt to increase workers' productivity. The workers' self-management meant the workers and their elected representatives control the corporation (Zwerdling, 1978 and Guzda, 1984). This is a radical change from traditional management. However, it has met with strong resistance in the United States. The top managers and the owners believe that employees lack the willingness and ability to manage themselves effectively and responsibly.

In spite of resistance, some European countries and some American corporations who are practicing employee self-determination and participation in management observed good results and achieved high productivity. This was mainly due to workers' democratic privileges and motivated by being part of the management team (Zwerdling, 1978 and Guzda, 1984).

Many other studies (Kanter, 1985 and 1989; Garfield, 1992; and Lawlarr III, 1992) argued that high productivity can best be achieved not by doing the old management better, but by adopting new and innovative management approaches that are more suitable for today's industrial world. They varied considerably in the new practices that they recommended, but they all stated that contemporary management had to move away from the top-down control practices. They emphasized the high employee involvement, cultural values and leadership in management as important factors for appropriate management practices for high quality and competitive advantage. These studies gave way to development of a new management approach, which is called total quality management (TQM).

## b) Total Quality Management (TQM)

Total quality management (TQM) is a process of developing quality characteristics. It involves technological, economical, social, political, environmental and ethical aspects of the existent knowledge, people, technology, capital and raw material. TQM integrates all of these elements in an organization and uses appropriate strategies, activities, and principles to produce high quality characteristics to satisfy people's needs.

### Main Principles of TQM

TQM places major emphasis on people, which include the producer, customer, supplier, and owner. They make the change and provide the continuous improvement, which is the main principle of quality management. It requires that people work as a team with full commitment, close cooperation and common objective. The common objective is the achievement of superior quality, which will satisfy all of the stakeholders. However, some argue that the main objective is to satisfy customers through quality products and services. They believe that if the customers are satisfied, everyone else will be satisfied.

Quality management processes combine and integrate fundamental management approaches developed earlier, but differ in principles and practices. In order to understand this process more fully, the major contributors of this development will be explained.

*Frontiers of TQM Movement*

There have been many contributors to TQM movement. The ones that are often noted in literature and followed by practitioners are covered in this section.

*W. Edward Deming (1981, 1982, and 1986).* The purpose of the Deming management method has been and continues to be the transformation and improvement of the practice of management, more specifically, the practice of management for quality. His major contributions to TQM have been an emphasis on statistics-based approach to solving quality problems, and an insistence that management, not labor, is the primary responsibility for the quality. He proposed his "Fourteen Points" to explain his management practices. He stresses statistical training, a consistency of purpose for continuous improvement, organizational pride, and self-esteem in workmanship. His fourteen points are principles of transformation to be embraced by top management to continually change and enhance an organization's ability to survive. Some of the fourteen points recommend behavioral practices aimed at changing the organization's infrastructure and cultural system. They suggest an open, trusting, and cooperative culture in which all employees from top to bottom perform to achieve the common goal of organization survival.

*Joseph M. Juran (1964 and 1988).* He approaches quality from a perspective of cross-functional integration. He divided quality management into planning, control and improvements and argued that this should be an integrated and continuous process. He is an advocate of customer-supplier partnerships in which companies seek long-term relationships. He also championed the idea of training groups of employees in problem-solving techniques, brainstorming, group dynamics, and teamwork. The major point of his training is to enable people to work in groups to determine cause and affect relationships of problems. Pareto analysis, which looks for the twenty percent of possible causes of eighty percent of all problems, is one of his tools.

*Armand V. Feigenbaum (1983 and 1986).* He originated the concept of total quality control (TQC) and argued that TQC must include everything that could be subjected to quality control including marketing, engineering, purchasing, supervision, finance, operations, and distribution. Feigenbaum's approach is given with his "Three Steps to Quality" which includes quality leadership, modern quality technology, and organizational commitment. The leaders and all the other members of the organization must be integrated and be responsible for quality of their product and service. Error-free performance should be the common goal. New techniques must be evaluated and implemented continuously. The quality should be a strategic element, and people should be trained and motivated for it. He also provided "Nineteen Steps" to quality, which mainly focused on the quality improvement.

*Kaoru Ishikawa (1984, 1985, and 1989).* He was the early champion and first to use the term total quality control in Japan. He developed the "Seven Tools" for total quality. These tools include pareto charts, cause and effect diagram (fishbone or Ishikawa diagrams), and statistical charts and diagrams. He also developed the "Quality Circles (QC)" process which has been very important for the total quality management. He argued that quality begins with education and ends with education. He also shifted his attention from process to customer orientation by including internal as well as external customers and suggested, "The next process is your customer." His work on QC was widely used in Japan and the other countries throughout the world.

*Philip B. Crosby (1979 and 1988).* He popularized the concept of "cost of quality" and "price of conformance" with his bestseller book; *Quality is Free* (1979). He believed that the only effective performance measurement is the cost of quality and that it is always cheaper to do the job right the first time. His attributes stressed quality as conformance to quality, the prevention of quality defects, and zero defects performance standards. Crosby maintains that there is absolutely no reason for having errors or defects in any product or service. He sees quality improvement as a permanent and lasting process.

Crosby believes that various Japanese companies properly applied "zero defects," using it as an engineering tool, with responsibility of implementation left to the management. The process was successful in Japan. However, it failed in the United States, because the responsibility was left to worker and was used as a motivational tool. Crosby's fourteen steps to quality focus on the continuous improvement process.

*Genichi Taguchi (1986).* He describes quality in terms of the loss generated by that product to society. This loss to society includes the time a product is shipped until the end of its useful life. His methods focus on the customer by using loss function. The key to loss reduction is not meeting specifications, but reducing variance from the nominal or target value.

Taguchi designed "on-line and off-line quality" methods that provide a unique approach to reducing product variation. "On-line" methods include the various techniques of maintaining target values and the variation about the target in the manufacturing environment. These techniques include statistical control charts. "Off-line" quality control involves the design of quality or quality engineering function and consists of system design, parameter design, and tolerance design functions. These three functions attempt to define design and process the quality.

## The Current State of TQM

Currently, many business executives, managers, academicians, consultants, and students have contributed considerably to the quality movement by writing books, articles, and doing research. Almost every public and private organization, military and government, developed programs and established seminars to improve their qualities. Some of the universities and colleges established total quality courses for both graduate and undergraduate programs.

The topics included in these studies can be grouped as follows: (1) Customer satisfaction including internal as well as external customers; (2) strategic planning and quality improvement; (3) tools and methods including statistical quality control, quantitative problem solving techniques, benchmarking, process improvement, reengineering of design, and marketing aspects of quality; (4) human resource development including training, leadership, motivation and reward systems; (5) behavioral issues including organizational structure, culture, collaboration, communication and team work; and (6) globalization and change making.

Total quality management is not founded on a single theory but a combination and integration of many traditional theories that developed before. It is similar to other integrative approaches; however, it differs in its practices and emphases. Starting with Deming and other innovators, the philosophy of total quality management is centered on the continuous improvement to satisfy customers' present and future expectations. There is great difficulty to know customers' needs and satisfy all of them at all times. However, it is assumed that the people involved in TQM will search for new ways, be innovative and make changes to achieve that necessary improvement in every part of management. The people's commitment, close cooperation and teamwork are required to achieve the continuous improvement necessary for quality. Thus, the people, including the whole stakeholders, play the key role in total quality management. In a way, total quality management emphasizing people's roles like participative management goes further beyond the traditional management approaches to provide more responsibility and authority to the bottom portion of pyramidal structured organizations. As Deming pointed out, this will break down the walls between the top and bottom of the management structure, eliminate fear, and provide trust among people.

Total quality management differs from the traditional management, mainly, in practices concerning organizational objectives, structure, authority, human relations, decision-making, ownership, philosophy of change, managers, and educational matters (see Table 3.1).

Total quality management has been applied by many public and private organizations, and by some of the departments of government. Although these practices differ in nature and emphasis, they include evaluating their vision, mission, and objectives. Some of the organizations include the quality improvement in their strategies and total quality objective became a part of the all management functions. The production and service departments established programs and projects to improve the performance of individuals and teams. These practices include cost-cutting operations, reducing waste, saving time, and increase quality through technological, process and service improvements.

Some of these organizations have good results with their quality programs and received the Baldridge Award. Some others are still trying to increase their activities to achieve better results. Many of those that did not get good results are still hopeful for their total quality programs. But many of the TQM practices have failed.

The next chapter covers the failure of the contemporary management practices as well as its success and discusses why, and how to change it.

**Table 3.1. Comparison of Traditional, Total Quality Management,
and True Democratic Management**

| Activities | Traditional Management | Total Quality Management | True Democratic Management |
|---|---|---|---|
| Authority | Top managers have full authority, with guidance from stockholders and board. | Top managers have full authority with guidance from stockholders and board. Some job related authority shifted downward. | Stakeholders have the full authority, rights and responsibility. |
| Hierarchy | Top-down, command and control principles are guiding principles. | Top-down, command and control principles are guiding principles; workers participate in job related issues in teams. | Democratic values and principles are the guiding principles for all management decisions and practices. |
| Organizational Structure | Rigid, top-down command and control principles. | Pyramidal, top-down control, limited participation of workers. | Horizontal Circular Network, full participation. |
| Ownership | Systems are owned by the stockholders and investors. | Systems are owned by stockholders and investors and some ESOP are allowed. | Systems are owned by all the stakeholders. |
| Decision Making | Top managers make the major decisions with the approval of stockholders and board. | Top managers make the major decisions with the approval of stockholders and board. Employees participate in job related minor decisions. | All the stakeholders participate in major decisions. |
| Employment | No job security, short-term employment is common practice. | No job security, short-term employment is common practice. | Job security is provided, long-term employment is common practice. |
| Human Relations | Rigid, structured and based on individualism. | Rigid, structured and limited flexibility in small job-related teams. | Flexible, open and real team relations as a whole system (like family). |

**Table 3.1. Comparison of Traditional, Total Quality Management, and True Democratic Management (*cont.*)**

| Activities | Traditional Management | Total Quality Management | True Democratic Management |
|---|---|---|---|
| Distribution of Outcomes | Top managers and stockholders get the high shares; salary gap is too high between top managers and the workers. | Top managers and stockholders get the high shares; salary gap is too high between top managers and the workers. | Top managers salaries are reasonable; salary gap is not too high between top managers and workers. |
| Objectives | High quality, established by top managers and approved by stockholders and board. | High quality, established by top managers and approved by stockholders and board. | Total quality; established by stakeholders. |
| Change | Fix, improve, and innovate when some elements fail. | Fix, improve and innovate continuously for quality. | Core factors have to be changed and improved as a whole and continuously for total quality. |
| Education | Specialized and emphasized technical education; training when it is necessary. | Specialized and emphasized technical education; training mostly technical oriented. | Technical and values education are integrated and continuously improved. |
| Environment | Polluting and depleting environment are not regulated and not controlled fully. | Polluting and depleting environment are not regulated and not controlled fully. | Polluting and depleting environment are not allowed at all. |
| Ethics | Morality and social responsibility are not promoted. | Morality and social responsibility are not promoted. | Morality and social responsibility are promoted and are a major task of management. |

# CHAPTER IV

## Success and Failure of the Contemporary Management Practices

*Management is the 85 percent of the problem.*
—W. Edwards Deming

ontemporary management practices provided great success and failures for many nations throughout the world. In order to understand its performance fully and evaluate it fairly, its success and the failures are examined.

### *The Success of Contemporary Management Practices*

After World War II, many nations tried to improve their management to increase their economic well. Management provided new market opportunities for products using existing technologies and promoted the development of new technologies. Development of each new technology provided new economic benefits to many nations throughout the world. For example, the industrial revolution fueled by the development of steam power, and the textile industry led the emergence of Britain as the leader of the global economy during the early 19th century. Later, the United States developed the railroads in the mid-19th century and transcontinental and international transportation including shipping, and later in the 20th century, airplanes, which helped integrate the U.S. as a leader into global economy. During the early 20th century, development of electricity and automobiles facilitated the integration of Australia, Canada and South Africa into the global economy. After World War II, developments of electronic and computers enabled Japan and other Asian countries including Taiwan, Singapore, South Korea and other NICs to enter into the global market.

From 1990 to 1992, economic growth measured in real GDP, in the industrialized countries averaged about 2.5 percent. During 1992 to 1996, developing countries averaged 6.5 percent of economic growth and developed nations averaged 2.5 percent (see Figure 4.1). During the next decade, however, the developing nations' economies are expected to grow between 5 and 6 percent per year. It is projected that as a result of this rapid economic growth, developing countries will produce more than 27 percent of total output (*WB@www.worldbank.org.*).

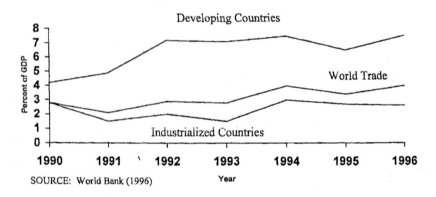

SOURCE: World Bank (1996)

**Figure 4.1. Real Global GDP Growth Rate 1990–1996**

Two-thirds of the radios made by Japanese manufacturing companies are produced abroad. Half of the stereos and color televisions sets are produced in South Korea and other nearby East Asian nations. Over 90 percent of South Korean exports of electronic equipment produced by affiliates of Japanese companies. The electronics, textiles and clothing are similar. These are not merely assembly operations. The production of components that require high levels of skill and/or technology is a more common undertaking in many developing nations. In the Philippines, for example, about 200 companies were operating in export-processing zones (EPZ's) in 1996, and employed about 50,000 workers. Most of these firms which are owned jointly, engaged in the manufacturing of electronics, microchips, semi-conductors, toys and garments. In 1996, the aggregate exports from these firms amounted to over 5.5 billion dollars, representing over 30 percent of the countries' exports by value. Between 1992 and 1994, developing nations received roughly 40 percent of all direct investment up from 20 percent in 1987, and expected to top 50 percent in 2010. The annual foreign direct investment from developed to developing nations has grown from 11.3 billion to 90 billion, and annual capital flows to developing nations increased from 100 billion to 350 billion during the period from 1985 to 1996 (International Finance Corporation 1996).

The developed nations including U.S., Japan, Germany, France, Italy and the UK provided 71 percent and some other 16 NICs nations produced 21 percent of the world's total manufacturing output in 1993 (Knox and Agnew, 1998). These nations employed about 20 percent of their workforce in manufacturing and manufacturing share constituted 26 percent of their GDP. Although the U.S. has retained its leadership as the world's major producer of manufactured goods over the past war period, its share in world output has been reduced from 40 percent in 1963, to 25 percent in 1995. In contrast, Japan has moved from fifth place with a share of 5.5 percent in 1963 to second-place with a share of 21 percent in 1995. This has been the result of increasing degree of globalization throughout the world economy. This interdependence is reflected by some important trends in manufacturing output; particularly the developing nations' growth of manufacturing. South Korea attained an annual average growth rate of almost 18 percent in the 1960s and 16 percent in late 1970's. As a result, South Korea surged up the list of developing market economies. The percentage of South Korea's labor force employed in manufacturing, increased from 9 percent to 29 percent during the period of 1960 and 1980 (Dicken, 1992). All four Pacific Rim countries have made enormous progress up the world league table of exporters. In 1993, Hong Kong ranked 9th in the world (up from 26th in 1979), Taiwan ranked 12th (up from 22nd), South Korea ranked 13th (up from 27th), and Singapore ranked 14th (up from 30th). These shifts have emerged from technological development through authoritarian management activities.

The 100 largest U.S. multinational companies had combined total sales in 1996 of $2,301,902 million; 40.3 percent of this was from international sales (*Forbes*, July 29, 1997). Total exports were $848.8 billion and total imports were $959.8 billions at the same year. It is estimated that $1 billion in exports creates approximately 22,800 jobs (Davis, 1989). Thus, increase in exports not only increase the nations per capita income, but would help to increase employment as well.

Collectively, the 500 largest U.S. corporations now employ in overseas labor force as big as their domestic labor force. Similar statistics applied to the largest Japanese corporations (Knox and Agnew, 1998). These data clearly indicate that authoritarian management practices increases the nations' technological, and economical conditions, which produce a higher total quality and competitiveness for their people. However, they also generate enormous problems, throughout the world. The following section covers some of the problems.

## *The Failure of Contemporary Management Practices*

Contemporary management practices have failed to satisfy all the stakeholders throughout the world. Although they generated great economic benefits for many nations as previous sections indicate, the distribution of these benefits are quite unequal.

During the last two decades, 64 percent of all male earnings in the U.S. went to the top one percent, and only 20 percent went to the workforce (Feenberg and Poterba, 1992). The top one percent received 90 percent of the total income. Salaries of CEO's of Fortune 500 went up from 35 to 157 times that of production workers (Blair, 1994 and 1995). CEO salaries tripled in France, Italy, and Britain and doubled in Germany during 1984-1992 (The Economist, Nov. 4, 1994). Female earnings followed with a 10 to 15 year lag. The distribution of earnings was starting to look more unequal than the male distribution of earnings (Thurow, 1996). The income share of the top quintile of households rose and bottom quintile declined. In the last two decades, only the top quintile of the workforce experienced real wage gains and all the others experienced a decline (Thurow, 1996). The declines in pension and health care insurance were even larger (Bloom and Freeman, 1992). In early 1990's the wage gap between the top and bottom quintile of the labor force was rising from 12 percent to 17 percent in OECD countries (*The Economist*, December 10, 1994).

Economic inequality generates political inequality and vice versa. People who have plenty of money can generate unfair political advantages through the media. People with political power can use it to generate economic advantages by using their influence. It is partly because of these kinds of exercises that most of the elected government officials are rich or become rich at the end of their political terms in many countries (Derber, 1998; Ackerman, 1999).

During the last two decades, massive layoffs did help many organizations to cut costs. But during this period, the stockholders' returns and the top managers' income increased (Will, 1991). Consequently, inequality between high-income groups and low-income groups has widened (Danziger and Gottschalk, 1995). The teams at the top benefited much more than their fellow employees. In 1991, top managers, earnings were 85 to 100 times as much as the average worker in the U.S.; comparative figures were 25 in Germany and 17 in Japan (Will, 1991). Since 1976 inequality between the real wages of workers and executives has soared in the U.S. Workers' wage index fell 14 percent by 1995, while that of executives' jumped 150 percent (Batra, 1996). This ratio increased to 690 in 2000 (U.S. News and World Report, 2000). The top 10 percent of population owned 82 percent of total financial assets, 91 percent of total corporate and business assets and 75 percent of the total wealth in 1997 (Brouwer, 1998). Because of these practices, fairness and inequality became major issues in the 1990's (Thurow, 1996; Galbraith, 1998; Mazarr, 1999; Gordon, 1996; Hendersen, 1996; and Blair, 1995).

Downsizing became the most common policy, while profits and earnings of shareholders increased (Baker and Mishel, 1995). Downsizing spread quickly to Europe and threatened Japan (German Information Center, 1994; and Simons, 1994). Downsizing and economic inequalities, which reduce the purchasing power of middle-class and low income families, generated social problems such as homelessness and divorce. Family structures were disintegrated worldwide (Lewin, 1995). The middle-class expectation of a rising standard of living and owning a house are disappearing. The middle-class is scared by the economic insecurity and they are losing their hopes for the future (Beatty, 1994; and Pearson, 1994). Even worse, 80 percent of the population believed that the country was run by the rich and for the rich (Phillips, 1993).

Many organizations still continue to downsize through restructuring, reengineering, rightsizing and lean and mean production techniques. During 1990-1995 announced corporate layoffs averaged about 500,000 and corporate profits after-tax averaged 293 billion dollars per year (Thurow, 1996). During the last three decades the private and employee pensions and the health insurance declined. Unemployment rate and Social Security tax increased, but the corporate tax rates declined in the U.S., Germany, France and Canada (Batra, 1996).

Downsizing leads to structural violence by denying part of the population the needed resources and the opportunities for a quality life and environment (Chasin, 1997). The less privileged may react to their situation by engaging all kind of crimes or show their anger at an unfair economic, political and social order against the poor and weak. Barbara Chasin shows that variety of inequalities and related violence exists in many developed countries.

It is estimated that the cost of price-fixing, pollution, bribes, work injuries, product defects, and re-works totaled several hundred billions of dollars per year, a significant portion of the total wealth of U.S. citizens (Etzioni, 1993). The interested employees, customers, local communities, and the public in general are clearly harmed (Batra, 1996; Chasin, 1997; Estes, 1996 and Derber, 1998).

It is argued that economic growth through contemporary management practices caused corruption. The governments of many developed and developing nations involved in variety of economic projects. Some of the government officials and their friends or relatives play crucial roles in selecting the nations and organizations for the economic projects. They influence the contractual agreements and other activities require these projects. Transparency International, based in Berlin, published a corruption index in 1995, ranking 41 nations in Asia, Europe and America, on a scale of 1 to 10; low score means high corruption. Among the 41 nations, 10 were identified as the most corrupt, with a score close to three or lower (Knox and Agnew, 1998).

Bribing is the major tool of winning the contracts, and getting the related materials through customs. Many government official in Mexico, India, Indonesia, Turkey and other NICs are accused of these activities (Garten, 1997). Friends and relatives of the ruling elite in these countries controlled business involved in economic growth. Thousands of low-paying, low-tech factories, which are producing clothing, shoes, electronics and toys for export, have brought this corruption. In other words, large portions of local resources are used for the multinationals' profits and small groups' income and wealth, in developing nations.

## *Authoritarian Management Practices Are the Main Source of Inequality of Income and Wealth*

It is well known that people have different capabilities and different desires. Some can learn faster and act more quickly and so on. Some like material or non-material values more than others. Hence, it should not be surprising that some people are more adept at earning income and accumulating wealth.

It is also clear that differences in intensity of work, the degree of risk taking, luck, inherited wealth, schooling and other types of training play an important role in income and wealth distribution. But the key source of unequal distribution of income and wealth within the nations is the authoritarian nature of the contemporary management practices.

The primary objectives of the contemporary management practices are still to maximize stockholders' profits. This objective has been in conflict with the interests of other stakeholders. While stockholders and top managers seek a quick return on the investments, employees want increased benefits and job security, and customer want high quality products and services at a low price. The organizations that seek to satisfy only the interests of stockholders and top managers could not satisfy the other stakeholders' interests. The organizations utilizing management practices toward this end will neither be able to establish equality among its stakeholders nor fully utilize their resources for quality.

Authoritarian management practices in industrial organizations control the major decisions of distributing their gains and costs. The level of employees' earnings and other benefits are determined by the top managers. The amount of profits, dividends, and price of the stocks partly depends on the amount of employees and their wages. In order to increase the interests of the top managers and the stockholders, the employees are laid-off and the wages are kept low.

The authoritarian management practices, which provide major decision making rights to a small group of people, could not achieve quality, liberty and equality simultaneously. The real world experiences show that the neglect of one or two of these objectives generate serious social, economic, and political problems that are not acceptable to many people. The authoritarian management practices may work well for a small portion of the population who control the management activities in the short-term. However, it may result in a catastrophe in the long-term (Albert, 993). History has many examples of this kind (Kennedy, 1987; and Braudel, 1994).

The recent collapse of authoritarian management practices in the Soviet Union and many other countries should be seen as a clear warning for the present practitioners of authoritarian management. Those newly democratized countries, especially who were looking to more democratized countries as a model, have to understand the serious problems in these nations. In order to eliminate these problems and have a secure and better future, the authoritarian management practices have to be changed.

## *Why Contemporary Management Practices Have to Be Changed*

There are many changes in contemporary management practices, which recently took place in the United States, Canada, Germany and Japan. Many institutions in these countries spend millions of dollars a year on quality improvement practices that do not improve their performance significantly and may even hamper it (Ernst and Young, 1992). Many experts (Brown, Hitchcock and Willard, 1994) provided some common causes for those failures. They argued that lack of management, commitment, poor timing, wrong education and training, and lack of short-term, bottom-line results are the common mistakes that practitioners make at the early stage because of their unfamiliarity with the basic precepts of total quality. Some major mistakes occur during the alignment stage because of the divergent strategies, inappropriate measures, outdated appraisal methods, and manipulative nature of rewards. They suggest that instead of focusing on the isolated improvement efforts, the entire organization must be aligned to total quality. Mistakes have been made in the integration stage, these mistakes include failing to transfer true power to employees, maintaining outmoded management practices, poor organization and job design, outdated functions of organization, finance, accounting, information and planning, and lack of their integration and failing to manage learning and innovation diffusion.

Studies of the contemporary management practices, here, support the conclusion of these studies about the total quality practices. For example, some organizations emphasize different portions of total quality management and leave out other portions. These practices do not have the totality of quality aspects, but a partial quality aspect. This is partially because of the short-term nature of the programs and partly because of the lack of total quality management knowledge by users. These studies and practices include development of a new mission statement, empowerment, quality through leadership, training and other elements of management. The practices of total quality elements do not differ much from the traditional management practices. The authority still belongs to top managers who are appointed or selected by the owners and the stakeholders. The managers make the key decisions including the production, employment and distribution of the gains and the pains of the organizations. The employees are not included in the main strategic decisions and the ownership of the organizations. The relationships between the managers and the workers are still structured, based on rank and related authority rather than open and friendly work environment. These types of practices, which were mainly based on short-term objectives, which do not include the full requirements of total quality management, will eventually not significantly change the present quality characteristics.

The contemporary management practices do not include environmental aspects such as resource scarcity, pollution, distribution of organization's return, and the management authority. Traditional management methods concerning ownership, employment and authority are still not resolved. Total quality cannot be achieved without solving the employment, authority, and distribution of return and cost problems that are at the center of management.

The importance of management for quality is well understood in today's societies. Institutions, small or large in size, nations developed or developing are all using contemporary management practices to increase quality. The people as workers, managers, owners, and consumers are looking for ways to improve management in their departments, institutions, and governments. Recent social, political, economical, technological developments at the global level increased the demand for more appropriate management for high total quality.

High-income societies demanded high quality goods and services. This demand is increased with the increased suppliers of the markets. Stiff competition to capture the market puts tremendous pressure on management to produce better quality goods and services almost at every level of every institution for everyone. Many experts, academicians, consultants and writers pointed out repeatedly and loudly that the present management practices in the United States could not satisfy this demand. They claim that the present management practices are too old and rigid to deal with today's needs, and achieve the high level of total quality to compete globally.

In order to satisfy this need, many quality experts, academicians, and practitioners started searching for the answer. They came up with the new management approach, commonly called "Total Quality Management" as we discussed in the previous chapter. Many studies (Brown, Hitchcock and Willard, 1994; Rosenbluth, 1992; Ernst and Young, 1990; Ackoff, 1994) and this analysis indicate that even the total quality management will not generate the high level of total quality. It deviates from the traditional management in many ways, but it does not go far enough to provide the much needed of management practices regarding the high total quality (see Table 3.1).

It is increasingly recognized that the current management practices and programs are not working well, and will not work in the 21st century. Contemporary management practices based on authoritarianism are both dangerous and wasteful in today's world. As information technology, global economic and ecological interdependencies and stakeholder demands increase and converge; the authoritarian management practices become obsolete. Continued autocracy has a high risk of revolt by the many poor against the affluent few. The overall success of business is threatened by non-competitiveness, bankruptcy, and a waste of human and other national resources. However, the radical changes in contemporary management practices present fear, risk of the unknown, and skepticism about the new. It is, therefore, necessary to understand the important aspects of why, where and how; contemporary management changes have to be made.

The recent changes in contemporary management practices through total quality management, employee involvement, empowerment and participation are centered on the "team work" in the organization. The common purpose of the teamwork is to increase the organization's productivity through close cooperation, communication, collaboration, and sharing the work among its members. The empirical studies support this argument. The teamwork through employee involvement practices provided more and better changes and innovation (Avishai and Taylor, 1989). Empowerment improved quality (Deming, 1986; and Juran, 1988); and employee participation in work-related decisions increased productivity (Denison, 1990; Levin and Tyson, 1990). Some organizations practiced employee involvement, performed better economically than controlled oriented organizations (Mitchell, Lewin and Lawler, 1990). They gained competitive advantages in the global market by moving toward participative management practices (Lawler, 1992).

However, many other studies proved that these management practices improve the economic performance of some organizations in the short term, but failed to reach expected possible outcomes in the long term for many other organizations in the U.S., (Brown, Hitchcock and Willard, 1992; Weiss, 1995; and Collis, 1998). These and other studies indicate that authoritarian command and control style practices are the main reason of this failure. The team concept that is employed by these practices has been partially utilized in the organizations. The employee's participation in work related issues in these teams are allowed to increase the productivity. But, they are not included in major decisions such as strategic planning, distribution of benefits and costs. Most benefits gained from productivity are shared by the other teams at the top, including top managers, stockholders or board members of the organizations. However, the costs of wrong decisions are often paid by the employees, customers, and the community (Will, 1991; and Etzioni, 1993).

The primary objectives of the contemporary management practices are still to maximize stockholders' profits (Friedman, 1970). This objective has been in conflict with the interests of other stakeholders (Evan and Freeman, 1993). While stockholders and top managers seek a quick return on the investments, employees want increased benefits and job security; and customers want high quality products and services at a low price. The organizations that seek to satisfy only the interests of stockholders and top managers could not satisfy the other stakeholders' interests. The organizations employing management practices toward this end will neither be able to establish a "real team" among its stakeholders nor fully utilize their resources.

During the last two decades, massive layoffs did help many organizations to cut costs, in the short term. But during this period, the stockholders' returns and the top managers' incomes increased (Will, 1991). Consequently, inequality between high-income groups and low-income groups widened (Danziger and Gottschalk, 1995). The teams at the top, benefited much more than their fellow employees. In 1991, top managers, earnings were 85 to 100 times as much as the average workers in the U.S.; comparative figures were 25 in Germany and 17 in Japan (Will, 1991). Because of these practices, fairness and inequality became major issues in the 1990s.

Many organizations are still continuing downsizing through restructuring, reengineering, and rightsizing techniques. These short-term oriented practices became a survival management for many organizations. However, they contribute to the causes of losing global competition for many American corporations (Hayes and Abarnathy, 1980; and Dertouzos, Lester and Solow, 1989). Many other empirical studies indicate that these practices may lead many American corporations to bankruptcy in the long-term (Jacobs, 1991).

Contemporary management practices, pursuing maximization of stockholders' and top managers' interests, cause other problems such as resource utilization and environmental hazards. It is estimated that the cost of price fixing, pollutions, bribes, work injuries, product defects, and reworks totaled several hundred billions of dollars per year, a significant portion of the total wealth of U.S. citizens (Etzioni, 1993; and Green and Berry, 1985). The interests of employees, customers, local communities, and the public in general are clearly harmed.

The recent failures of socialist and communist countries and the serious problems of many capitalist countries clearly indicate that authoritarian management practices cannot satisfy the needs of many people throughout the world. The authoritarian management practices provide major decision-making rights to a small group of people and will not achieve quality, liberty and equality simultaneously. The real-world experiences show that the neglect of one or two of these objectives generate serious social, economic, and political problems that are not acceptable to many people. The authoritarian management practices may work well for a small portion of the population who control the management activities in the short-term. However, it may result in a catastrophe in the long-term (Albert, 1993). History has many examples of this kind (Kennedy, 1989; and Braudel, 1994).

The recent collapse of authoritarian management in the Soviet Union and many other countries should be seen as a clear warning for the present practitioners of capitalist authoritarian management. Those newly democratized countries, especially who were looking to more democratized countries as a model, have to understand the serious problems in these nations. In order to eliminate these problems and have a secure and better future, the democratization process has to be accelerated with a new strategy.

The contemporary management practices, guided with authoritarian principles, are old, rigid and unfair. They are not responding to today's fast-changing needs of customers, knowledge employees, technologies and the hyper-competitive global market. Many prominent authors such as Alvin Toffler (1980), Robert Reich (1991), James Brian Quin (1992), Peter Drucker (1993), Margaret Blair (1995), James O'Toole (1995), Lester Thurow (1996), Michael Hammer (1997) and other thinkers (Renesch, 1992; and Gibson, 1997) indicated that traditional management practices are reaching the end of the road, and they will not work in the 21st century. Many empirical studies support this argument. Most top managers, business experts, employers, and the public, in general, believe that contemporary management practices have to be changed for total quality and competitiveness (Collis, 1998). The need for fundamental change of contemporary management practices is clear. However, there is still no clear vision "where" and "how' to change. The following section addresses the issue of where and how to change.

## *Where and How to Change?*

The authoritarian management practices were challenged before, decades ago. Elton Mayo (1933), Mary Parker Fallett (1924), Douglas McGregor (1960), Rensis Likert (1967), and Warren Bennis (1966) argued that human and social factors have to be included in management for organizational effectiveness and for a democratic way of life. Recently, Slater and Bennis (1992) have repeatedly argued that "democracy," which often is defined as "people's rule," is the only management system that can successfully cope with the changing demands of contemporary civilization, in business as well as in government. They use the term democracy as a system of values including full and free communication relying on consensus. Russel Ackoff (1994) described organization in his book, *The Democratic Corporation*, as a social system, which serves the interests of its stakeholders and increases its variety of both means and ends, which are the essence of democracy. That is, each of the stakeholder groups has a right not to be treated as a means to some end, but must participate in determining the future direction of the organization in which they have a stake (Rawls, 1971). Most recently, William Halal (1996) wrote a book *New Management: Democracy and Enterprise are Transforming Organization* that attempts to integrate principles of democracy in corporate management.

These and many other studies are emphasized in balancing the interests of all stakeholders of organizations through democratic management practices. The democratic management practices hoped to generate a sense of community around a shared vision, and a set of values that will decentralize authority and provide rights and responsibilities for all the stakeholders as a "real team" in the organization. This process would motivate, facilitate and enable all the stakeholders to increase the total quality of the organization. However, the "process of how" is not yet clear.

The process of changing the old management practices has been very difficult and raised some important questions (O'Toole, 1995). First of all, changing the old practices that have been used for many years and generated great wealth for many people in the U.S., and in other countries may require a new thinking and learning and may take a long time (Gibson, 1997; and Senge, 1993). In today's competitive global market, the success of the past has no implication for success in the future. The business world has changed so much that the practices of yesterday's success are almost guaranteed to be practices for failure tomorrow (Hammer, 1997). Secondly, the top managers and the investors, which control and share a large portion of the organization's returns, would not give up these rights and privileges. However, the source of these rights and privileges used to be the investors' capital and the top managers' knowledge and skills. In the present business world, the knowledge employees became the critical asset for the knowledge organizations creating the most competitive advantage (Drucker, 1993; Nonaka and Takeuchi, 1996; and Thurow, 1996). Just like the stockholders and top managers, knowledge employees want to share the rights and privileges for their critical resources. Thirdly, it has been argued that democratic management is not practical or efficient because of its slow decision-making process and loose control of workers' productivity. This argument has lost its validity. The recent advancements in information technology and increased knowledge of employees have made it possible to make decisions faster and more effective through speeded and wider information, learning, debating and direct voting of a larger group (Snider, 1996; *The Economist*, June 17, 1995). Information technology provides opportunities for reaching and integrating better resources and knowledge and, at the same time, distributing them for larger groups. This will increase the effectiveness of the decisions. The knowledge employees will be motivated to utilize their energies and minds for the objectives of the organizations more fully if they are included in the "real team" with the rights to participate in major decisions. Finally, the basic objective of democratic management is to balance the quality (wealth), equality (equal opportunities), and liberty (economic and political freedom) for all the people. How could this be possible for the stakeholders of contemporary organizations? Establishing the balance among these objectives has been the most difficult process of the management practices in the past and imbalances caused the fall of many great powers (Kennedy, 1989). It is still difficult to balance these objectives in an organization. There is no theory to balance these objectives for all the stakeholders of the organization. It is only democratic values that, if implemented appropriately in the management practices, are able to balance these objectives through compromise and trust of the individuals in an organization. As the advancements in information technology and knowledge increase, it is also necessary to increase value-based education to make it possible for practicing democratic management in the 21st century.

Many organizations including Hewlett-Packard, IBM, Xerox, Semco, General Electric, AT&T, Preston, Chaparral Steel and Japanese high-tech organizations in Japan and in U.S. and some organizations in Germany and in other countries have been employing some of the principles of democracy in their management practices. They achieved relatively higher productivity and competitiveness in the global market (Halal, 1996; Martin, 1996; O'Toole, 1995; and Ozaki, 1991). However, none of these organizations has been utilizing democratic principles fully. The democratic principles have to be employed fully and as a whole, rather than partially and in pieces, to generate higher productivity (Blair, 1994 and 1995).

There is no economic or political theory to provide an acceptable balance of these objectives other than true democracy. Most people understand the value of democratic management, but do not have the power yet to out power the practitioners and supporters of authoritarian management. The main power that will eliminate the authoritarian management and give rise to democratic management is the integration of technology and ideology. Technologies, which are founded on hard sciences, provide the main force needed for democratization. However, without the ideology, technology may not lead to democracy. Ideology based on human values provides the direction with continuous improvement. However, if technology and ideology fall apart, continuous improvement in the wrong direction may lead to catastrophe.

True democratic management is the only alternative that can achieve the quality, liberty, and equality that most people want to have throughout the world. Democratic management does not give the authority of decision making to a few or group that controls the destiny of an organization or nation. They are biased toward themselves or their group who provide them that authority. They also make serious mistakes that involve many people (McNamara, 1996). In civilized societies, organizations, and nations, people should control their destiny. This can be achieved by the true democratic management practices. In democratic management, the people through consensus or majority make the decisions to balance quality, liberty, and equality objectives.

# PART TWO:

## TRUE DEMOCRATIC MANAGEMENT PRACTICES FOR DESIRABLE TOTAL QUALITY

P art Two develops true democratic management practices including authority, organizational structure, ownership, decision-making and employment. It also explains how true democratic management, can enable people to achieve the desirable total quality and competitiveness through generating real team relations in an organization.

# CHAPTER V

# True Democratic Management Practices

*It is the management of thinking, deciding,*
*acting, sharing and winning independently together.*

D emocratic management or governance is not well understood by
many people throughout the world. Most of the governments and
public institutions in the Western nations claim their governance is
a democratic one, because they have elections every four years. Even the
most authoritarian governments are ruled and controlled by one or a few
dictators or their representatives claim that they are democratic. There are
even some people who do things to hurt some others by making decisions
and taking harmful actions within the contemporary democratic governance.
Even in the industrial organizations, some managers claim that they practice
democratic management because, they are elected by the board of trustees
or some other groups. However, they usually are elected by top managers.

None of these practices represent the democratic management in its
true meaning. In the following sections we will define the true nature of the
democratic management through explaining its objectives and major practices.

# The Nature and Objectives
# of True Democratic Management

The true democratic management is usually defined as the "people's management." In true democratic management, people make the decisions freely and by themselves rather than someone else making the decision for them. In true democratic management people are sovereign, and have rights to participate in management in all aspects of human life (March and Olsen, 1995; Slater and Bennis, 1990; and Cohen, 1971). In true democratic organization, people include all the stakeholders who can affect or are affected by the organization's activities and objectives (Freeman, 1984). The stakeholders usually include top managers, stockholders, employees, customers, local community and the nation's government.

The major true democratic management activities include authority, organizational structure, ownership, decision-making, and employment in an organization. The top managers, stockholders and the employees are the key sources of the organization. They invest capital, knowledge, and other resources in the organization and are directly involved in every aspect of management. The other stakeholders, including customers, local and government participate in management through their representatives.

The major objective of democratic management is to satisfy all of the stakeholders' needs and wants through achieving high and balanced total quality and competitiveness. We have shown in Chapter IV that the contemporary management practices have failed to achieve this objective. They are neither able to achieve high total quality nor able to balance the quality, equality and liberty among the stakeholders. They may satisfy the stockholders' and top managers' needs and wants, but not the employees, customers and the public in general.

The contemporary management practices of many organizations and nations tried to achieve one or more of the total quality aspects. For example, in Socialist or Communist economies, the equality aspects have been emphasized, often neglecting the aspects of liberty and quality. The empirical results indicate that emphasizing one or more aspects of total quality and neglecting others may cause organizational bankruptcies and national downfalls. The recent collapse of the Soviet Union is often attributed to emphasizing equality, but neglecting liberty and quality aspects of total quality. On the other hand, equality problems of income and wealth in the U.S., and many other capitalist countries, are indications of imbalances of total quality aspects in these countries. The management's main objective in these countries is to satisfy the needs of the owners, shareholders and the board of trustees through maximizing profits or sales (Baumol, 1959; Morris, 1998; Estes, 1996 and Derber, 1998). The maximization of profit or sales provided high income for the top managers and high return for the investors. Satisfying the employees' needs came mostly second. Frequently, many organizations reduced work forces, pensions, health care benefits, and eliminate retiree benefits. The public responsibility is considered informally. In reality, polluting air and waters and destroying land, which generate great cost to public, are common practices of contemporary management (see Chapter IV).

Top managers and the investors, have full liberty, which is provided and protected by the government to satisfy their needs, often by harming employees and the public. Because there are no limitations for distributing the organizational gain, the top managers and investors manage to receive high salaries and other benefits. They fully appreciated the high quality and the economic and political freedom. But the employees receive the small share of the quality and pay most of the costs through unemployment and other cuts of their benefits. The salaries of top managers are relatively high and the gap between them and the employees are increasing as discussed in Chapter IV. Although this kind of management practice provides high quality (economic wealth), it also generates sever inequalities and limited economic and political freedom of the employees and the public.

The development of total quality cannot be established at the expense of any stakeholders in an organization or a society. All the stakeholders involved and affected by the total quality have to be fairly and sustainably satisfied. Only then, total quality and competitiveness reaches the highest level in the global market through motivating stakeholders and utilizing their resources fully.

Without total freedom and total equality there can be no total quality. The true democratic management plays the key role in developing total quality and competitiveness in the global market by providing equality and full liberty. The true democratic management provides opportunities to develop a common objective through direct participation, open discussion and communication, debating and voting freely for all the stakeholders. The stakeholders, with a common objective, will be motivated to seek, learn and develop superior knowledge, skills and values for achieving their prime objective: total quality.

The true democratic management provides rights and responsibilities for all the stakeholders to utilize their knowledge and skills fully for their objective. The rights to participate in major organizational decisions, including distribution of gains, motivate all the stakeholders, especially the employees, to generate monetary values. Democratic management provides help for the local communities' social and economic needs. The community, which receives help from the organization, would support the activities and the interests of the organization. Almost all the successful organizations have good relations with their community (Peters and Waterman, 1982).

The true democratic management provides opportunities to establish close relations with the government concerning legal and ethical aspects of their operations. The laws governing these issues, should be developed jointly and applied fairly to preserve the public interests. The government should provide appropriate trade laws to preserve free and fair competition domestically and globally. The government helps to promote and develop new technologies, and transfer them to the organizations. The success of Japanese competitiveness in the global market is partly attributed to this kind of close relation between government and the organizations (Masaaki, 1986; and Ozaki, 1991).

True democratic management provides opportunities for the organization as a producer and customers to work closely for the mutual benefits. The organization should act with a realization that the customers are the main reasons for their existence. The customers provide the demand for the production. True democratic management considers interests of every stakeholders and seek ways to act together to increase each other's benefits.

The stakeholders with equal rights, responsibilities and opportunities to participate in management will be able to make better decisions and be motivated and united to do their best for the achievement of the high total quality.

## *Major Practices of True Democratic Management*

The major practices of true democratic management included are authority, organizational structure, ownership, decision-making, and employment. These practices together, establish the foundation of the true democratic management. They have to be utilized as a whole in order to achieve high level of total quality in balance and competitiveness.

## *Stakeholders' Authority*

Authority can be defined as the right to control all of the management activities in an organization. Throughout the history of management development, the owners and the top managers, including the president or CEO of an organization, have this authority, as we have shown in Chapter III. In a pyramidal organizational structure with many layers, the authority flows from top to bottom as a guiding principle of management practices. This kind of management is often called authoritarian.

The authoritarian management practices are based on "authority". The authority of decisions making of important issues in an organization, belong to one person or a few people close to top manager. They rule from top of the pyramidical hierarchy and others implement the decisions. They retain all of the authority and responsibility as a ruler, and the rest of the employees have to comply. The top managers are not elected by the employees. They are usually selected or appointed by the owners or stockholders through board of trustees that are also selected by the president and the stockholders. Therefore, the top managers are mostly responsible to those who selected them. They make all the major decisions for production, distribution, employment and all the other important management activities. Their main objective is to satisfy the needs of the owners, shareholders and board of trustees through maximizing profits, or sales.

Although this kind of authority have generated relatively high quality for the citizens of the United States and the other industrialized countries, they also generated sever inequalities between privileged groups and rest of the employees as discussed in Chapter IV. The management authority which does not provide equal rights and freedom for employees could not motivate a large group of the employees who are the main source of the quality and the competitiveness. Decisions that are limited to one or a few person could not be effective and could not be supported by most of the employees. Thus, they will not generate the higher total quality and competitiveness in a global market.

In true democratic management, "authority" mainly belongs to all the people of an organization who work there. This is possible through group decision making of all the stakeholders. They participate in decision making by direct voting on major issues through utilizing information technology (*The Economist*, June 17, 1995; and Snider, 1996). The debating, learning and voting directly on important issues were possible with the new information technology. Modern technology allows democratic decision making in a shorter time, lower cost, and easy implementation. Most importantly, the level of total quality and competitiveness will increase with decreasing authoritarian authority and increasing employee participation (Likert, 1967; Denison, 1990; and Lawler, 1995).

Recent advances in information technology and increasing knowledge and skills of the work force, are shifting the balance of authority, from the top managers to the workers at the factory floor. Rigid authoritarian practices are being discarded in favor of employee participation in management. The contemporary command and control managers are becoming coaches and counselors in democratic management. The central theme of this change is partnership, rather than master and servant relationship. Many corporations in the U.S., including Preston Corporation, Steelcase, Inc., Semco, IBM and Hewlett-Packard are trying to give some limited authority to their employees (Garfield, 1992). Some other countries that are giving relatively more authority to their employees are getting better results than the U.S. In Germany, employees are considered long-term stakeholders in the companies. The employees in the German organizations that employ at least 2,000 employees have the right to elect half of the members of the supervisors' board. These boards, select and oversee the activities of the managing board, which makes the day-to-day management decisions, and represents companies externally.

The authority is shared in many Japanese large corporations through group decision-making, long-term employment and father-son-like relationships of management to employees. Their success in global competition is often attributed to their management practices, which share the authority with their stakeholders (Masaaki, 1986; Nakane 1970; Sen, 1982; Ozaki, 1991; and Ouchi, 1981).

## *Horizontal Circular Network Organizational Structure*

The pyramidal organizational structure is most commonly used in contemporary management practices. The president is at the top of the pyramid. The other layers from top to bottom include top managers, middle managers, team leaders and workers. The size of the layers commonly depends on the size and the nature of the work of the organization. This kind of organizational structure is suitable for the authoritarian management practices. It is rigid, the communications and human relations are based on the rank and order. The command and control flow from top to the bottom positions. The people at the top layers are considered the most important, and at the bottom are the least important for the management. The people at the bottom, which include most of the employees, do not trust the top managers. Top managers feel the organization belongs to them, and the employees are there because of the top managers. Top managers' objectives are to maximize profits and the workers' objectives are to maximize wages. These objectives are in conflict. Because of the different objectives and rank, the pyramidal organizational structures cannot generate the unity and trust among the people of the organization, but divides them as, "us" and "them." Therefore, they cannot achieve the highest total quality and the competitiveness.

Many of the organizations are trying to increase profits, reduce costs, and improve the efficiency of the organization with massive layoffs. Many layers of bureaucracy have been eliminated, and huge cuts were made in middle management. However, the collective attempt by American corporations to become "lean and mean" did not produce the desired results. Many of these organizations have failed to recognize that the root cause of the problem is not simply the size of the bureaucracy, but the fundamental structure of the organization (Garfield, 1992; and Mills, 1991).

In true democratic management the organizational structure is a horizontal circular network that distributes authority to employees and other stakeholders. This kind of organizational structure increases communication, coordination and provides a close relationship among the stakeholders, which are important for a high level of total quality and competitiveness (Byrne, 1994; Davis, 1989; and Mills, 1991). The horizontal network structure includes the president, vice presidents, middle managers, workers, and representatives of the other stakeholders. The president is at the center of the network. He is elected by all the employees of an organization. The vice presidents and representatives of the other stakeholders are at the first circle around the center. The vice presidents are directly linked to the president and to middle managers. The middle managers, which are located at the second circle, are linked to each other and to workers in that section which is located on the third circle. The workers are linked to each other in each section. Thus, all the human resources are directly related to each other in the organization. The vice presidents are elected by the employees of each group, and the middle managers by the employees of each section. The workers are selected by the middle managers and the employees of that section, and approved by the vice president of that group and by the president (see Figure 5.1).

The horizontal network structure eliminates both hierarchy and functional or departmental boundaries. It makes teams the main building blocks of the organization, limits supervisory roles by making the team manage itself, and gives the team a common purpose and responsibility for the total quality and the competitiveness. It maximizes stakeholders' contact at every work level, and adds knowledge and skills to team work, through close communication.

The horizontal circular network structure allows people to move easily and fluidly within the organization. The employees are also rotated from function to function in a relatively shorter time to maximize flexibility and encourage new thinking. Information technology has made it possible to link people anywhere in the organization, and the world. Through information technology, companies are linked directly to their suppliers, distributors, and customers.

With ongoing fast change in global market, decisions are made both at the front line and the top management level. In order to be successful in contemporary competition, information had to move quickly and people had to be given the freedom to function in a flexible environment. The pyramidal structure, which is inherently rigid and inflexible, is bound in time-consuming bureaucracy. The flexibility required to produce the most needed innovation cannot be achieved within the rigid and controlled pyramidal structure. The pyramid may be adequate for producing standardized goods and services that may not require innovative knowledge and skills. The horizontal network structure provides opportunities for creativity and innovation by permitting intuitive as well as systematic searching. The free and full com-

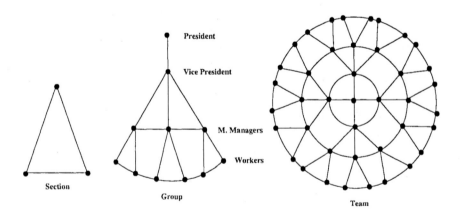

**Figure 5.1. Horizontal Circular Network Structure**

munication without fear and coordination among stakeholders will provide the best opportunities for a high level of quality and competitiveness. Many organizations including Hewlett-Packard, AT&T, General Electric, Xerox, Motorola and Kodak are moving toward horizontal network structure by reducing the layers of management to increase their performance (Halal, 1996; and Martin, 1996).

## *Employee Ownership*

The ownership of a productive system or a wealth is the natural desire of human beings, because wealth is the power for a good material life. The amount of wealth and income indicates, in some degree, the economic and professional success of a person. In fact, the capitalist system, encourages everyone to become a capitalist which will increase the economic wealth of a nation (Smith, 1994). However, the capitalist countries can only produce few capitalists relative to large populations of poor. Since the 1970s in United Sates of America, inequality of wealth and income has increased dramatically, while average wealth and income for middle-income earners barely kept pace with inflation, and those at the bottom of scale actually fell in real terms. Inequality of wealth widened with the gaps between haves and have-nots escalating to levels experienced during the Great Depression (Galbraith, 1998).

Many economists and researchers claim the causes of this inequality might be the skill-biased technological change, economic globalization, new production practices, declining union membership and "winner-take-all" markets. Although, these suspected causes of inequality are perceived to be the forces of the private, free-market economy, the real causes of this inequality has been the contemporary management practices which is controlled by the wealth owners, not the autonomous forces of technology and the globalization as we have seen in Chapter IV. This kind of management practice that is controlled by the owners, favors the owners. It cannot motivate the workers for the high quality and competitiveness, but limits their performance and generates negative feelings toward owners and their organizations that might be very costly and risky for everyone.

In democratic management, the organization belongs to everyone who invests knowledge, capital and other resources in it for high level of quality and competitiveness. The ownership of shares by all stakeholders provides opportunities to utilize critical resources of physical, and human capital, more productively, thus sharing the risks and returns of the investments. Ownership of private property is the central mechanism by which incentives are created for the productive use of resources in a free market economy. True democratic management provides opportunities for everyone to be the owner of their work place rather than generating work for a few upper management owners.

The contemporary management practices, which provide the ultimate power and rights to capital holders lead to under-investment by other stakeholders, and thus diminish potential corporate wealth generation (Blair, 1995). The organizations should not be regarded as bundles of physical assets that belong to shareholders, but also specific human capital that all stakeholders contribute as specific assets. This, includes not only shareholders, but also, long-term employees who provide specialized knowledge and skills for the organization, suppliers, customers, or others who may also make specialized investments.

In light of recent stiff global competition, many organizations are redefining themselves in terms of their basic or core competencies, and pursuing policies to develop specific knowledge, skills and values as a "critical resource." The employees who embody them are the competent carriers who provide collective learning, and coordinate diverse production skills, to develop high total quality, and competitiveness of the organization (Lawler, 1992; Monks and Minow, 1995; Hoerr, 1985; and Blair, 1995).

The ownership practices, have been taking place in many organizations in the form of partnership, profit sharing, gain sharing and employee stock ownership plans (ESOP) (Adams and Hansen, 1992; and Blair, 1995). In 1991, over 12 percent of the work force participated in employee ownership plans in the U.S. It is estimated that profit sharing or gain sharing compensation plans cover about one-fifth of the private work force (Mitchell, Lewin and Lawler, 1990). Employees, collectively, held more than $150 billion worth of corporate equity in the early 1990s (Blasi and Kruse, 1991). As of 1992, employee ownership in public organizations accounted for 43 percent of the ownership equity. It is estimated that more than one-quarter of all stock market companies would be owned by their employees by the year 2000 (Joseph and Blasi, 1992).

Employee ownership has saved many companies from bankruptcy and has increased productivity in the U.S. However, without changes in management practices, employee ownership practices alone seems to produce a one-time increase in productivity, and does not increase the rate of growth of productivity over time (Kruse, 1993). They increase quality, if they combined with programs that provide participation in management (Conte and Svejner, 1990). The employee ownership has to be combined with the voting rights just like other shareholders, to generate maximum impact on firms' performance. It induces quality because they share and control some of the costs of poor quality. The managers cannot constantly monitor their employees, but instead motivate them to think like owners (Stiglitz, 1974).

Only a few of the employee representatives are allowed on the board of directors in some organizations in the U.S. Even where the employees are the dominant shareholders, only a few companies had employee representatives (Blasi and Kruse, 1991). Some other countries including Germany, France and Japan, who are given relatively more voice to their employees, get better results than the U.S. In these countries, employees considered long-term stakeholders of the companies and permitted them to participate in major management decisions. This kind of practice, has to be increased to include employees, in major decisions of management practices, which will increase total quality and competitiveness of the organization.

## *Group Decision Making*

There are no diseconomies to knowledge. The more participants are involved in decision-making the larger the information and knowledge required for better decisions. The major decisions of industrial organizations are made by top managers in contemporary management practices. The president of an organization consults with the vice presidents and with the board members, in most cases, for major decisions. The people, including the other employees who implement the decisions and will be effected by the decisions concerning their economical and operational issues, are excluded from the decision making process. The top managers also exclude other stakeholders from the process of decision-making including the representative of suppliers, customers, the community and the government who will be affected by these decisions. Most importantly, they exclude the employees who will not only be affected by these decisions, but they will implement them. The success of these decisions mainly depends on the employees' support and implementation.

The decision making process in true democratic management include all the stakeholders including top managers, the board of directors, the representatives of the shareholders, employees and the representatives of the suppliers, customers, community and the government. This type of group decision-making provides wide knowledge, information and support of all the stakeholders. The decisions that are based on wider knowledge, information and supported by all the stakeholders generate better results.

However, decisions requiring special knowledge such as engineering, financing, marketing, and so on have to be analyzed and decided within that group or section first, and forwarded to vice presidents who will discuss them with their own groups. If there is a problem with a decision, they will work with the related people before presenting it to the president, for the final approval. When decisions are presented to the president, they are mostly complete, and the president usually approves them. However, if there is a problem, it has to be worked out with the related people before the final approval. The president provides the final checking of the feasibility of the decision, for overall interests of all the stakeholders. Most of the high-tech Japanese organizations have been utilizing this type of decision-making process to reach consensus (Nakane, 1970; Sen, 1982).

Decisions made by consensus of large groups, using wider knowledge and information will be more effective than those decisions made by one person or smaller groups. Those who participated in decision-making will probably support and have the desire to implement it. Individuals who are given authority to influence decisions will have more responsibility to implement it. This will increase total quality, and competitiveness of the organization through cost cutting activities, increasing learning and innovation, and utilizing available resources and individuals' knowledge and energies more fully, and effectively (Lawler, 1992).

Contemporary management practices in most organizations in the U.S. involve major decisions by one person, or a small group of top managers and implemented by other employees. Eighty percent of America's 1,000 large corporations are ruled by one person as a chairman and CEO. He or she controls the meeting of the directors, who theoretically monitoring his/ her performance on behalf of shareholders. CEO's attitude is, "it is my company, and it's my board." Their decisions are often biased toward themselves, and the shareholders. They satisfy their personal and the shareholders' interests, often at an enormous cost to other stakeholders. During the late 1980s and early 1990s, large amounts of workers lost their jobs due to downsizing of many organizations (Mirvis, 1993; Harrison, 1993; and Byrne, 1994). Most American firms have cut back on health care benefits, reduced pensions, and eliminated retirees' benefits (Peterson, 1994). Many of these corporations increased the income of their CEOs and the dividends of their shareholders. During the period of 1980 and 1992, the average pay of the top 1,000 U.S. corporations' CEOs increased from $625,000 to $3,882,000. In 1991, CEO's earned 85 to 100 times, as much as the average workers; these figures, were 25 in Germany, and 17 in Japan (Will, 1991). Because of the unfair decisions of contemporary management practices, most of the employees do not trust their own managers. The American public believes that leaders of large organizations care more about their own interests, than the well being of stakeholders (Collis, 1998).

The shareholders of many organizations are looking for short-term returns for their investments rather than long-term returns. Top managers, who are often appointed for short-term bases, make decisions for short-term interests. The widespread focus on short-term interests has been a major contributor to the loss of international competition by many U.S. corporations (Hayes and Abarnathy, 1980; Dertouzos, Lester and Solow, 1989).

The contemporary authoritarian decision makers often argue that workers do not have enough knowledge and skills to participate in major decisions. They also argued that including large groups of workers in decision-making would be slow and impractical. Both of these arguments have lost their validity in the current competitive business world. In the contemporary global markets, the knowledge and skills are the key factors of total quality and competitiveness (Drucker, 1993; Toffler, 1990; Quin, 1992; Senge, 1993; and Nonaka and Takeuchi, 1995). The employees with the knowledge and skills that play an important role in production, can also contribute in major decisions, and they want to participate in decision-making. Most importantly, recent advancements in information technology made it relatively much easier and faster to access new knowledge, ideas, skills and information in large volume. The debating, learning and voting directly on major issues as a large group is possible now with the information technology. This process, which used to be difficult and impractical before, is possible now, and will become easier, faster and less expensive and more efficient in the 21st century as advancements in information technology increase (Snider, 1996; and *The Economist*, June 17, 1995).

In Germany, the workers and other stakeholders are included in decisions through "supervisory boards" of which half of them are elected by the employees (Schneider-Lenne, 1992). Most German companies also have "work councils" made up of employees, and union representatives that management must consult about certain major business decisions. Other stakeholders also have representatives on the supervisory board, and participate in decision-making. In Japan, group decision-making process is one of the key practices of their management. The employees have a central role in group decision-making, although it is more a cultural phenomenon that results in a formal legal arrangement (Nakane, 1970; and Sen, 1992). The group-decision making of participative management practices, has been the ultimate advantage, and perhaps, most important competitive advantage of the Japanese automakers (Womack, Jones and Roos, 1990). Many American automakers including NUMMI, GM and Toyota increased their productivity about 40 percent by using Japanese management practices. Group decision-making was the most important among these practices (Levin, 1995). These practices have also been exercised in England and other countries. It is quite clear that, participative decision making in an organization increases total quality and competitiveness. The group decision-making activities have to be increased for high level of quality and competitiveness.

## *Long-Term Employment*

Employment is essential for the human existence. In true democratic management the human resources are considered to be the most important factor of production. They provide employment to generate value and are part owners of their organization. In true democratic management the employees have both the right of their employment and responsibility to generate value to support their employability and their investment. Therefore, true democratic management provides opportunities for all the employees to be productive and competitive through long-term employment. The long-term employment provides opportunities for continuous learning, and increases knowledge and job security that satisfies employees' needs and motivates them for high total quality and competitiveness.

The human resources constitute the ultimate asset of the organizations. Capital and natural resources are passive factors of production. Human beings are the active agents who generate, accumulate and utilize capital, exploit natural resources, and build organizations (Harbison, 1973). Human resources, provide the most important sources including energy, skills, knowledge and talent for the organization. The human resources that have these capabilities are the most critical competitive advantage for organizations. It is, therefore, the most important responsibility of both the organizations, and the people who work there, to develop these capabilities and utilize them fully. As global competition intensifies, the organizations have to provide opportunities for their employees, and the employees have to learn new knowledge, and skills continuously, to survive and be competitive. Continuous learning requires continuous and long-term employment. However, the organizations and the employees have also the responsibility, to generate enough monetary value to support, long-term employment.

The true democratic management provides opportunities for the employees to learn and educate themselves for the needs of global competition.

Contemporary competition requires superior skills, knowledge and innovation. These competencies cannot be learned from the textbook alone, but from on-the-job learning, learning by doing, by working together and by experimenting. The work itself is a learning process in the knowledge of organizations. In order to maximize the organization's wealth the employees have to contribute fully. This is possible with long-term employment, which provides continuous learning. True democratic management provides opportunities for acquiring, creating, storing and spreading knowledge and using it to change the work that is done (Barton, 1992). The only sustainable, competitive advantage is the ability to learn faster than one's competitor (Arie de Geus, 1988), which is possible with the long-term employment.

Long-term employment provides opportunities for employees to learn continuously and faster. Knowledge workers must be employed on a long-term basis because their work is inherently complex, innovative, and requires long-term learning, and stability for continuous improvement. Frequent layoffs, generate short-term cost reductions, but may decrease long-term value generating capability of the organizations. They may even generate delays, and plateau on the learning curve that may cause learning disabilities that are fatal in organization (Senge, 1993; and Martin, 1996). Long-term employment is also necessary for employees to satisfy most of their needs, security, self-respect and self-actualization (Maslow, 1964). Job security and good pay are the essential needs for the employee's life, and long-term employment provides opportunities to satisfy these needs.

On the other hand, in true democratic management the employees have to develop knowledge, skills and values and utilize them to generate values to support their employability, and the existence of the organization. The long-term employment empowers employees to be creative, use their brains, take initiative, and make improvements in the work process. The employees have to develop knowledge, and skills as fast as technological development to compete in global market. Job security does not mean generating obsolete thinking, rather an incentive to generate more value, and share the risk of employability. Thus, every employee has the right to share the returns and, at the same time, have the responsibility to maximize the value of the organizations. Consequently, both the individuals' and the organizations' benefits will be maximized, by linking employee rights and responsibilities through long-term employment. The long-term employment, will also generate, high morale and a real team relations that increases the employees' total quality and competitiveness (see Chapter VI).

In true democratic management, the managers and the employees have to make every effort to secure every individual's position. In case of financial difficulties, or for technological reasons, the losses will be shared by all the stakeholders. If some positions, sections or groups cannot be operated economically, these employees should be reeducated and retrained to transfer to other groups into which they can fit. If this is not possible, these employees should be helped financially, and in other ways to find new employment. There will be no firing, unless an employee fails to perform his/her job responsibilities, for reasons other than health. Long-term bases of employment will make it possible for the organization to re-educate and retrain its employees continuously. It will also eliminate costs of strikes, absenteeism, rehiring and negative impacts of firing on the remaining work force. Thus, the organization's total quality and competitiveness will increase.

Two-thirds of Japanese high tech organizations have been using lifetime employment practices. Global competitiveness of many Japanese organizations is partly attributed to their employees who are employed for a lifetime. Many organizations in Germany employ their workers on a long-term basis. These organizations have achieved a high level of total quality and competitiveness in the global market. Some American organizations, including Hewlett-Packard, Semco, Preston, Chaparrel Steel, IBM, Motorola and many other high tech organizations, see their employees as the most critical assets for their total quality and competitiveness. They try to increase their employees' knowledge, and skills through continuous learning, experimenting and working that requires long-term employment. This way, employees have opportunities to generate monetary value for their employment and the success of their organizations. This kind of long-term employment practice should be encouraged to utilize employees' knowledge and skills potential fully, which will increase the total quality, and competitiveness of the organization in the global market.

The key management practices including authority, organizational structure, ownership, decision-making and employment in an organization have to be designed based on democratic principles. Democratic principles of equality (equal opportunities) and liberty (economic and political freedom) provide rights and responsibilities for all stakeholders to utilize their minds and energies effectively, efficiently and ethically for achieving the high level of total quality and competitiveness in global market. The next chapter explains this process.

# CHAPTER VI

# True Democratic Management Generates Desirable Total Quality

*Relation is the essence of everything that exists.*
—Meister Eckhard

True democratic management practices including stakeholder's authority, horizontal circular network organizational structure, employee ownership, group decision-making, and long-term employment provide the foundation for close human relations in an organization. Close human relations are crucial for the real team organization to maximize peoples' and organizations' total quality and competitiveness.

Close human relations in a team help to achieve the high total quality and competitiveness through generating common objective. Close human relations provide an environment to develop real team relations. The institutions with the real team relations have common objectives among its stakeholders. The following section will explain the nature of the real team relations and show how it can achieve the highest, sustainable and balanced total quality and competitiveness through utilizing true democratic management practices.

## Characteristics of Real Team Relations

Human relations are the interactions of people in a team. The people's interactions may occur physically like actions and behavior and non-physically like emotions and values. The team includes two or more people, like a family, a basketball team, a department, an organization, a nation and the world. The people in a team are interrelated and interact to achieve the common goal of the team. (Roseberg and Birdzel, 1986). Each team could be divided into smaller teams and also linked to other teams which together they can develop a larger team. For example, an organization as a team includes smaller teams such as employees, shareholders, customers, suppliers, community and the government. The employees can also be divided into smaller work teams based on the nature of the work. The organizations may develop larger teams through joint ventures and alliances to increase their total quality. Sometimes, even all of the industrial organizations in a nation can establish a team for their mutual benefits like the Ministry of International Trade and Industry (MITI) in Japan. The European Union (EU) and the United Nations (UN) represent larger teams. They all have a common objective of satisfying the needs and wants of the people they represent.

Many theoretical and applied studies have indicated that close human relations in a team increase the total quality and competitiveness of individuals and the team (Manz and Sims, 1980 and 1995, Purser and Cabana 1998, Argyris, 1957; Likert, 1967; McGregor, 1960; Ouchi, 1981; Peters and Waterman, 1982, O'Toole, 1985; Kanter, 1985; Ozkanli, 2002; Womack, Jones, and Roos, 1990). Almost every major U.S. organization has been seriously considering work teams. There are many books and articles on the subject of teams (Shonk, 1992; Horr, 1989; Hackman, 1984; Masaaki, 1986; Dumaine, 1990; Katzenbach, 1998; Parker, 1990; Kayser, 1990; Tichy, 1990; Garfield, 1992; and Nirenberg, 1993). However, neither of these studies nor their real world applications capture the main characteristics of close human relations in a team. They emphasize the limited relations between managers and workers or among workers for work related operational issues. They also attempted to analyze human relations in the organization by working within the existing structure as we discussed in Chapter III. These kinds of tools and techniques do not provide the environment for close human relations.

True democratic management practices through stakeholders' authority, horizontal network organizational structure, employee ownership, group decision making and long-term employment provide environment for all the stakeholders to establish a real team. In real teams close human relations help to unite the stakeholders and generate a common objective, which in turn the common objective enable the team to achieve the highest total quality.

Figure 6.1 conceptualizes the process of achieving the highest total quality in teams through close relations. In this figure an arrow represents the scale and the direction of the goal. The arrow (S) represents the objective of stockholders and (E) represents the objective of employees. Their contributions to an organization's objective are represented by the arrow. As we can see in Figure 6.1a, the goal attainment is $V_1$ which attained by summing up the $S_1$ and $E_1$. As the objectives of stakeholders and the employees get closer and closer to each other as indicated in Figure 6.1b and Figure 6.1c, their goal attainment gets larger $(V_2 > V_1)$ and larger $(V_3 > V_2 > V_1)$. In case of common objective as indicated in Figure 6.1d, their goal attainment becomes the largest $(V_4 > V_3 > V_2 > V_1)$.

The close human relations in a team can occur in many ways such as helping and supporting each other through open communication, continuous learning and sharing knowledge, skills and the outcomes of the team. A member of the team may even reduce his/her quality to provide help and support for the other members that may increase the total quality of the team. Close human relations in a real team may result in a chain reaction that has multiple impacts on team's total quality by increasing individual's total quality simultaneously in a chain reaction.

By working in close relations one gets the value of each other's knowledge, skills and emotional support almost instantaneously at the right place and just in time. Close human relations provide free, open and honest discussions and debates of the pros and cons of different alternatives. Close relations generate variety of amplifying effects that in turn facilitate a more through exploration and interpretation of actions, ideas, knowledge and skills. Close relations also mean people think and decide fairly, act humanly through caring deeply and fully by utilizing all possibilities and abilities. People in close relations share equitably and reasonably without any favoritism and biased ness. Close relations in a team require team members to give and take physical and emotional help and support freely and responsibly.

The team acting and behaving with close relations generate a unity among its team members with a philosophy of "one for all, and all for one". This is what we call a "real team." The people in a real team try to obtain the best of the existing knowledge, skills and values and search new ways

*Democratic Management*

and means to increase their qualifications for contributing the team's total quality and competitiveness. In a real team people care for each other genuinely, trust each other fully and love each other sincerely. The members of the real team act like a good family who help each other, love each other and protect the interests of the home. They act like good soldiers who die

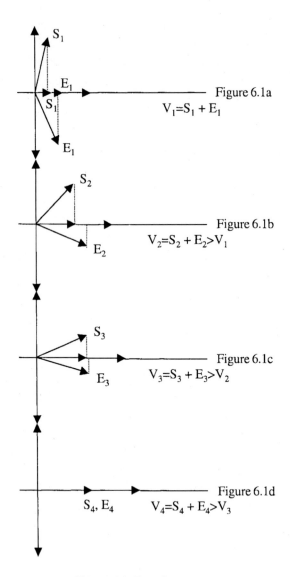

Figure 6.1a
$$V_1 = S_1 + E_1$$

Figure 6.1b
$$V_2 = S_2 + E_2 > V_1$$

Figure 6.1c
$$V_3 = S_3 + E_3 > V_2$$

Figure 6.1d
$$V_4 = S_4 + E_4 > V_3$$

**Figure 6.1. Goal Attainment**

for his/her battalion when it is necessary or good citizens who treat other citizens like the way he/she wants them to treat him/her or like caring brothers and sisters. These characteristics represent some of the close relations in a real team.

It takes the real team relations to raise the total quality and competitiveness of a team. In a real team, like a good family, the human relations influences individuals' and the families' total quality and the competitiveness. The parent's physical support for their children through providing capital, a good house, clothing, food and an education and by loving and caring for them allows them to excel in their studies and their life. On the other hand, the children's responsibility for housework and respect for their parents increases the parents' total quality. These kind of cooperative relations among the family members generate trust, confidence and security among the family members and reduce the conflict among team members. The parents who communicate with their children openly and fully, provide good care, and are fair and honest with them, establish the unity for the whole family. The united family works cooperatively, share the gains and the pains of the family, and support each other fully to increase their and the family's productivity and competitiveness. These kinds of parent-child relations constitute the foundation of the real team. The "real team" families are successful and happy.

Japanese culture's high level of total quality and competitiveness in global market are often attributed to their utilization of the human relations of the household for their management practices (Nakane, 1970; Sen, 1982). These relations are explained by the traditional terms of *ayabunkobun* in which *ayabun* means the person with the status of *oya* (parent) and *kobun* means the person with the status of *ko* (child). The child receives benefits or help from the parents and in return the child provides services to the parents whenever the parents require them (Nakane, 1970). On the other hand families with poor human relations among its members such as poor communications, no cooperation and no support for each other either in physical or non-physical terms, and do not share the gains and the pains of the family, can not generate trust and the unity among its members. This kind of family may fall a part and may not be productive and happy at all. The contemporary family crisis and high divorce rate in the United States are partly the result of poor human relations in American families (Hassett, 1981; London, 1987; Wallerstein, 1989; Lickona, 1991).

# *True Democratic Management and*
# *Real Team Organization*

Human relations in an organization should be designed like a good family, the real team. The stakeholders, are internally or externally related to organization. Their internal relations to each other in the organization includes all the employees and external relations include the stockholders, customers, suppliers, community and government essential for the total quality and competitiveness of each member and the organization. The pioneers of human relations or behavioral management studies strongly argued that human relation of workers and managers at work place are essential for their productivity, as we discussed in Chapter III. Most recently TQM emphasized the teamwork as a major determinant of high productivity and competitiveness. However, none of these practices dealt with the human relations issue fully and utilized it for their management practices. Most of these practices were involved in work places as a small team and focused on the workers' relations, concerning how to do a specific job more productively. These relations are mostly limited to workers' communication, cooperation and participation in work related issues, which may increase the team's productivity. However, the relations involving major issues such as authority, organizational structure, ownership decision- making and employment distribution of the gains and pains of the organizations have not been included in work-related teams. These are the most important issues in management practices as we discussed in Chapter V for the total quality and competitiveness of the organization. In their absence, none of the organization can provide the environment for real team relations; and without real team relations the organization cannot maximize the total quality and competitiveness.

The real team relations can be achieved through practicing true democratic management. True democratic management practices provide necessary environment for close human relations by providing equal rights, opportunities and responsibilities for everyone in the organization. The horizontal circular network structure and ownership of the organization generate close relations and trust among the members. Full participation in major decisions and job security of the employees through long-term employment are essential for the close relations in the organization. The organization has to establish close relations among its stakeholders like a good family.

In true democratic management, authority belongs to the stakeholders. Contrary to authoritarian management practices, the employees including top managers, middle managers and the workers have equal authority in major decisions of the organization. This process eliminates the superiority and inferiority feelings among the employees. In contemporary management practices the managers, because of their positions and rank, have the authority to order or down grade other employees. True democratic management differs in that responsibility and rights of the employees are the basic guiding principles and everyone has them. The responsibility and rights of everyone is equally important. The responsibility of the custodian and the president is equally important for the close relations and total quality and competitiveness. They also have equal rights concerning the major decisions and other democratic management practices. These rights and responsibilities generate good feelings, mutual respect, and good family relations among employees rather than master-servant relations of people in contemporary organizations. The network-circular-horizontal organizational structure of democratic management provides opportunities for employees to act and interact with each other without boundaries and walls which exist in contemporary management practices. This kind of organizational structure makes it easier for employees to approach each other directly, easily, freely, and fluidly. This atmosphere provides opportunities for an open and full communication and cooperation among employees.

The ownership in the organization plays a crucial role in determining the nature of the human relations in that organization. Historically, the owners have been managed or controlled the management practices of the organizations they owned. These kinds of management practices have been the main cause of master-slave or master-servant relations that describe existent human relations in many organizations. In order to establish good family relations and replace the master-servant relations, the stakeholders, and most importantly the employees, must become an owner of their organization. Employee ownership provides incentives for employees to interact with each other like a partner rather than a master and servant. The partnership helps to eliminate the superiority and inferiority feelings among the employees. They are all equally focused on the goals of the organization. Ownership will provide opportunities to eliminate the workers feelings toward owners that they exploit workers for profit and the owners' feelings that the owners are making their living because of the owners' investment. The ownership eliminates the "we" (the workers) and "they" (the owners and their top managers) relationship and generates unity and the real team relationship among all the stakeholders. The ownership provides opportunities to eliminate the income and wealth inequalities among the employees who bring harmony and increases the motivation and sharing for all the employees to do better for each other, the organizations and for themselves.

Participative decision-making eliminates the slogans and the feelings of the workers that top managers are favoring themselves and the investors concerning the distribution of gains and the pains of the organization. Although, providing ownership opportunity for the employees may partly reduce the unfairness of sharing the gains and pains, without workers full participation in decision making they will not be able to erase these feelings completely.

The full participation in decision-making provides equal partnership for workers, which in turn generates support for implementing decisions. The workers may communicate openly and cooperate fully to implement decisions whose outcomes would be shared by everyone. The organizational decisions, which include participation of all stakeholders, may generate trust and unity among all participants. The more knowledge, information, and support generate not only better decisions, but good relations among the stakeholders.

Another factor that generates real team relations in organization is long-term employment. Long-term employment generates high total quality and competitiveness in an organization through providing opportunities for close relations among workers and managers.

Long-term employment is not a right but also a responsibility for employees to generate economic value to support their long-term employability. This kind of employment relations decrease downsizing and increase job security, which in turn eliminates negative feelings toward top managers whose employees' jobs are under their control rather than at a mercy of the top managers. It also eliminates superficial respect toward managers rather it establishes genuine and mutual respects among the all employees. Long-term employment also eliminates the fear of workers toward their managers because they cannot fire them based on cost cutting or any personal hard feelings. The employees without fear of losing their job and making mistakes, will take risks and communicate more openly, cooperate fully and be more productive and competitive.

The responsibility to support employability provides opportunities for everyone to seek new knowledge, skills and support to increase their total quality and competitiveness. The open communication, full cooperation and sincere help is required to obtain new knowledge, skills and support from each other. Employees will be motivated to establish the real team relations that will help everyone to generate mutual benefits as a giver and as a taker to support their employability. This kind of relation, which is partly the source and the result of long-term employment, increases the total quality and competitiveness of individuals and the organization.

True democratic management practices, through stakeholder's authority, horizontal network circular structure, employee ownership, group decision making and long-term employment provide the main building blocks of real team relations in an organization. The people's authority and horizontal structure erase the command and control hierarchy in relations and establish the open and full communication in an organization regardless of rank and profession. The ownership and group decision-making eliminates the superiority and inferiority among the people and make everyone feels equally important to the organization. Finally, the long-term employment provides security and incentives for all the employees to develop the best knowledge, skills and values for desirable total quality and competitiveness of the organization.

# PART THREE

---

# DEMOCRATIZATION OF MANAGEMENT AND ITS CORE FACTORS

*Everything changes. Nothing remains without change.*
—The Buddah

Although management practices have been changing, they are not changed enough to provide a true democratic environment in any contemporary institution. In order to democratize contemporary management practices, fully, it is also necessary to democratize its key determinants including educational, political, economical, technological and global factors as a whole. This part explains the process of how to democratize management and its core factors in long as well as in short term.

# CHAPTER VII

## Democratization of Management

*Everyone doing his best is not the answer. It is first necessary that people know what to do. Drastic changes are required. The first step in the transformation is to learn how to change.... Long-term commitment to new learning and new philosophy is required of any management that seeks transformation.*
—W. Edwards Deming (1986)

Democratization of management both in state governments and in industrial organizations has been a global phenomenon in recent decades. Many of the governments and organizations of developed and developing nations have been trying to change their management practices for high level of total quality and competitiveness. However, the process of "how" to democratize management practices has not been understood well. Many less democratized countries that abolished their authoritarian governments are trying to democratize their management activities by benchmarking the more democratized countries' management practices. On the other hand politically more democratize countries including United States, Western European countries and Japan are having serious socio-economic problems because of their authoritarian management practices in their industries. It is therefore, necessary to understand the democratization process within a broader global system.

## *Democratization Process*

History of management development indicates that management is continuously changing as we have discussed in Chapter III. In order to be successful in today's hyper-competitive global market the management must be agile and responsive. This can be done through not only changing major practices of management but also changing its key determinants including educational, political, economical, technological, social and global factors which we call core factors. All these changes have to be made by the people who are involved in these activities. Therefore, people have to change their minds first. The best way of changing people's mind can be achieved through education. Education is not only the key factor of changing management practices, but it is also the foundation of all other factors for democratizing contemporary management practices. All these factors have to be changed together interdependently and as a whole for a successful democratization.

The process of democratization of management is a key competency that must be built into institutions as a way of continuous understanding, thinking, deciding and acting. The management must not wait for the democratization to happen by surprise or should not assume it will not happen. Democratization comes from planning. There are always questions about how can we prepare for changes we cannot predict. The only answer to this question is to plan for the best and make changes toward that goal. One must conceptualize the best even though it is uncertain and work towards it.

David Held (1996) and many other studies' authors including Ackoff, 1994; March and Olsen, 1995; LaMarsh, 1995; Senge, 1993; Mazarr, 1999; Minkin, 1995; Halal, 1996, Makridakis, 1990; Gibson, 1997; Thurow, 1996; Dalziel and Schoonover, 1988; Connor, 1992; Peters, 1992; Slater and Bennis, 1990; O'Toole, 1995; Martin, 1996; Lebow and Simon, 1997; Drucker, 1995; Smith, 1995; Marshall, 1995; and Sen, 1996 provide a variety of models for democratization. These models lacked one or more of the core factors of democratization. Democratization requires change, and change does not just happened. It is driven by core activities, which are mainly educational, political, economical, social, technological, and global. Their democratization is explained in the next section. The core activities have to be integrated, and coordinated for stable and successful democratization. These activities can move towards the future on many paths within the upper and lower boundaries, as indicated in Figure 7.1. If the core activities are planned, coordinated and integrated toward true democratic management, democratization of contemporary management activities can reach the upper boundaries, the high level of democratization. The time needed to reach this level will depend mainly on the present conditions of core factors. If the conditions of core factors are relatively more democratic, at present, the time to reach the high level of democratization will be shorter. On the other hand, if the present conditions of core factors are authoritarian, it will take a relatively longer time to reach a high level of democratization.

If there is no plan to change the core activities toward true democratization, authoritarian management activities may stay the same. In this case democratization may occur through revolution or with a total breakdown of the core activities such as organizational bankruptcies and national collapses. Many of the contemporary organizational bankruptcies in the United States are those who cannot make necessary changes in their authoritarian management practices. On the national level the former Soviet Union, and many empires in the past collapsed because of their rigidities in their management practices (Kennedy, 1987).

The present authoritarian conditions of core factors may become more authoritarian by the time authoritarian management practices follow the lower boundaries. In this case democratization may be very difficult even with the revolution, because the core factors are not favorable for the democratization. In this case it will take a long time to educate people about democracy and change their minds for democracy. The current conditions of the core factors in many underdeveloped nations who utilize authoritarian management practices for many years and have no plan to change these practices are good examples for this case.

The area covered by the upper and lower boundaries and the time between present and future periods cannot be clearly defined. This transition field provides uncertainty and confusion. Democratization toward true democratic management through making appropriate changes in core activities may eliminate most of the uncertainty, risk and confusion. The following sections discuss these changes.

## *Democratization of Core Factors*

Democratization of contemporary management activities is complex, continuous and a cumulative process. Its core factors include educational, political, economical, technological, social and global activities that are interdependent and influence each other as shown in Figure 7.2.

It is necessary to democratize all the core factors simultaneously. If only one of them, for example, political activities democratize, but other

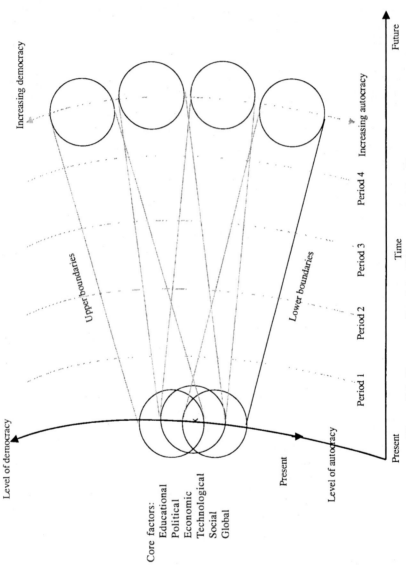

**Figure 7.1. Conceptualization of Democratization Process**

factors are not democratized, democratization of management activities will be minimal or stay the same as we have seen in Figure 7.1. In order to have a successful democratization of management activities, it is necessary to democratize all of its key determinants at the same time.

Education plays an important role in this process. It develops technical and values knowledge that helps people become effective, efficient and ethical. People's knowledge is essential for their political, economical, social, technological and global activities.

All of these activities are rooted in the knowledge of people who practice them. Thus, the change of these activities toward true democratic management has to start with democratization of the educational programs at schools and other institutions. Details of this process involving management activities are explained in Chapter VIII.

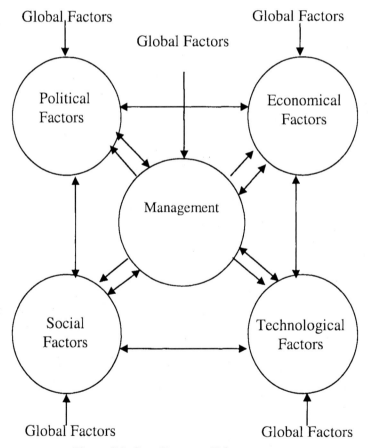

**Figure 7.2. Core Factors of Management**

Political activities at local and national level include the political parties, political institutions and their resources such as capital, and capital goods. Their main objective is to prepare and elect people for the offices of local and national institutions. Elected officials designed laws and regulations and implement them for the well being of the people. Elected officials establish governments for local and national offices to manage political and other activities of the institutions.

The most important institution is the nation's government. The government plays the key role in management activities of all other institutions such as medical, economical, educational and military sectors. In general, the nature of the government's management may also determine the nature of the management activities of other institutions in the nation. Democratic governments most likely make democratic law and regulations, rather than authoritarian laws and regulations. Most of the real world experiences indicate that democracy started with political democratization and then spread on the other activities. In order to democratize management, it may be faster to start democratization of political activities. Political democratization may influence economical, technological and social activities through adopting democratic laws and demonstrating their effects. Details of political democratization are in Chapter IX.

Economic activities include establishing industrial organizations, its organizational structure, employment, ownership, and distributing its gains, as we discussed in Chapter V. Democratization of these activities is directly related to political activities. Democratization of political activities may establish democratic governments through elections. Elected officials may design laws that favor all of the stakeholders through encouraging true democratic activities in an organization. On the other hand, they may favor the stockholders, because of the stockholders' financial and political support of the elected officials such as the case in United States (see Chapter IX). Therefore, to democratize political activities it is necessary for the democratization of economic activities (see Chapter X).

Democratization means change and technology is the major force for making a change. Technology is a key factor to produce goods and services. The nature and quality of goods and services, depends in great extent, on the nature and quality of technologies. Democratization of technology can be achieved through developing and utilizing appropriate technologies that are consumed by the people and are friendly to the environment. Those technologies that are produced for military purposes are often destructive for the people and the environment. They do not contribute in the economy

as much as those commercialized technologies. Although the military technologies are supposed to be used to protect the nation's liberty and sovereignty
their practical applications indicate that they are used mostly for the colo-
nialism that harmed many people throughout the world.

The appropriate or democratic technologies serve all the people and
contribute to economic development without harming others and the environment. Technologies also help people to communicate, learn and diffuse
democratic ideas, values and principles that might be helpful for democratization (see Chapter XI and XII).

Social values are one of the key factors of influencing the management
practices. These values such as love, respect, trust, truthfulness, fairness,
tolerance, responsibility, unity and freedom are accepted universally (see
Table 8.1). People utilize and want them for their life and happiness. However, people's needs and wants are different for their life and happiness.
Some people want material values like money, land and capital products
more than any other values. Some of these people do not have any limit to
their needs and wants. They want as much as they can get. The large
amount of rich people and the degree of their richness are clear indications
of the existence of their unlimited desires for their materialism. On the other
hand some people want to help people as much as possible through dedicat-
ing their life for the others' life, like Mother Teresa and Mahatma Gandhi.

There are, of course, a variety of values between these groups that
people have. However, without a common set of values, institutions become an unstable collection of individuals who cannot coexist easily.
Individuals or small groups that are extremely materialistic can even destroy themselves and their society. History is full of these kinds of examples
(Kennedy, 1987). It may not be an exaggeration to say that our individual
survival as an organization and a nation depends in great extent on our
shared values (Trompenaars and Turner, 1998; Harrison and Huntington,
2000; Sen, 1999; Kinkead, 1959; Kidder, 1994; Deal and Kennedy, 1987).
Democratic values provide such a common value that it allows us to interact successfully. Without such common values, we risk being a destructive
community, nation and global society. It is, therefore, imperative to democratize human values through democratizing education for true democratic
management (see Chapter VIII).

Global factors, including all the international activities such as political,
economical, technological and social play important roles in a nation's democratization. When these activities occur between two or more
organizations and nations, the democratization process spreads around the

globe through demonstration effect. The experience of democratization of one or more institutions and nations becomes a benchmark for others to follow. This process provides some useful insights for the followers and shortens the time for their democratization.

Globalization provides opportunities for people, institutions and nations to select the best of the knowledge and actions required for democratization. As globalization increases, people, institutions and nations tried to equalize their differences in their core activities and harmonize their lives towards democratization (see Chapter XIII).

All of these core factors influence each other's democratization interdependently and positively if the necessary policies are planned and applied simultaneously. Consequently democratization of contemporary management activities becomes reality. The following chapters explain this process in more detail.

# CHAPTER VIII

## Democratization of Management Education

*Modern civilization can survive only if it*
*begins again to educate the heart.*
—E.E. Schumacher

Although the political, economical, social, technological and global activities are the main determinates of management activities, education is the foundation of all of these activities. Education develops knowledge that forms the bases of management decisions and actions. Education, in great measure, forms the technical and values knowledge of people. Technical knowledge mainly helps people to determine the bases of what and how to do things. The behavioral values provide values, which in great measure determine the moral bases of people for determining mainly why to do things. Technical and values knowledge together make us who we are and the kind of people should seeks to create. It is, therefore, necessary to understand the nature of contemporary education and then provide some ideas for its democratization.

### Nature of Management Knowledge

Knowledge may be defined as a capability of knowing what to do, how to do, and why. People, individually, and as a group including a family, an organization and a nation develop and use knowledge to satisfy their physical and emotional needs and wants. Knowing what to do includes the knowledge of selecting and developing things like a profession, product and service. This kind of knowledge determines the physical characteristics of the things like nature, quantity, size, color, price, weight and speed. Knowing how to do includes the knowledge of doing things like developing, producing and distributing goods and services. It is the know-how, which includes all kinds of technologies, capital equipment, process, rules, principles and activities. They can be expressed in verbal statements and other analytical formulas. Knowledge of knowing what and how, can be seen, taught, and transmitted to individuals. They can be standardized, measured, shared and stored for future use. This kind of knowledge is called "explicit knowledge" or technical knowledge in the literature. Utilization of technical knowledge for management is commonly known as scientific management that is discussed in Chapter III (Taylor, 1911).

Knowing why provides the reasons and means for doing things. It influences every human decision and action for selecting, producing and distributing goods and services. It includes the social values, ideas, intuition, imagination, and beliefs. They constitute the non-physical part of knowledge. Unlike technical knowledge, values knowledge also known as behavioral knowledge, cannot be seen, standardized and measured easily. Values cannot be stored physically, but they are embodied in the individual's mind and heart, and reflected in human thoughts, decisions and actions. We call this "values knowledge." It is known as tacit or behavioral knowledge in literature (Polanyi, 1966; Nonaka and Takeuchi, 1995).

Social values are the economical, political, social, technological and ethical characteristics of values knowledge. These characteristics, unlike the physical characteristics of goods and services, are non-physical like love, truth, fairness, freedom, and goodness (see Table 8.1). Utilization of values knowledge for management is called "values knowledge management." In this study we focus on social values that are universally accepted (Rushworth, 1994).

Values knowledge and explicit knowledge determine the whole body of knowledge. Values knowledge constitutes mainly the ideological aspects and the explicit knowledge constitutes the technological aspects. They are complementary to each other. The social values are at the center of every human decision and actions. The vision, mission, and objectives of humans are rooted in these values. Human actions start with these values and end with these values such as goods and services (see Figure 8.1). Although the end products are mostly involved in explicit knowledge, they are guided by

**Table 8.1. Some Universal Values**

| | | |
|---|---|---|
| Adaptability | Democratic | Participative |
| Affirmative | Dependable | Peaceful |
| Altruism | Diligence | Persistence |
| Artistic | Dignity | Politeness |
| Attentive | Discipline | Punctuality |
| Attitude (good) | Efficiency | Quickness |
| Awareness | Empathy | Rational |
| Balanced | Enthusiasm | Realist |
| Beauty | Equality | Reasonableness |
| Benevolence | Fairness | Reliability |
| Boldness | Faithfulness | Resilience |
| Brave | Flexibility | Respectfulness |
| Candid | Goodness | Responsiveness |
| Caring | Gracefulness | Resourcefulness |
| Charisma | Harmony | Safety |
| Cheerfulness | Helpfulness | Security |
| Civility | Honesty | Self-discipline |
| Collaborative | Hopefulness | Sensitivity |
| Collectively | Hospitality | Sincerity |
| Commitment | Humility | Solidarity |
| Communicative | Humor | Stability |
| Compassionate | Impartiality | Steadfastness |
| Competitive | Insightfulness | Tactfulness |
| Consciences | Integrity | Thoughtfulness |
| Consistency | Just | Thrift |
| Constructive | Kindness | Timeliness |
| Coolheadedness | Liveliness | Tolerance |
| Cooperativeness | Love | Trust |
| Cordial | Loyalty | Trustworthiness |
| Courageous | Lawful | Unbiasedness |
| Creativity | Liberal | Unity |
| Courteous | Modesty | Visionary |
| Decency | Openness | Warmth |

the values knowledge. The social values radiate from the center outward like an invisible force and play an important role to produce physical goods and services with explicit knowledge. The explicit and values knowledge constitutes a whole body and soul. One cannot function meaningfully without the other. The explicit knowledge is the knowledge about the object or phenomenon, and the values knowledge is the knowledge that is used to handle what is being focused. Values knowledge assists the explicit knowledge to accomplish the vision, mission, and tasks (Lebow and Simon, 1997).

## *The Importance of Knowledge for Management*

Although both explicit and values knowledge are important for management, the explicit knowledge dominated the knowledge in contemporary management practices. Scientific management, which plays an important role in the development of management, is solely based on explicit knowledge. Frederick W. Taylor (1911) and his followers argued that the explicit knowledge has to be used in every aspect of management for productivity, as we discussed in Chapter III. The managers have to select the best knowledgeable workers and train them for a specific job. On the other hand, Elton Mayo (1933) and his followers argued that behavioral sciences are also important for productivity. The followers of both groups expanded knowledge management in these fields to include a variety of disciplines including sciences and liberal arts courses to broaden the management knowledge (George, 1972; Wren, 1972; Roth, 1993; Crainer, 2000).

During the last two decades, knowledge became the most important factor for determining the comparative advantages of an individual, organization and nation. The management experts write about knowledge for management. Managers and employees try to increase their knowledge throughout the world. The recent hyper competition in the global market and the advancements in information technology have generated new interest and more emphasis on the importance of knowledge in management.

Alvin Toffler (1990) claimed that knowledge is the source of the highest quality power and the key to the power shift that lies ahead. He argued that knowledge is the ultimate replacement of other resources. Robert Reich (1991) argued that the only true competitive advantage would reside among those; he calls "symbolic analysts," who are equipped with the knowledge to identify, solve and broker new problems. James Brian Quin (1992) pointed out that organizations' economics and its producing power depend mainly on its intellectual capabilities rather than its assets such as land, plant, and equipment. He stated that knowledge based intangibles, like technologies know-how, personal creativity and innovation, are the main factors of determining the value of most products and services. Peter Drucker (1993) argued that knowledge is not just another resource alongside labor, capital and land but the only meaningful resource today. He claims that "we are entering the knowledge society and the knowledge workers will play a central role." Every organization in the knowledge society has to be prepared to abandon knowledge that becomes obsolete and learns to create new knowledge. Thomas Stewart (1997) sees knowledge as an intellectual capital, which is the chief ingredient of what we buy and sell, the raw material for the work. It is the most important asset of organizations to generate wealth. They all indicated in their books that the future belongs to people who are endowed with knowledge.

Some other management experts emphasize the learning and creating aspects of knowledge as a competitive advantage. Peter Senge (1990) argued that the "learning organizations" has the capacity for both generative (active) learning and adaptive (passive) learning as the sustainable resources of competitive advantage. Nonaka and Takeuchi (1995) argued that knowledge creation is the most important factor of competitive advantage. He claims that the ability of Japanese organizations to create knowledge is the key for their competitiveness in the global market. Prahalad and Hamel (1990) argued that the core competencies of corporations mainly depend on their collective learning especially, on the coordination of their production skills and integration of multiple streams of technologies. Teece, Pisano, and Shuen (1991) developed the concept of "dynamic capabilities" as the ability of an organization to learn, adapt, change and renew overtime. They indicated that knowledge is a tool, which involves search identification, and problem solving at the organizational level. Stalk, Evans, and Shulman (1992) expanded this view by integrating all kinds of training and support of all involved networks, including design, operations and distribution of products.

Jeromy Rifkin (1993) argues in his book, *The End of Work* that the advancements in information technology displace more jobs than they create. He suggests the massive advance in education to renew and acquire new knowledge is a solution to this problem. Bill Gates (1995) says that in a fast changing world education is the best preparation for being able to adapt. The knowledge in the form of automation and information, which replace low knowledge or skill, repetitive jobs, is the most critical asset for productivity. Arie deGeus (1997) argues that knowledge displaces capital as the scarce production factor, which is the key to corporate success. Those who had knowledge and know-how to apply it would henceforth be the wealthiest members of society. He stated that the only sustainable competitive advantage is the utility to learn faster than one's competitor.

Rose and Nicholl (1997) argues that the speed at which the world is changing demands an ability to learn faster and provide the essential core skills of learning fast and thinking creatively. Knowledge is doubling every two to three years in almost every occupation. People who are not aggressively and continuously upgrading their knowledge and skills are not staying in the same place. They fall behind and are replaced by people with new knowledge. The new strategic resources are ideas and information that come out of knowledge people.

Many academic institutions as well as corporations start emphasizing knowledge that enhances the competitiveness. Some universities and colleges are establishing alliances with corporations to customize instructions and work as a team with corporate educational staff (AACSB, Newsline, 1997). Many corporations establish their own universities like Arthur D. Little's School of Management and collaborate with other universities locally and globally to emphasize global competitiveness. These programs focus on management of organizational learning and creation of knowledge as a team rather than as an individual. Their objective is to integrate individual or partial knowledge into common practice by the whole community, which is called knowledge creation or community learning.

Many organizations establish new positions like chief of knowledge officer (CKO) or chief of learning officer (CLO) indicating the importance of knowledge in management. These officers manage the learning, transferring and utilizing existing knowledge and provide opportunities to innovate new knowledge through alliances with other global and local institutions to increase the organization's competitiveness. The commission for a Nation of Lifelong Learners report that over the next decade, 75 percent of the American workforce will need significant retraining (*Fortune*, January 12, 1997).

Parallel to explicit knowledge, values knowledge has also been tried for utilization in management. The studies, generally known as the behavioral or human relations, approach to management argued that people are the key to productivity (see Chapter III). According to advocates of this group (Mayo, 1933; Fallett, 1949; Maslow, 1943; Argyris, 1957; McGregor, 1960; and Herzberg, 1968), explicit knowledge in the form of technology, work rules, and standards do not guarantee good job performance. Instead, success depends on motivated individuals who were committed to organizational objectives. Only a manager's sensitivity to individual concerns can foster the cooperation necessary for high productivity. They believe that successful management depends largely on one's ability to understand and work with people who have a variety of backgrounds, needs, perceptions, and aspirations.

The progress of the humanistic approach to management from the human relation's movement to organizational behavior has greatly influenced contemporary management theory and practices (George, 1972; Wren, 1972; Roth, 1993; Crainer, 2000). Recently, Slater and Bennis (1989; 1990) argued that it is the system of values in the form of democracy that can successfully cope with the solving demands of contemporary civilization in business, as well as in government. Many other researchers' works indicate that those corporations who are utilizing values knowledge achieved, relatively, better results for productivity and competitiveness (Terpstra, 1978; Deal and Kennedy, 1982; Peters and Waterman, 1982; Blanchard and O'Connor, 1995; Lebow and Simon, 1997; Trompenaars and Turner, 1998). Furthermore many studies indicated that utilization of values knowledge for management was the main determinant of Japanese economic growth and competitiveness in the global market (Sen, 1992 and 2001; Ozaki, 1991; Nonaka and Takeuchi, 1995). Recently, Nissan in Britain and NUMMI in America achieved such outstanding productivity results by utilizing the Japanese management system that utilizes values knowledge more extensively, relative to U.S. and Western nations (Womak, Jones, and Roos, 1990). These practices clearly indicate that universal values knowledge increase productivity and competitiveness.

There is general agreement among many management experts and practitioners that the knowledge is the main source of competition. The individuals, organization and nations competing in global market have been looking for ways to increase their knowledge capabilities for generating comparative advantages in the global market. However, the review of the existing management studies and practices indicate that efforts to create and utilize new knowledge had been concentrated mostly on the explicit knowledge (see Chapter III). Utilization of values knowledge for management has been neglected. It seems that the importance of values knowledge for productivity and competitiveness is still not well understood by many management practitioners. The following section provides some insights for this purpose.

# *Values Knowledge is Crucial for Management Practices*

Values knowledge plays a very important role in every aspect of management. It provides reason, beliefs and means for developing visions, missions and objectives of individuals and the organization. It also guides people to achieve them. Every managerial decision and action required for producing, distributing and consuming goods and services start and end with the values knowledge (see Figure 8.1). Values knowledge provides the means and reasons for determining human objectives and guides human actions to achieve objectives successfully. The decision for selecting and developing product or service, technology and other elements of production including

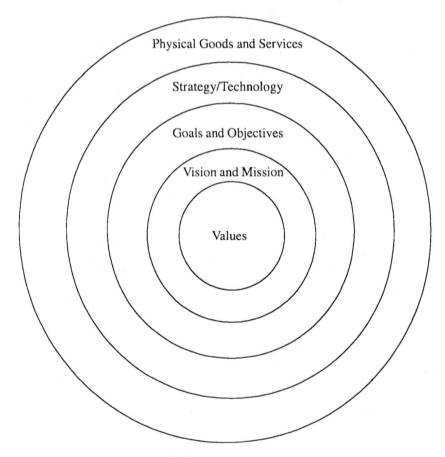

**Figure 8.1. The Role of Values in Management**

employment, teamwork, human relations and productivity are heavily influenced by the values knowledge. Although the free market economy has been used as a main reason for these decisions, the decision-makers-values knowledge provides the foundation and guidance for them. Values knowledge provides a sense of common direction for all employees and guidelines for their day-to-day work.

People in every society hold certain values about themselves, their families, organizations community and nation (Terpstra, 1978; Trompenaas and Turner, 1998). The individuals' social values determine the norms and culture of a society and provide balance and continuity for their existence. The culture of the family, organization and nation is relatively stable when their values are similar.

When the social values of people in family organizations and nations fail to match, the unity and stability will be lost in that society. They will not be able to achieve common objectives and cannot generate motivation for successful results.

The people who are utilizing values like honesty, fairness and caring make decisions toward objectives that these values represent. On the other hand, people who are self-centered and do not care for others, but care only for their own interests, make decisions to favor their own benefits. These kinds of decisions generate inequalities and related problems among employees in an organization. As we discussed in Chapter IV during the last two decades, the top managers of many organizations in the United States have made decisions to lay-off many employees. These layoffs cause many employees financial and social hardship, while the top managers' and stockholders' income increased. The values knowledge of decision-makers has played the key role for these kinds of decisions concerning who will gain or lose and by how much.

Technologies are developed and utilized together with ideologies. Without ideologies technologies cannot be developed and utilize meaningfully. Chinese ancient technologies were not utilized and did not advance because of their ideologies were dominated by social values rather than material values (Peyrefitte, 1992). Without values knowledge, the technology becomes a random force, which may eventually destroy its owners, others and the society in general. Without values knowledge, human beings use technology like untrained animals, which can even kill others for their own interests. The values knowledge leads and controls technology through providing reasons and means for it. With the absence of values knowledge, technology dominates decisions and directs human beings, organizations and nations toward unknown events. Some of these unknown events including global warming, environmental hazards and nuclear weapons build up may generate catastrophic results for everyone in the world in the long-term.

Social values provide the inner foundations for sustainable competitiveness of all organizations. They determine the people's interaction with each other that produces sustainable comparative advantage for any organization or nation. People who have values like diligence, punctuality, timeliness, agility, responsibility, cooperativeness and discipline, get better results and achieve higher competitiveness relative to others who do not have these values. People in an organization who have values like sharing gains and pains, and caring for each other establish trust, mutual friendship and good relations with each other. People who have good relations with their teammates commit themselves to achieve common objectives. People with democratic values like fairness, openness and respect for others generate good relations and unity among the team members, which motivate them to generate desirable total quality and competitiveness.

The organizations that utilize values, knowledge as a team, create comparative advantages for the organization and provide a better life for its employees as explained. All the stakeholders in an organization, including managers, stockholders, employees, and customers in the community, act like partners. They ultimately try to achieve the common goal for desirable total quality and competitiveness. They prosper and live better because of the organization, but so should the others affected by its activities (Freeman, 1984). The people's partnership would be a true collaboration with the active engagement of all parties bringing the best of whom they are, what they know, and what they can do to that collaboration. The people who have the democratic values act ethically and show each other love and appreciation as they interact. The democratic values generate the greatest source of human motivation to work productively and happily (Likert, 1967; Lebow and Simon, 1997; and Halal, 1996). Teamwork, which has been practice as a new tool for productivity and competitiveness in organizations, must be rooted in genuine respect and understanding. Relationships among team members must be grounded in democratic values. Neglect of what is genuinely human is a major reason why so many people in American business now feel more victimized than helped by the latest management practices such as restructuring, reengineering and downsizing (Hayes and Abernathy, 1980; Etzioni, 1993; Collis, 1998; and Estes, 1996).

The social values like truth, beauty, goodness and unity structure all of human life and provide the foundations for sustainable human and corporate excellence (Morris, 1997). This is because they are the deepest touchstones for the ultimate individual fulfillment and happiness. Values knowledge is genuinely human and important for all the management issues. As long as human beings do work in organization, produce and consume products and services of the organizations, the values knowledge must be the most important issues and must not be forgotten.

## *Developing and Utilizing Values Knowledge for Management Education*

The main sources of values are the family, organization, nation and the globe. Every individual in each of these institutions develops their own values interdependently and continuously. Each individual in a family influences the other families in the community or organization to develop organizational values. The organizations influence each other and families in their community to establish national or regional values. Every nation also influences each other to establish shared universal values (see Figure 8.2).

Education in schools, family, workplaces community, government, media and religion organizations are the key for developing values (see Figure 8.3). In order to adapt, improve and integrate values knowledge for management the education in these institutions has to be emphasized. The contemporary management (business) programs at universities and colleges are the main source of the management education. The management training programs of the organization also contribute to management education. However, currently none of these programs includes values knowledge. As seen earlier, all these programs are dominated by the explicit knowledge. Some of management programs at universities and colleges include business ethics and morality in business, as an elective.

But, these courses do not treat values knowledge by integrating them with the functional course of management such as marketing, finance, operations and others (Weiss, 1998; Martin, 1989). It is generally assumed that the values knowledge is a liberal arts subject and has to be included in the liberal arts core of the management programs. However, even the liberal arts program does not cover values knowledge specifically, but include it in some course like philosophy, sociology, religion and others. There is no attempt to treat values knowledge fully and integrate them in management functional course.

Recently, Assembly of American Collegiate School of Business (AACSB *Newsline*, 1997) insisted that management education must be based on the liberal arts and required that about 50 percent of the coursework must be in liberal arts. However, the courses students take in the liberal arts subject appears to have little or no relations to their studies in management. On the other hand, if any integration has been made, liberal arts become a list of skills that are instrumental to management functions (Porter and McKibbin, 1998; and Davis and Botkin, 1994).

Liberal arts programs must be redesigned to include the specific and broad values knowledge courses, including universal values. These courses have to be integrated with the management course to establish the background of values knowledge of the management education. Every functional course has to be designed together with the values knowledge and their practical utilization have to be illustrated together in the real world applications as a whole. There are general exceptions among many educators that those "who have been trained to think upon one subject or one subject only, will never be a good judge even in that one" (Newman. 1992). Management education is incomplete without a broader integration and utilization of the explicit and values knowledge together as a whole.

Values knowledge has to be also included in training programs of the contemporary organizations. These programs have to be established to train all the employees at work places. Many of the contemporary training programs at the workplaces are concentrated on explicit knowledge. These organizations neither teach nor promote values knowledge at work places, formally. It is assumed that employees know values knowledge and they utilize it appropriately. There is neither any requirements nor incentives for the utilization of values knowledge.

The organizations have to design values knowledge training programs together with the explicit knowledge training programs. The organization should cooperate with colleges and universities for the design and teaching of these training programs. The organizations should promote values knowledge at work places through incentives and by other means. Most importantly, values knowledge has to be integrated into the management policies, rules and regulations of organizations. They have to be required, legalized and controlled by management.

The training programs for values knowledge has to start with top managers and must be followed by everyone else who works at that organization. Top managers have to utilize and practice values knowledge and be a model for the other employees. However, learning and practicing values knowledge is everybody's job at work places. Everyone should learn, implement and be responsible for establishing values-knowledge-based management practices at work places.

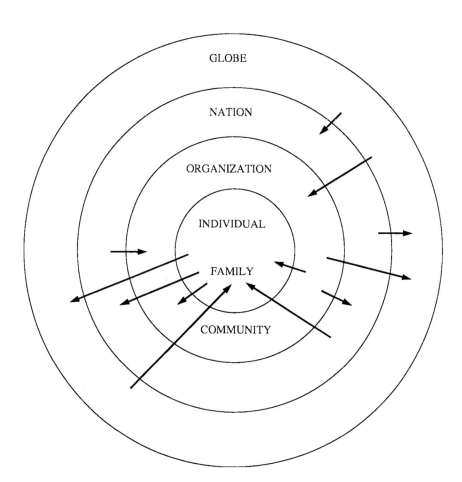

**Figure 8.2. Source of Values**

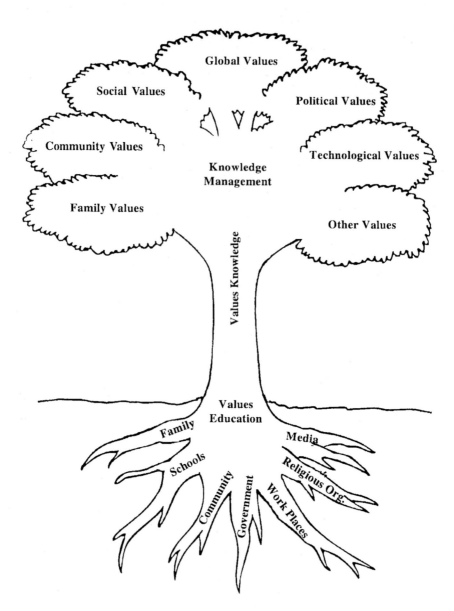

**Figure 8.3. Determinants of Knowledge Management**

Values knowledge has to be a part of the education at high schools and secondary schools. The contemporary high school and secondary schools in the U.S. do not include values knowledge in their programs (Kilpatrick, 1992; and Reavis, 1992). The main reasons for this negligence are that school administrations, teachers and parents could not agree on what values to teach and how to teach them (Lickona, 1992). This argument has lost its validity. It has been demonstrated that values knowledge can also be transferred like explicit knowledge. NUMMI's workforce was comprised of 80 percent of the old GM workers. They simply relearn the basic values to operate in the team through utilizing Japanese management practices (Womak, Jones, and Roos, 1990). Similar practices took place in Britain and many other nations. These examples indicate that the universal values can be transferred and adapted to the local conditions. Thus, the values knowledge can be taught at any organizations regardless of their origins. Furthermore, globalization provides new opportunities for individuals, organizations and nations to transfer, learn and adapt universal values. As we enter into the 21st century, a global society is becoming a reality and sharing its values knowledge a possibility. In a shared values environment individuals, employees and managers start to act in ways that teach the people around them what the new values are and which ones are acceptable. The values knowledge education has to be started at home, at schools, workplaces and utilized for all the management activities. The fastest learner and user of the values knowledge might be the most productive and competitive of the future (Drucker, 1994; and Rose and Nicholl, 1997).

Developing values knowledge management education may take a long time. The seriousness of contemporary problems caused, in great measure, by the authoritarian management practices, require immediate changes in management education. These changes have to be taken at home, schools and work places (see Chapter XIV).

The educational activities can be changed first by the people who influence the management education the most. This should start through educating teachers and managers in democratic education at every institution including government, organizations, and family. The government officials including the president and his/her advisors have to be educated in democratic values. They have to start reading the world's great thinkers, from the West, including Plato, Aristotle, Kant and Dewey, and from the East, including Confucius, Laotzu and Buddha, who have all been strong advocates of giving conscious attention to value formation and focusing human energies on living a happy life. These thinkers tried to answer questions such as

"What is a good and noble life?" "What do people need to be truly happy?" and "What do people need to keep from self-destruction?" Broadly speaking, their answers to these questions is to know what a good life is and to work to conform oneself to that ideal—an educational task. Secondly, the leaders should read the recent publications pointing out the seriousness of the problems that authoritarian management has generated. Some of these materials are provided in the references.

Although values knowledge management education is the key for democratization of management, the core activities such as political, economical, social, technological and global have to be democratized to accompany value knowledge management education for a successful democratization of management. The following chapters cover the democratization of these core activities.

---

# CHAPTER IX

# Political Democratization

*There is one thing more powerful than all the armies of the world;*
*and that is an idea whose time has come.*
                                                                —Victor Hugo

P olitical democratization plays an important role in industrial
democratization. In fact democratization process mostly starts first
with the political democratization and spreads to other areas. The
historical analysis of democratization supports this argument (Haggard and
Webb, 1994; Haggard and Kaufman, 1995; and Huntington, 1991). The
United States, Western European countries and Japan have tried to
democratize their political institutions first. Many less democratize nations
and others, that abolished their authoritarian governments, are trying to
democratize their management activities by benchmarking against more
democratize nations. The following sections explain the contemporary
democratization activities, and the problems associated with them and provide
some solutions.

## *Recent Democratization Activities*

In the last two decades, many governments and organizations throughout
the world have been experiencing profound changes in their management
practices (see Table 9.1). Most of these changes involved the widespread

*Democratic Management*

## Table 9.1. Nations Start Democratization

| Nation | Date | | | | | | | |
|--------|------|------|------|------|------|------|------|------|
| | 1790 | 1848 | 1900 | 1919 | 1940 | 1960 | 1975 | 1990 |
| United States | X | X | X | X | X | X | X | X |
| Canada | | | X | X | X | X | X | X |
| Switzerland | X | X | X | X | X | X | X | X |
| Great Britain | | X | X | X | X | X | X | X |
| France | X | | X | X | | X | X | X |
| Belgium | | X | X | X | | X | X | X |
| Netherlands | | X | X | X | | X | X | X |
| Denmark | | | X | X | | X | X | X |
| Piedmont/Italy | | | X | X | | X | X | X |
| Spain | | | | | | | | X |
| Portugal | | | | | | | | X |
| Sweden | | | X | X | X | X | X | X |
| Norway | | | | X | | X | X | X |
| Greece | | | X | | | X | | X |
| Austria | | | | X | | X | X | X |
| Germany, West | | | | X | | X | X | X |
| Germany, East | | | | X | | | | X |
| Poland | | | | X | | | | X |
| Czechoslovakia | | | | X | | | | X |
| Hungary | | | | | | | | X |
| Bulgaria | | | | | | | | X |
| Romania | | | | | | | | X |
| Turkey | | | | | | X | X | X |
| Latvia | | | | | | | | X |
| Lithuania | | | | | | | | X |
| Estonia | | | | X | | | | X |
| Finland | | | | X | X | X | X | X |
| Ireland | | | | | X | X | X | X |
| Australia | | | | X | X | X | X | X |

Table 9.1. Nations Start Democratization (*cont.*)

| Nation | Date | | | | | | | |
|--------|------|------|------|------|------|------|------|------|
| | 1790 | 1848 | 1900 | 1919 | 1940 | 1960 | 1975 | 1990 |
| New Zealand | | | | X | X | X | X | X |
| Chile | | | X | X | | X | | X |
| Argentina | | | X | X | | | | X |
| Brazil | | | | | | X | | X |
| Uruguay | | | | X | X | X | | X |
| Paraguay | | | | | | | | X |
| Mexico | | | | | X | X | X | X |
| Colombia | | | | X | X | X | X | X |
| Costa Rica | | | | X | X | X | X | X |
| Bolivia | | | | | | X | | X |
| Venezuela | | | | | | X | X | X |
| Peru | | | | | | X | | X |
| Ecuador | | | | | | X | | X |
| El Salvador | | | | | | X | | X |
| Nicaragua | | | | | | | | X |
| Honduras | | | | | | | | X |
| Jamaica | | | | | | | X | X |
| Dominican Republic | | | | | | | | X |

trend away from authoritarian management practices toward democratic management (Haggard and Kaufman, 1995; Fukuyama, 1992; and Dankwart, 1990).

Beginning in the late 1970s and early 1980s, many Latin American countries including Argentina, Brazil, Peru, Mexico and Chile started establishing democratic governments. During the 1980s, some Asian countries including South Korea, Taiwan, Thailand, the Philippines, and Turkey, Pakistan struggled to establish civilian governments. In the late 1980's, authoritarian governments in Eastern Europe and in the Soviet Union collapsed mainly because of their poor economic performance. These activities, which Samuel Huntington (1991) called the "third wave," put pressure on many of the

authoritarian governments of Africa and the Middle East for democratization. Rustow Dankwart (1990) calls this development "global democratic
revolution."

In the early 1990s, and presently, many of theses countries are still
trying to improve their political democratization. Others are abolishing authoritarian management practices and making reforms toward political
democratization (Haggard and Webb, 1994). The democratization activities
are increasing with a fast growth rate (see Figure 9.1).

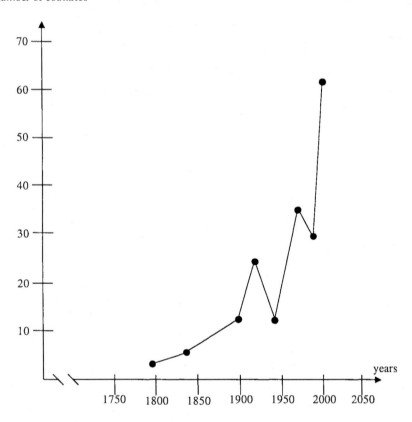

**Figure 9.1. Growth of Worldwide Democratization**

Parallel to political democratization, there have been even more dramatic changes toward industrial democratization in these countries. They have been privatizing their businesses, organizations, adopting more liberal trade policies, and seeking broader collaborations with other nations for economic growth. The governments and business organizations seek better management practices, to increase their competitiveness through globalization (Carnoy, 1995; and Budge, 1996).

Political factors play an important role in industrial democratization. Top managers of elected governments ordinarily seek opportunities to increase the economic performance of their economy. These elected officials who cannot provide economic growth and prosperity for their citizens often fail to win in the next elections, and sometimes necessitate early elections or military takeovers, mostly in developing countries (Haggard and Kaufman, 1995; Fukuyama, 1992; and Dankwart, 1990). Many developing countries try to democratize their governments by adopting new policies and laws to liberalize their trade activities and privatize their national industries. They establish new policies for joint operations, transfer of new technologies, and knowledge.

Political democratization promotes economical and other democratization activities. More democratized nations such as the United States, Western European countries, and Japan have been transferring economic and technical resources for their economic and technological developments. Recent alliances of the North American Free Trade Agreement (NAFTA), the European Economic Community (EEC), and the Association of South East Asian Nations (ASEAN) were mainly established for these purposes. Relatively more democratized governments have historically had to develop institutions and pursue policies that reflect the democratic vision and, at the same time, they tried to create a suitable environment for capital accumulation (Bowles and Gintis, 1986). In the information age, governments shape the policies for domestic business organizations and foreign business enterprises to interact through new policies. These policies often promote democratization for better collaborations and joint operations. Less democratic governments often adopt new policies in alignment with more democratic countries' policies to increase their trade as well as political conditions favoring democratization. For example, many West European countries including Bulgaria, Romania, Turkey and others have been trying to democratize some of their political, economical, and other activities to become a member of the European Union. These kinds of collaborative activities encourage and increase political democratization globally.

In spite of considerable amount of political democratization throughout the world, the contemporary political practices are still authoritarian and partially authoritarian which is commonly called representative political democracy. Both of these political practices have provided enormous opportunities for developing relatively high level of total quality and competitiveness for many nations and organizations. But, they also cause very serious problems that are covered in the following sections. In order to eliminate these problems and establish better conditions for developing higher total quality and competitiveness, the current political activities have to be changed. The last section of this chapter provides some guidelines for the change.

## *Authoritarian Political Practices and the Problems*

Authoritarian political practices have been based on authority. The authority of decision making of important issues belongs to one person or a few people. They manage from the top of the pyramidal hierarchy and others implement their decisions. They retain all of the authority and responsibility as a ruler, and the rest of the people have to comply. The rulers are not elected by the people. They are usually selected or appointed by special groups that have the political, economical or militaristic power. They are mostly responsible to these groups and work mainly to satisfy their needs.

The authoritarian political management has been practiced in governments of the Soviet Union, many African, Islamic, Asian and Latin American countries and have generated severe economic, political and social problems. The intensity of these problems grew to such a level governments of the Soviet Union and Eastern European countries collapsed in the late 1980s. The management objectives of these governments were to achieve equality and quality at the expense of political and economic liberty that is the essence of communism. They have neither achieved the equality nor quality to satisfy their people.

The governments of many other countries practicing authoritarian management were experiencing similar problems. During the last two decades, many Latin American countries, including Argentina, Brazil, Peru, Mexico and Chile; some Asian countries including South Korea, Taiwan, Thailand, the Philippines, Pakistan and Turkey, struggled to establish democratic governments (Haggard and Webb, 1994; Haggard and Kaufman, 1995; Neher and Marley, 1995; Luckham and White, 1996). In the early 1990's and presently, many of these countries are still trying to improve their democratization. Others are abolishing authoritarian management practices and are making some democratic reforms toward democratization. They are hoping that establishing representative democratic management will help eliminating many of their political and economical problems and satisfy people's needs and wants better. However, representative democratic management practices have also generated very serious inequality problems in many industrialized countries (see Chapter IV). The following section explains these practices and shows how these practices and the authoritarian management practices support each other and favor the politicians, owners and the top managers.

## *Representative Democratic Management Practices and the Problems*

The representative democratic management practices are partly based on "democracy," which means "people's rule." President Lincoln described the democracy as "government of people, by the people, for the people" in his Gettysburg address of November 1863. In this sense, the contemporary democratic management practices are not a real democracy at all; they are a representative democratic management. In the representative democratic management practices, people exercise their political rights indirectly through elected representatives. The representatives have the authority to make the major decisions. The nature of the representatives and their elections may vary. Members of the United States Senate represent the people of their states, and members of the House represent the people within their congressional district. The President of the United States is considered the representative of all the people, and elected by the electoral delegates, but not by the majority of people's vote as we have seen in the recent presidential elections. The candidate can win the popular vote, but cannot be the President without winning the majority of the electoral delegates. On the other hand the candidate can win the majority of the electoral delegates without winning the popular vote. In short, in the United States, the delegates elect the President, not the people.

In some countries, each political party leader selects the representatives for each province and after that, the people in that province select the representatives for that province. The party leaders are elected by the party delegates of each province, rather than by the people. The representatives then elect the President at the parliament; they are not elected by the people. The representatives then elect the Prime Minister and the President at the parliament. The people in these countries cannot elect the President or the representatives directly. This kind of management may be called a semi-representative democracy or a semi-authoritarian management since the party leaders have a strong influence on the representatives. If representatives do not vote according to the wishes of the party leaders, they may not be elected by the party leaders in the next elections. This kind of practice has caused so many political and social problems that the military has intervened many times in recent decades to restore law and order and helped return democracy in many countries (Haggard and Webb, 1994; Haggard and Kaufman, 1995; and Dahl, 1989).

Representative management has been practiced in the governments of Western Europe, North and South America, Australia, New Zealand and Japan. The governments of these countries have provided a relatively higher degree of quality and liberty. The high quality was achieved mainly through the authoritarian management in the industrial organizations. The representative management of government and the authoritarian management of the organizations have supported each other in many ways. The representatives make it possible through laws and regulations for organizations to act freely and to determine the profit level and its distribution through free market. The corporate or capital tax policies have not changed the ultimate outcomes (Batra, 1996; Galbraith, 1998).

The representative democratic management of government and the authoritarian management of private organizations work well to create quality (income and wealth). However, they generate economic and political inequalities between the privileged group (representatives, top managers and the shareholders) and the employees and the people. The high quality helps the representatives, politically and economically. The high level of economic growth has always played a positive role for the elections. The poor economic growth caused many representatives to lose elections. Consequently, the representative management of government helped the authoritarian management of industrial organizations, in many ways, to achieve high profit.

They provided full freedom of business through a free market with a limited tax. The authoritarian management of industrial organizations supported many representatives by financing their election expenses. They work in harmony to achieve a high level of quality and freedom for themselves and for the small portion of the population who are associated with them. On the other hand, the large portion of the population did not have the high quality and the liberty as much as the privileged groups.

The government of the U.S.A decreased the income tax rates for the high-income group from 70 percent to 40 percent during the period of 1980 to 1995. They argue that lowering tax rate for the rich will increase the personal saving rates. In reality the personal saving rate fell from 8.2 percent to 4.3 percent during the same period (Batra, 1996). As income tax rate of top-bracket decreased from about 70 percent to about 40 percent during the same period the investment rate did not increase, but decreased from about 12.5 percent to about 10 percent. When the high income groups of 5 percent of the population, can achieve their target savings, regardless of the income tax rate, they do not raise their savings, but they spend the extra income of the consumption of luxury goods, such as gold, art objects, antiques, yachts, financial and commodity speculations (Veblen, 1934; Galbraith, 1998). The government has favored the industrial organizations by reducing their corporate income taxes during the period of 1955 and 1985 from 27.3 percent to 8.4 percent but the investment rates increased only 2.4 percent during the same period. It was clear that the government's hope for increasing investments through corporate tax cut did not come through; but it did help corporations to increase their profits. This fact hase never changed the minds of politicians for asking further corporate tax cuts (Makin and Ornstein, 1994). The government also helps to cut taxes on capital gains. All of these cuts did not help to promote savings, and investments, but helped the high income and the wealthiest to increase their income and wealth. Almost all other taxes such as sales, excise, and Social Security—which are regressive—hurt the poor the most. These policies generate further increase in inequality gap between rich and poor groups.

History shows that authoritarian management practices of governments, which generate extreme inequalities, are the main causes of the collapse of the governments and civilizations. In ancient Egypt, India, China, Europe, and Japan gross disparities of income and wealth demolished their societies. It causes peaceful rebellions, bloodshed and violence (Kennedy, 1987). In modern eras inequality has caused speculative battles, poverty and depressions. It destroyed Soviet Communism and threatens capitalist nations. Political democratization toward true democracy is not an option, but imperative for the solutions of the world's political, economical and social problems.

## *Democratization of Political Activities*

Practicing some of the ideas and principles of democracy in modern world has started two hundreds years ago in the United States. Although many developing nations have been following the experiences of the United States and the other countries, these political practices have not changed enough to accompany recent changes in economy and technology. The political democratic process including party establishment, appointing and selecting candidates for the public offices and the election process itself are too old, unfair and can not provide opportunities for electing the best candidates. Even in the United States, which is supposed to be the leader and the originator of the modern democracy, the political activities are not working well. The most recent presidential election between the Republican candidate George Bush and Democratic candidate Al Gore have clearly demonstrated that American political activities are not working well at all, and they have to be changed.

The contemporary political activities in the United States are designed for the conditions that existed in America for more then two hundred years ago. The relevant political, economical, technological, social and global conditions have been changing drastically. The people are much more knowledgeable today than two hundred years ago. They observe and understand that this is not a real democracy. Most people are unhappy about the political activities and they want to change them. But, they expect the government to make the changes. They are right on this expectation; if the government belongs to the people, it should do what the most people want them to do. However, practical experiences do not show this at all.

Unfortunately, most of the contemporary democratic governments throughout the world do not represent the interests of the majority of their people. Most of the government officials try to satisfy the needs and wants of the party officials, corporations, and wealthy elite that play major roles for their elections. The economic powers of the elites and elite organizations control the political activities. Only the candidates of elites are able to win the election. The other candidates who do not support the interest of the elites cannot win, because they do not have enough financial resources for the expensive campaigns. Thus, this political democracy becomes a rich man's democracy. Although the poor and the middle classes are in the majority, the candidates that they elect are the candidates of the elites. People who understand this game do not even vote. They lose their hopes in politics and live like a second-class citizen in their own country.

The governments of elite groups manage the national affairs mainly for the interest of elite. Their selfish interests become the national interest. The interests of majority of people, such as the security of employment, safety of workplaces, safety and quality of goods and services, social and economic equality, protection of the environment and other public issues become secondary. The basic civil right laws, environmental and consumer legislations were laid down during the 1960s and early 1970s in the United States. Over the last three decades there has been almost no changes on these laws. During the last two decades the electoral process has increasingly come under the control of business organizations' lobbyist and political action committees that have used their superior financial resources to manipulate public opinion to influence candidates. The political activities reinforced the economic inequality and generated a vicious circle. Most people believing that elections are being controlled by "special interests," have stopped participating in political activities, reinforcing the domination of the same interests (Derber, 1998).

Managing the political activities in the United States is similar to the management activities of industrial organizations. The top managers of government including the President, Vice President, Senators and the Representatives try to satisfy the interests of their own and the interests of their financial supporters of rich people and the elite organizations. The elites and the elite organizations becomes like stockholders who invest in electing the political candidates, just like the stockholders who invest in corporations and play important role in selecting their top managers. In return, top managers try to maximize the interests of stockholders, sometimes, at the expense of other stakeholders such as employees, consumers and the community. Just like the top managers of industrial organizations, the top managers of political parties and government officials try to satisfy the interests of their stockholders (elites and elite organizations) first, and the interest of the public, sometimes at the expense of the public. Thus, in reality, the contemporary political activities establish governments that represent the interests of special interest groups, rather than representing the interests of the general public. Consequently, the current political and economic inequalities generated mainly by the contemporary political activities, increase rather than decrease.

Contemporary political activities do not provide any real opportunity for most of the qualified candidates unless they join the elite groups and support their interests. As a result contemporary political activities cause many qualified candidates to stay out of politics. Thus, the best candidate, not from the most diversified large groups rather from a small group, which represents mainly the elite.

Unfortunately, most of the people are biased toward themselves, friends, relatives and others who provide financial or other supports for them. Most political officials in many democratic countries are helped by corporations and wealthy people. In turn, political officials pay back to the corporations and wealthy people through influencing the laws and regulations by favoring their interests. They also help their relatives and friends by using their political influence. These activities caused sever inequality and corruption problems in many countries throughout the world. In order to eliminate these problems political activities should be democratize. The political activities should not be controlled by corporations and the rich. The political parties should belong to everyone. The necessary financial and other resources necessary for political activities should be provided to everyone equally. Otherwise, the corporations and people who have the money control the political parties.

The people should select party officials and delegates directly. The delegates should not be elected by national leaders of the parties or any other party officials. The political parties and the candidates for any public office should not get any financial aid from the corporations and rich people. Republican presidential candidate John McCain and Green Party presidential candidate Ralph Nader, strongly argued that candidates for public offices must not get any financial aid from the corporations and from the wealthy people in order to have a fair election. Their ideas not only provide opportunities to have a fair election for the public offices, but also will eliminate part of the inequality and corruption problems.

Democratically elected representatives for local and national governments should not make all the decisions on behalf of people. People, should vote for important issues directly by themselves. In many Scandinavian countries people make important decisions by themselves through referendums. These referendums are made five or six times for every year. These kinds of referendums can be increased to allow people to make decisions for themselves and by themselves. This is the real democracy and can be done easily and economically in this information age.

Unfortunately, most well qualified people do not get into politics, because they do not have enough money to contribute to a party and support the campaign activities. Even some of those with enough money do not get involved in politics, because the contemporary political activities are not fair and clean. There is a lot of "give and take" and "scratch my back and I will scratch yours" deals which are taking place in contemporary political activities. Providing public financial support for the candidates and eliminating corporations and rich people's influences from political activities will encourage many qualified people to run for the public offices. This will increase the chances of having more people in politics with a greater commitment to democracy. Consequently, this process may increase democratization and productivity in general.

The current political activities in the United States mainly allow only two parties to win major elections. The other "alternative" parties are not included in the presidential debates. The new parties like Green Party do not have the similar financial resources like the other two major parties. They cannot win without getting the same financial support of the two popular parties. Changing the current financing system of political parties and the elections will provide equal chances to run elections fairly and successfully.

The President and the Vice President have to be elected by the Representatives and the Senators. Electing the President by the house or parliament like the European political democracies will make it easier, cheaper and more convincing. Besides, the President should not be given the power that he/she has presently. It is too dangerous, unproductive and undemocratic to provide a person such enormous rights and responsibilities. Democracy provides rights and responsibilities to all the people not a person. The President's rights and responsibilities have to be transferred to the house, like in European democracy.

Similarly the present Senators and Representative have to join together and form only one group as Representatives of the people. Their numbers and the rights and responsibilities of their positions have to be reduced through allowing people to make some of the important decisions by themselves through voting directly. Utilization of information technology for the election and decision-making will allow more people to provide inputs for political activities. Large inputs from large group of people will increase democratization and the productivity of the institutions (see Chapter XIII). As the utilization of information technology in political practices increase, the participation of people into the elections and decision-making will increase. Consequently, the movement of democratization toward real democracy will be accelerated and enlarged. This way, people will make decisions for themselves, by themselves, rather than someone else making decisions for them.

As the numbers of people participating increases and their knowledge increases, the chances to reach true democracy will increase and become reality. Otherwise, the current political activities that have been practiced for two hundred years will never result in real democracy. The current political activities are generating and accumulating many political, economical, technological and social problems that need fixing, both cooperatively and democratically so the future of humanity will be protected. Delaying political democratization will increase the current political problems that may cause revolutions.

However, only the political democratization alone cannot solve the current problems. Economical democratization has to be accompanied with political democratization for a successful democratization process. The next chapter explains the economical democratization.

# CHAPTER X

# Economical Democratization

*New economies should be free, fair and sustainable.*

Economic activities including production, and consumption of goods and services play a key role of satisfying people's needs and wants. The degree of quality, equality, and liberty aspects of total quality depends, mainly, on the nature of economical activities. Economic success is crucial for political success and for the success of management. Therefore, the management of organizations and nations is given high priority to achieve economic success.

The capitalist countries, including the United States, Western European countries, and Japan who are using "free market" (capitalist) economics, have relatively higher total quality in terms of Per Capita Income (PCI) or Gross Domestic Product (GDP) per capita. Presently, most of the developing nations and the big ten nations (BINs) including South Korea, Mexico, Brazil, Turkey and other newly industrialized countries (NICs) have relatively high GDP through utilizing free market economics (Garten, 1997; Knox and Agnew, 1998). The former Soviet Union, which represents state-owned communist economies, was not able to achieve a high level of economic success and consequently collapsed. Presently, Russia and its former states are trying to establish free market economics. However, the contemporary economic activities are generating severe inequality and low productivity problems. In order to eliminate these problems the contemporary economical activities have to be democratize.

# Contemporary Economical Activities
# Generate Inequality

Economic freedom in the form of capitalism has not achieved complete equality. In the United States, during the last two decades, 64 percent of all male earnings went to the top one percent, and only 20 percent went to the work force (Feenberg and Poterba, 1992). The top one percent received 90 percent of the total income. Salaries of CEO's of *Fortune* 500 went up from 35 to 157 times that of production workers (Blair, 1994; and Rose, 1994–95). CEO salaries tripled in France, Italy, and Britain and doubled in Germany during 1984–2001 (*The Economist*, November 4, 1994). Female earnings followed with a ten-to-fifteen-year lag. The distribution of female earnings was starting to look more unequal than the male distribution of earnings (Thurow, 1996). The income share of the top quintile of households rose and the bottom quintile declined. In the last two decades, only the top quintile of the workforce experienced real wage gains, and all the other experienced a decline (Thurow, 1996). The declines in pensions and health care insurance were even larger (Bloom and Freeman, 1992). In the early 1990's the wage gap between the top and bottom deciles of the labor force was rising from 12 percent to 17 percent in OECD countries (*The Economist*, July 24, 1994).

Downsizing became the most common cost cutting policy, while profits and earnings of shareholders increased (Baker and Mishel, 1995). Downsizing spread quickly to Europe and threatened Japan (German Information Center, 1994; and Simons, 1994). Downsizing and economic inequalities, which reduced the purchasing power of middle-class and low-income families, generated social problems such as homelessness and divorce. Family structures were disintegrated worldwide (Lewin, 1995). The middle-class expectation of a rising standard of living and owning a house are disappearing. The middle-class is scared by the economic insecurity, and they are losing their hopes for the future (Beatty, 1994; and Peterson, 1994). Even worse, 80 percent of the population in America believed that the country was run by the rich and for the rich (Phillips, 1993).

The representative democratic management practices in political activities and the authoritarian management practices in the industrial organizations have supported each other in many ways. The elected political representatives make legal laws and regulations for the management of industrial organizations to act freely to determine the profit level and its distribution through free market. The corporate or capital gain tax policies have not changed the way business is done.

The representative democratic management of government and the authoritarian management practices of the industrial organizations worked well to create quality (income and wealth) for the privileged group. The high level of economic growth has always played a positive role for the elections. The poor economic growth caused many representatives to lose elections. Consequently, the representative management of government helped the authoritarian management of private organizations to achieve high quality (high level of profit).

The authoritarian management of organizations supported many representatives by helping them to finance their election expenses. They work in harmony to achieve a high level of quality and economic freedom for themselves and for the small portion of the population who are associated with them. On the other hand, the large portion of the population did not appreciate the high quality and liberty as much as the privileged groups. Although these practices have generated inequalities, they did not cause serious problems in the past, since the economic growth and the general level of quality was relatively better than other countries, including communist and developing nations. Besides, the citizens of the other countries have been looking for opportunities to have similar quality and freedom. Presently, many developing countries and former communist countries of Eastern Europe and Soviet Union are trying to adopt this kind of representative management for their governments and the authoritarian management for the industrial organizations. These countries have to understand the problems of free market economic to avoid the similar problems which exist in the U.S. and other industrialized countries.

## *Free Market Economics Is Not Free*

The "invisible hand" of Adam Smith's free market economy, which has been the guiding principle of the capitalist nations' economic activities, became the "visible hand" of contemporary management activities by generating political and economic inequalities. Both the authoritarian and representative democratic management practices are clearly favoring the rich through political and economic activities, and generating inequalities among the people. It is quite clear from the results of the contemporary management activities that Adam Smith's economic theory that "as each economic player acts for his/her own-self interest, wealth will naturally increase and society as a whole will prosper" is not working. Only the investors and the top managers who control the major managerial decisions are prospering. The others, which include most of the employees and the customers, which constitute the larger portion of the people, are apparently not prospering as much as the rich group. Some portions of the population are even suffering. . As we have seen a system that favors the self-interest of the group, sometimes is at expense of the employees. Smith argued about this self-serving issue in his earlier book, *The Theory of Moral Sentiments*. According to his view, human desires and self-interests had to be regulated in a social framework where people could pursue profit, status and health as long as they acted within certain principles of justice, such as the protection of individual's right to life, liberty and property. Thus, Smith was able to justify of personal interest within a social and economic frame. However, the actual facts of life indicate that the personal desire of the top managers and investors did not represent the personal desires of the other groups. This was also pointed out by Karl Marx (1818–1883) by indicating that capitalism would destroy itself as workers became increasingly at a mercy of a very few. He also understood that economics deeply connected with philosophy and social activities (culture). Although the economics involve both the quantifiable (explicit knowledge) and non-quantifiable (values knowledge) concepts of production, their distribution effect on society and governmental influence on economy are not covered well. Contrary the Smith's optimism about economic growth, David Ricordo (1772–1823) and other neo-classists worried about the poverty, and unemployment during the economic slowdown. Following the German historical and the Austrian marginal utility schools, the American institutional school of economics led by Thorstein Veblen (1857–1929), considers economics a social science rather than an abstract analytical science. However, during last fifty years most of the American Nobel Prize economists have tried to quantify social economic phenomena with a theoretical economic model. The European Nobel Prize winners led by John Hicks (1972 winner) have stressed that economics is contextual and not a pure science. John Hicks and Wassily Leontief (1973 winner) were critical of the American economists' idealized free market. They indicated that capitalist economics had and needed to have planned dimension. British economists, led by Keynes stressed government intervention as a necessary tool for prosperous society. Contrary to British economists, the American economists have placed more emphasis on free enterprise. However, none of these studies dealt with the inequality problems that generated by the economic activities. Tools of economy have been used to create wealth but its distribution left to the users, more specifically to the top managers who make and control the distributional decisions.

In America, the Republicans have traditionally represented the interests of the rich group, while the Democrats have been more liberal since Roosevelt's New Deal, which supported the workers and farmers. This type of general laissez-faire economics mixed with Keynesian approach of employment and Paul Samuelson's tax cut policies, have never eliminated the inequality problems, but they increased it, as we have discussed earlier.

The practices of economics have never been utilized as a social science in the United States' governments and its industrial organizations. Like the analytical models, it left distribution issues to the discretion of the users, politicians and the top managers in the industrial organizations. Thus, contemporary economics without social concerns and integration provides opportunities for self-interested individuals and groups to control most of the wealth. Recently, Shinichi Inoue (1997) noticing the limitations of the contemporary economics as a pure natural science discusses the need of a fresh philosophical basis for a new economics. Joan Robinson (1971), and Hazel Hendersen, (1996) made the similar claim earlier, by arguing the necessity of new paradigms because of the economic crisis caused by dependence on defense spending for past war employment and the inability to account the real cost of natural resources with the laissez-faire economics. Furthermore, the 1992 Nobel Prize winner, Gary Becker, argued that economic justice with profound insights of the human behavior are impossible to quantify. The economic activities based on analytical tools and models that are oversimplified, cannot represent the actual social activities (social values) of the society. The use of analytical models are static, they do not include the future impacts of the economic activities on the society. Therefore, they are useful for managerial decisions, but not reliable. In fact, most of the managerial decisions rely on the managers' judgment. Since, the managers' judgment favor their own-interest and the interests' of their main representatives (the investors, shareholders, the owners) the governments should intervene to correct the situation through relevant laws, rules and regulations.

## *The Role of Government in Economics*

In theory, free market economics should rule without any interference when there is a private sector. However, in practice, we have seen that "free market is not free." It is guided by the management of economic and political power holders. The governments make the laws to help the industrial organizations to create wealth. The management of industrial organizations distributes the generated wealth by favoring themselves and the investors. They also support political power holders through financial contributions for elections campaigns, and other means of pay back for political support. These kind of "scratch my back, I scratch your back" activities between political powers and economical powers that generate wealth cause severe inequalities in a society. The government sometimes interferes to stop rising inequalities, but only in extreme cases (antitrust cases). The inequalities could have been much more than if the market had been completely free. Without government intervention it is possible that one or a few people could have all the nation's income and wealth. In the free market, once the wealth accumulated, opportunities to generate more wealth multiply, since the accumulated wealth leads to income earning opportunities that are not open to those without wealth.

One may think the free market economy provides opportunities to distribute economic gains according to their measured talents (knowledge, skills and desires). However, in reality the top one percent of the population in the United States have 40 percent of total net worth, but they do not have anything like 40 percent of total IQ. There simply are not individuals with an IQ 1,000 times larger than those of other people. According to the recent statistics one can be in top one percent IQ with thirty-six percent above the average (Jensen, 1981). Even starting with equal distribution of purchasing power, free market economies quickly convert equalities into inequalities, mainly because everyone faces unequal opportunities even if they have similar qualifications. Historically, many governments find it necessary to interfere in the market to reduce the inequality rising with a variety of programs (Bailey, Burtless and Litan, 1993).

Bismark, Churchill and Roosevelt adopted social welfare policies to save the free market economy by protecting the middle class. These kinds of government policies have been reducing the inequalities that free market generates and maintain its continuity. However, most of the governments of the authoritarian and semi democratic nations do not go far enough to reduce inequality to a "reasonable level" that may be fair for everyone according to their measurable talents. On the other hand, if governments interfere too much they may harm the incentives to generate wealth.

Thus, the question of what is a reasonable level of inequality and how much government interference is optimal never gets answered. There are no satisfactory answers to these questions and there will not be one in the future either. Even the social market economies left these questions to the judgment of management. It assumes that management act with good social values to pursue the interests of both self and others. If managers do not act with good values to satisfy the needs of themselves, their constituents and others, the inequality problem and fairness issue will not be resolved. Even acting with good values many top managers has made serious mistakes to harm themselves and others. Thus, the contemporary management practices, which are controlled by a few people or a group, cannot determine the optimal interference and reasonable inequality.

The true democratic management in government and the organizations is the only alternative to achieve a reasonable and acceptable inequality level. Relevant decisions are made by all people, rather than a small portion of the organization and the nation. The decisions made by larger group of people are not necessarily always better than the decisions made by a relatively small group. However, the decisions will be much fairer because the decision makers represent both themselves and others in that organization and that nation. They pursue their self- interest as well as others' interests. Inequality will be caused only by the differences of the level of individual's knowledge, skills, values and work that is natural and fair. Thus, the inequality generated by the contemporary management practices will be eliminated through democratization of economical activities.

## *Democratization of Economical Activities*

The inequalities in capitalist countries, generated by the free market economies, cannot be eliminated by the contemporary management of their governments. The governments of capitalist nations ordinarily do not interfere in free market economies. Even, if they interfere, in the case of severe inequality or quality problems, they cannot find the optimum level of interference to eliminate inequality without hurting the quality. The capitalist economy provides, relatively, high quality with a full freedom for certain elites and elite organizations that have the economic and political power. The rest of the population does not have the similar political and economical opportunities that these groups have. Only the small portion of the population appreciates the high quality and the political and economic liberty fully from the free market economics. The free market is free for them and controlled by them. The majority of the people have lower quality and limited economical and political liberty and consequently have suffered from the inequality problems.

On the other hand controlled socialist economics did neither achieve high quality nor political and economical freedom. Having less inequality, without quality and liberty, did not satisfy most of the people. Consequently, the government of socialist nations had severe economical and political problems. Many of them were collapsed and presently trying to survive through adopting the capitalist or mix economies.

It is clear from the real world experiences that neither the capitalist economies nor socialist economies are able to provide a desirable level of quality, equality and liberty for the majority of the people. Both of these economic systems failed because they were controlled by the authoritarian management practices. The political and economical activities are dominated by the elites and the elite organizations. They favored themselves and their immediate supporters through controlling the management of political and economic activities as we have seen in Chapter IV.

The market is made up of people who produce, consume and distribute goods and services. The free market is free if it provides equal opportunities for those people who are engaged in production, consumption and distribution process without harming others and the environment. If the market favors a few or one group over the other groups and harms the environment this is not a free market, but a controlled market. The contemporary capitalist market is not a free market in this sense, but a controlled one. As we have seen earlier, it's controlled by the small group of population that has economic and political power. The real free market does not allow these groups to control economic activities. The individuals and organizations may have superior qualities to provide comparative advantages in a free market economy, but they cannot have monopolistic advantages concerning their economical, political and technological powers. The real free market economy provides equal opportunities for everyone to compete and cooperate for producing the high quality and equality. The monopolistic power in economic activity does not provide equal opportunities for utilizing the all resources, including the people. Consequently, with a limited economic freedom producers cannot achieve the high quality and equality.

The contemporary economic activities have to be democratized for high quality and equality. The postwar economics of Germany and Japan are referred to as a "miracle" applied "social market" economies, rather than completely free market economy. In social market economics, the individual's freedom is essential but the true and fair competition can only occur if the framework for guaranteeing freedom for the individual is secured. In other words, the labor management relations have to be arranged in such that all the workers have to participate in decision making concerning the economical as well as social laws including employment, payments, savings and building infrastructures and decentralizing industry. Ludwig Erhard, economic minister of West Germany during the period of 1949–1963, implemented a wide range of policies that are based on the Lopke's new economics of human citizen. Erhard, in his 1957 book, *Woshlstand fur Alle* (Happiness for All), emphasized the need to overcome the inherent tensions between the haves and have-nots in society. This would be possible by guaranteeing fair competition with policies of banning cartels, ensuring fair pricing, rent control, and supporting people with disabilities laws. Implementing such policies through the management of both the government and the industrial organizations were the bases of Germany's "social market economics" which is free and fair relative to American economic and management practices.

In Japan, the free market economy has been used with the Japanese social values as a "social market." The social market is still a free market economy but it is fairer than the American economic and management practices. While Adam Smith emphasized the pursuit of self-interest and regarded self-interest to be the driving force behind economics, the Japanese economics and management practices pursue the interests of both oneself and others (Ozaki, 1991; Inoue, 1997). They have been doing this by providing long-term employment, group decision making and sharing the pain and the gain. These activities increase the good relations among the people and the productivity and competitiveness of their organizations and Japan.

Both Germany and Japan have been using the free market, laissez-faire economy, but they are mixing it with the social responsibilities to generate "social market" economy. In America, Henry Ford increased the workers' wages to sell his cars to them. This process increased the well being of the employees and the productivity of Ford Motor Company. The employees were enabled to buy the Ford's product. It also increased the workers' motivation to do their best for the company. There are other corporations in the United States that exercise social market principles by being responsible for the social issues of the employees, communities and the public in general. The Hewlett-Packard, and Lincoln Electric are some of the American companies that use the free market economy with fair social responsibilities.

These activities in Germany, Japan and the United States indicate that, the free market economic activities can be integrated with the fair social activities to be more productive and competitive for everyone in that society. These activities can be increased through democratizing contemporary economic activities. There have been few suggestions for this model. Shinichi Inoue argues that while economics will continue to be based on the "free market," the interpretation of the "free" can be different from that normally accepted in the capitalist countries in the West, where freedom centers on the rights of the individual. In contrast, in the Buddhist economy freedom ensures when all personal desires are mastered. In this view a Buddhist approach involves understanding that economics and a moral, spiritual life is neither separate nor mutually exclusive. Buddhist economics avoids conflict with nature and operates in a way that is spiritually rich, socially fair and beneficial and environmentally friendly. It shows us how to move beyond the unfortunate compartmentalization of our lives to a more holistic vision of life. The Buddhist economic view, reflected in Japanese management, emphasizes caring for others as the basis of one's actions. It stresses hard work and motivates people to help others. Kazuo Imamori who founded Kyocera Corporation (high tech) and DDI (telephone company) encouraged his employees and fellow managers to focus on the need for spiritual and ethical basis for making a profit (Inoue, 1997).

The Buddhist economics have been influencing the Japanese economic activities throughout the history by integrating the spiritual and material wealth. In Buddhist economy happiness can be increased by reducing one's desires; in contemporary economics the happiness can be increased through increasing wealth (happiness = wealth/desires). Buddhist economic philosophy argues that, the self cannot live independently but only in relation to other people. Both physically and psychologically, humans are dependent on other human beings as well as on the natural environment. When we recognize that our lives interconnected with others, thoughts of appreciation toward others and the earth will naturally arise. Our self-centered desires conflict with the fact of being interconnected with others. We cannot give up our self-desires, but we can adjust them to the others and to the natural need of the earth resources. If our desires do not have the limit, we cannot continue peacefully without destroying the humanity and destroying the earth.

All of these activities played very positive roles in reducing inequalities and increasing quality in both Germany and Japan. These activities also indicate that democratization of economical activities depends in great extent to the true democratic management activities through providing authority to all the stakeholders and adopting ownership plans, long-term employment policies, group decision process and sharing the gain and the pain of the economic activities. These economical activities are also the main elements of true democratic management. Thus democratization of economic activities is necessary for the democratization of management.

# CHAPTER XI

# Democratization Through Technological Development

> *We must ask of technology that not only does it make*
> *money for its owners, but also, is it good for people,*
> *the environment, and the resource base.*
> —George McRobie

Educational, political, and economic democratization requires change and technology is the major force for these changes. The success of educational, political, and economical activities of a nation, mainly depends on the success of its technological development. Technologies in the form of explicit knowledge (know-how, capital equipment and methods) generate capital, goods and services to satisfy people's needs and wants. Politicians through government and industrial organizations have been promoting technological development to increase the nation's economic well being and maintain its political and social stability. Technology has been the major force for productivity and competitiveness of the organizations and nations (Solow, 1957; Jorgenson, 1969; Fabricant, 1954; Denison, 1969, Sen, 1982; Porter, 1990; and Marber, 1998).

Many organizations and nations throughout the world have been continuously trying to develop new and better technologies to increase their economic and political competitive advantages. United States, Germany and Japan have developed the high level of economic growth through developing the superior commercial technologies. They also have, relatively more, staple and more democratic political activities. United States became the world most powerful nation-militarily by developing the superior military technologies through developing strong economy. On the other hand, the former Soviet Union developed superior military technologies and became one of the super military powers of the world. But without the economic well being that people needed, the governments could not maintain the political stability and it did collapsed. Russia dismantled most of its military technologies and is now concentrating on the commercial technologies to establish both the economic growth and the political stability. Thus, technologies may play an important role in nations' economic and political affairs. It is also clear from the real world practices that the nations that develop better technologies have better economic, more stable, and more democratic political processes.

Technologies also influence social values of a nation. During the technological chain process nations' social values change going through developing intermediate, advance and frontier technologies. This happens through changing the knowledge and skills that require for these technologies. For example, during the development of textile technologies people wanted to have better quality of cloths. During the development of advance technologies people not only want good quality of cloth, but good quality of cars, TVs, music sets, etc. Presently, at the stage of frontier technologies, people became more materialistic through consuming new technological goods like computers, cellular telephones, and others. People's consumption and needs increase and they become dominated by the materialistic values, as new technologies are developed. However, it is difficult to say that people's social values are also increased. Contrarily, many argue that people's values such as care, trust, honesty, integrity and fairness are disappearing. At the stage of frontier technologies which require relatively more collectivity and cooperation people are becoming more self centered and a "me" society rather than a "we" society. They think of their self-interests and forget others.

The desires and the pressures to satisfy the people's materialistic needs and wants generate violence, corruption, and social injustices all over the world. Individual managers of organizations and the governments are concerned with their own interests. Even the government officials of the most developed nations indicate openly that we operate based on our national, political and economical interests. The social problems such as hunger, health care, homeless and corruption are growing globally without even a plan to deal with them. The solutions to environmental problems, including air and water pollution, land destruction and resource depletion have to be considered as a social problem that can only be solved by the true democratic management practices which utilize technologies with the social conscientious.

Technological democratization requires the development of appropriate technologies to generate equitable political, economical and social outcomes. This can be explained through studying the technological development process and its impact on the educational, political, and economical democratization. The following sections address this issue.

## *The Concept of Technology*

The concept of technology can be defined as knowledge (know-how), methods and equipment, which are applied to produce goods and services to satisfy human needs. Webster's dictionary defines technology as "that branch of knowledge which deals with the industrial arts." Edwin Mansfield (1968), one of the major writers in this field, defines technology as a society's pool of knowledge regarding the industrial arts. The technologist, including scientists, engineers, and managers, generally view technology in a framework of techniques and processes used in the flow from raw materials through to final goods and services. In this study technology is defined as an explicit knowledge (know-how, capital equipment and methods) and skills used to generate capital, goods and services to satisfy people's needs and wants.

The modern technologies can be divided into three categories. First, those which are scientifically simple and relatively more labor-intensive and less capital intensive like textiles, food processing, light metallurgy, light machinery and construction which are called *intermediate light technologies.* These technologies are scientifically unsophisticated, organizationally simple, and mechanically easy to operate and require low labor and managerial skills with a limited capital investment. Second, those scientifically more sophisticated and relatively less labor-intensive and more capital intensive like iron and steel, heavy chemicals, heavy machinery, heavy electronic equipment, and metallurgical processing which are called *advanced heavy technologies.* These technologies require relatively high scientific and managerial skills, trained labor, and a complex organization, heavy capital equipment, long-range capital investment, high risk and a large amount of research and development activities. Finally, those technologies which are still being standardized, improved significantly, and which general knowledge is not universally available, like aerospace and computer technologies; these are called *new or frontier technologies* (Sen, 1982).

The change in technology in the form of capital equipment, knowledge and skill is called technological development or technological progress. The technologist views technological development in a framework of techniques and processes used in the flow from raw materials through to final goods and services. However, the economists consider technological development as a whole factor in generating a nation's economic output. Increases in output, which are not due to increases in inputs, are referred to as "technological progress." (Solow, 1957; Jorgenson and Griliches, 1969; Denison, 1969). Several studies indicate that about 90 percent of the long-term increase in output per capita in the United States was attributable to technological change, increased educational levels and other factors not directly associated with increases in the quantity of labor and capital (Fabricant, 1954; Solow, 1957). However, it is not yet possible to isolate the contribution of technological development, precisely, in quantitative terms from the other factors.

The most important part of the role of technology in economic and political development cannot be understood without considering its relations to the social factors. Thorstein Veblen (1919) and Clarence Ayres (1944) emphasized the importance of technological innovation for economic development through its impact upon social institutions and human development. Simon Kuznets (1953) strongly reinforced the view that a nation's economic growth is based on advanced technology and the institutional and ideological adjustments it demands. Kuznets has emphasized the inadequacies of capital investment as a measure of economic growth. The most important capital of an industrially advanced nation he considered is not its physical capital but its human capital. Its scientific and technical knowledge result from improved education and training. It might even be possible for technological progress to increase output rapidly "without any addition to the stock of capital goods." Capital investment, therefore, cannot be regarded as the one strategic factor. The growth of applied scientific knowledge must account, in large parts, for rapid rates of economic growth in recent centuries. Though it has obviously been closely related to broader educational, political, and economic factors, it is this fact, which has been "the strategic factor" (Kuznets, 1973). This view has been supported by an increasing number of other economists and is adopted in this study.

## *The Process of Technological Development*

Technological development is a continuous and cumulative historical process. According to the technological life-cycle (TLC) hypothesis, technologies go through different stages, like the product life-cycle (PLC) (Kuznets, 1953 and Vernon, 1966). According to this hypothesis, technologies and the products have a finite life-cycle similar to the life-cycle of animate objects; each begins, exist for a time and dies. The technology maybe outmoded or changed its geographical location, but continuously propagates and facilitates new cycles through its multiple effects. This is generally known as a chain or linkage effect (Hirschman, 1970).

The chain effect involves generating a series of related technologies. The development of one technology in a given sector often produces a technological disequilibrium among related sectors. For example, a sector produces high quality goods, often demands high quality of raw materials, intermediate goods, parts, components, and other inputs. In order to satisfy this higher quality demand, related sectors must raise the level of their technologies. The chain effect also occurs through supplying new technologies with an increased and accumulated knowledge, and experience from standardized technologies. Every new technology propagates additional ones and widens the technology frontier. Historically, the intermediate technologies like textiles are developed in the early links of the modern technological chain. The adjacent links to intermediate technologies are the advanced technological such as iron and steel, electronics, and automation technologies. The links at the end of the technological chain include the frontier technologies, such as aerospace and information technologies. Historically, most advanced nations have developed intermediate technologies before developing advanced and frontier technologies. The techniques and economic characteristics, stated above, make it quicker, cheaper and easier to develop less sophisticated technologies earlier and more sophisticated technologies later. For the same reasons, presently, developing nations are also proceeding in the same way.

A country can have a modern technology by proceeding through all the stages of the technological life cycle described earlier. Most of the developed nations follow this pattern, which we call that of being *originators*. An alternative possibility for a nation to develop technologies is through globalization. Most of the presently developing nations are adhering to this pattern, which we called that of being *followers*.

## Originators' Technological Development

Originators support all activities of basic knowledge across the broadest front to produce most of the technologies, by going through all of the stages of technological development. In other words, the originators integrate the elements of technologies forward from invention to standardization. A nation following this pattern, aims to maintain a position in all advanced fields of military, economic, and political importance. The United States of America, Great Britain, Germany, France, and other Western European nations are the major originators (Oldham, Freeman, and Turkcan, 1967). However, none of these nations originated all of the technologies that they have used. When a new technology is standardized by one or a few of these nations, it is often transferred by others.

Developing technologies through transferring them is possible among the advanced nations because the necessary conditions for the transformations of these technologies exist in these nations. These conditions are mainly technical, managerial, political, and economical in nature. The knowledge involved in these technologies has been accumulated in these nations. They have already established high-level scientific institutions, universities, scientific libraries, and information services, basic and applied research and development centers, and laboratories. They produce a considerable amount of skilled manpower, including scientists, engineers, managers and technicians (OECD, 1967). This high quality manpower is already engaged in scientific and technical education, training and popularization of basic knowledge through the mass media. They have already applied the basic knowledge in agricultural and industrial production and services. They have established many industrial organizations. These organizations have already developed and utilized all the management activities including productions, engineering, marketing, financing, human resources and others. These nations, have already been actively producing similar technologies, and accumulated enough technical knowledge and experience to undertake the development of new technologies by themselves.

These countries also enjoy similar demand conditions that stimulate a wide range of innovations and transformation of new technologies. Their economies are well developed to provide necessary capital for the investment in technological organizations. They can provide high wage rates that promote high income and savings for new technologies. The high income generates a strong demand for the quality of new products. These economies are in the age of the high mass-consumption stage (Rostow, 1969). These economic conditions are accompanied by favorable social conditions, including a high level of education, communications, business enterprises, acceptability of new ideas, organizational effectiveness and relatively more democratic and more stable political conditions.

Because these conditions are highly developed in advanced countries and there are no major technological, economical, political or relevant gaps between these countries, the process of developing standardized technologies through transferring them in the form of patent agreement, licensing or joint ventures occurs in a relatively short time. We call these nations *early followers* or *originators* because of this short imitation time and because they are also innovators of some other technologies. Their technical capabilities and resources permit early identification of significant international development and facilitate the actual transfer of technology.

However, when these conditions are not close to each other and a considerable gap exists between originators and followers, technological development takes different routes and generates different results for different countries. We call this *late followers pattern.*

## Late Follower's Technological Development

There has been a large gap between advanced and developing nations concerning technical, managerial, economical, political, as well as other conditions (Pearson, 1969, Knox and Agnew, 1998). The technological gaps between advanced nations and developing nations developed after the industrial revolution of the Western world, when the first modern technologies, notably those in textiles, standardized during the 1750–1850. Many developing countries did not have enough technical, managerial, and economic capabilities to transfer these technologies in the form of patent agreements, licensing, or joint ventures. Rather, they became consumers of the products of these technologies in the form of imports in the early stage of their technological development. However, a nation, which seeks economic development, will have to try to build up its own modern technologies to produce these goods. In order to achieve this objective, developing nations import standardized technologies and then adopt and assimilate them into their home markets. This is generally known as the import-substitution strategy (Alexander, 1967). Late follower nations establish less sophisticated technologies at the early stage and other technologies at the later stage according to their technical, managerial and economic conditions. They have to improve these conditions for developing more sophisticated technologies later. We call these nations late followers, because it takes a relatively longer time to develop modern technologies. However, they may eventually, become an originator such as an advanced country like Japan.

The process of technological development may be explained in the context of the technological life cycle theories (Akamatsu, 1962; Alexander, 1967 and Sen, 1982). According to these theories, the late follower's technological development goes through different stages, which require globalization. When originators standardized new technology, according to the technological life cycle, they make every effort to export their products to other countries. Consequently, when the products of standardized technologies invade the developing country's markets, they import the standardized technology, and related capital equipment, knowledge, and operation methods, and employee engineers, technicians and managers from the advanced countries. At the same time, they promote the development of agriculture and rich domestic raw material technologies for export. These technologies are very important to generate necessary foreign currency for purchasing imported technologies as well as for other imported items. During this stage, the follower country has a considerable amount of market for the products of these technologies and enough income generated by the agricultural products and by the raw material to afford the consumption of the products of imported technologies. Most importantly, they have plentiful low-wage labor to generate comparative advantages in these technologies.

## Equalizing and Shifting Comparative Advantages

At the early stages of technological development, the comparative advantage is on the originator's side. Therefore, the late followers take necessary measures to increase their technical, managerial and economic conditions to catch up with the originators. At this stage, the late follower's government may play an important role in employing highly qualified engineers, technicians and managers from the originator countries and send native engineers, managers and students to originator nations for further knowledge and skills. Furthermore, they may establish pilot projects for training engineers and workers to improve technical and managerial conditions. As the late follower's technological and managerial conditions improve, imported standardized technologies gradually are adopted, assimilated and diffused into the domestic market. Thus, the indigenous technologies improve while related knowledge and skill (experience) are accumulated. As Thorstein Veblen (1959) argues for the "late comer thesis," this transformation is not a simple borrowing or carbon copy; they start innovating while transferring, just like Japan did for its early stage of technological development (Sen, 1982). Presently, the big ten nations (BTNs) including South Korea, Mexico, Brazil, Turkey and Newly Industrialized Countries (NICs) are developing modern technologies by using this strategy.

The absorption of one branch of technology will generate demand for processed raw materials, intermediate goods, and light machinery, which in the first instance will be met by imports. Gradually, the size of this demand may become sufficiently large to stimulate domestic production and thereby creating additional demand for the standardized technologies. At the same time, the developed technology creates a backward and forward linkage effect, which propagates further technological development.

If the follower country's market is large enough, to establish light industry they eventually create sufficient demand for the products of heavy industry, such as iron, steel production, and the heavy chemicals. Finally, the developing nations may have a market sufficient to install machine making and machine tool industries, involving still more specialized and complicated knowledge and skill.

During this process, the follower's supply conditions improve to keep up with an increasing demand. Consequently, the employment, wages and income increase as skill and productivity of the labor force grows. The follower's technological, as well as managerial, economical and political conditions improve further and become closer to those corresponding conditions of advanced countries. The followers start catching up with originators and close the technological gap. The Japanese technological development level during the late 1970s and early 1980s and the BTN's current technological developments, represent these conditions (Garten, 1997).

During the early stages of technological development, most of the new industries in the follower's country are likely to remain relatively less efficient relative to similar industries in the originator countries. They survive in their early production, mainly because of the low-wage comparative advantages, and government protection of the home market.

But in the long term, the followers close the technical and managerial gaps that separate them from the originators insofar as the intermediate technologies are concerned. The comparative advantages shift to the followers, mainly because of the plentiful low-wage labor. Thus, they can produce similar products less costly and start exporting to other followers as well as to originators. Consequently, the originator's output of these products will tend to slowdown while their exports decrease, and imports increase. As a result, the direction of trade in the products of relatively simple technology completely changes. The follower (which used to be the importer) becomes the exporter and the originator (which used to be the exporter) becomes the importer of these products. Thus, technologies developed through globalization change the direction of trade and increase its volume.

Eventually, the early follower's comparative advantages will decline, because the late followers establish the simpler technologies in the same way as the early followers did, and acquire the comparative advantages. As a result, both production and export trends of a particular follower country may change by first going up, with the growth of production for the domestic market. However, these trends go down as late followers follow the same process.

During the historical development of technologies, some of the early followers become advanced nations like Japan, some of the late followers develop standardized technologies and move into the development of more sophisticated advanced technologies like the BTN's and NIC's. However, the nations with poor technological, managerial and economic conditions cannot develop modern technologies either by themselves or through globalization. They may just import the limited amount of products of standardized technologies like Bolivia, Liberia, Sierra Leon and other less developed countries (LDCs).

Thus, the nations develop their technologies in the span of the technological chain, as their comparative advantages shift. As a result, the technological development generates enormous impacts on the participant nations economical, political and social activities. The next section explains these impacts.

## *The Impacts of Technological Development*

Technological development plays the key role in nations' economic and political development by way of increasing productivity and competitiveness in terms of gross domestic product and per capita income. Free and fair economic and political activities are necessary for the high benefits of the technological development. Otherwise, technological development with inappropriate economic and political activities may generate adverse affects on nations' developments. However, all of these activities and the impacts of technological development depend on the nature of the management activities in an organization and nation.

### Positive Impacts of Technological Development

After World War II, many nations tried to develop their technologies to increase their economic well-being. Development of each new technology provided new economic benefits to many nations throughout the world. For example, the industrial revolution, fueled by the development of steam power, and the textile industry led the emergence of Britain as the leader of the global economy during the early 19th century. Later, the United States, developed the railroads in the mid 19th century and efficient transcontinental and international transportation including shipping, and later in the 20th century, the airplanes, which helped, integrate the U.S. as a leader into global economy. During the early 20th century, development of electricity and automobiles facilitated the integration of Australia, Canada and South Africa into the global economy. After World War II, developments of electronics and computers enabled Japan and other Asian countries including Taiwan, Singapore, South Korea and other BTNs to enter into the global marketplace.

From 1973 to 1992, economic growth, measured in real GDP, in the industrialized countries averaged about 2.5 percent. During 1992 to 1996, developing countries averaged 6.5 percent of economic growth and developed nations averaged about 2.5 percent (see Figure 2.1). During the next decade, however, the developing nations' economics are expected to grow between 5 and 6 percent per year (WB, 1996). It is projected that as a result of this rapid economic growth, developing countries will produce more than 27 percent of total world output (*WB@www.worldbank.org*).

Two-thirds of the radios made by Japanese manufacturing companies are produced abroad. Half of the stereos and color television sets are produced in South Korea and other nearby East Asian nations. Over 90 percent of South Korean exports of electronic equipment produced by affiliates of Japanese companies. The electronics, textiles and clothing are similar. These are not merely assembly operations. The production of components that require high levels of skill and/or technology is a more common undertaking

**Table 11.1. Manufacturing in Some NICs, 1960–1993**

| Country | Share of world manufacturing output | | Average annual growth in manufacturing | | Share of total labor force in manufacturing | |
|---|---|---|---|---|---|---|
| | *1963* | *1993* | *1960–70* | *1980–93* | *1960* | *1993* |
| Hong Kong | 0.08 | 0.22 | — | 4.8 | 52 | 19.8 |
| Singapore | 0.05 | 0.25 | 13.0 | 5.1 | 23 | 26.7 |
| South Korea | 0.11 | 1.16 | 17.6 | 8.4 | 9 | 24.1 |
| Taiwan | 0.11 | 1.30 | 15.5 | 8.9 | 16 | 27.1 |
| Brazil | 1.57 | 1.68 | — | -2.4 | 15 | 15.9 |
| Mexico | 1.04 | 1.25 | 9.4 | 6.7 | 20 | 15.9 |
| Portugal | 0.23 | 0.26 | 8.9 | 8.9 | 29 | 24.9 |
| Greece | 0.19 | 0.23 | 10.2 | 0.8 | 20 | 20.2 |

*Source*: Knox and Agnew (1998)

in many developing nations. In the Philippines, for example, about 200 companies were operating in export-processing zones (EPZs) in 1996, and employing about 50,000 workers. Most of these, firms that are owned jointly, engaged in the manufacturing of electronics, microchips, semiconductors, toys and garments. In 1996, the aggregate exports from these firms amounted to over 5.5 billion dollars, representing over 30 percent of the countries' exports by value. Between 1992 and 1994, developing nations received roughly 40 percent of all direct investment up from 20 percent in 1987, and expected to top 50 percent in 2010. The annual foreign direct investment from developed to developing nations has grown from 11.3 billion to 90 billion, and annual capital flows to developing nations increased from 100 billion to 350 billion during the period from 1985 to 1996 (*International Finance Corporation* 1996).

The developed nations including the U.S., Japan, Germany, France, Italy and the UK provided 71 percent and some other 16 BTNs and NICs produced 21 percent of the world's total manufacturing output in 1993 (see Table 11.2). These nations employed about 20 percent of their workforce in manufacturing and manufacturing share constituted 26 percent of their GDP. Although the U.S. has retained its leadership as the world's major producer of manufactured goods over the post-war period, its share in world output has been reduced from 40 percent in 1963, to 25 percent in 1995. In contrast, Japan has moved from fifth place with a share of 5.5 percent in 1963 to second-place with a share of 21 percent in 1995. This has been the result of increasing degree of technological development throughout the world economy. This is reflected by some important trends in manufacturing output, particularly the developing nations' growth rate (see Table 11.2). South Korea attained an annual average growth rate of 18 percent in the 1960s and 16 percent in the late 1970s. As a result, South Korea surged up the list of developing market economies.

The percentage of South Korea's labor force employed in manufacturing, increased from 9 percent to 29 percent during the period of 1960 and 1980 (Dicken, 1992). All four Pacific Rim countries have made enormous progress up the world league table of exporters. In 1993, Hong Kong ranked 9th in the world (up from 26th in 1979), Taiwan ranked 12th (up from 22nd), South Korea ranked 13th (up from 27th), and Singapore ranked 14th (up from 30th). These shifts have emerged from technological development.

Collectively, the 500 largest U.S. corporations now employ an overseas labor force as big as their domestic labor force. Similar statistics applied to the largest Japanese corporations (Knox & Agnew, 1998). These data clearly

## Table 11.2. World's Manufacturing Output

| Rank | Country | Total Manufacturing Value Added (US $ millions) | Percent of World Total | Manufacturing as share of GDP | | Manufacturing as share of Labor force | |
|---|---|---|---|---|---|---|---|
| | | | | 1965 | 1993 | 1965 | 1993 |
| 1 | United States | 1,481,700 | 27.7 | 29 | 18 | 36 | 18 |
| 2 | Japan | 1,023,048 | 19.1 | 32 | 30 | 30 | 23 |
| 3 | Germany | 565,603 | 10.5 | — | 23 | 48 | 26 |
| 4 | France | 271,133 | 5.1 | — | 20 | 39 | 17 |
| 5 | Italy | 250,345 | 4.7 | — | 20 | 40 | 21 |
| 6 | United Kingdom | 201,859 | 3.8 | 30 | 21 | 48 | 20 |
| 7 | Russia | 200,237 | 3.7 | — | 49 | — | 27 |
| 8 | China | 147,302 | 2.7 | — | 45 | — | 13 |
| 9 | Canada | 103,690 | 1.9 | 23 | 18 | 34 | 17 |
| 10 | Spain | 100,672 | 1.8 | 25 | 23 | 31 | 20 |
| 11 | Brazil | 90,062 | 1.7 | 26 | 25 | 15 | 16 |
| 12 | South Korea | 85,454 | 1.6 | 18 | 29 | 9 | 13 |
| 13 | Mexico | 67,157 | 1.3 | 21 | 22 | 20 | 16 |
| 14 | Netherlands | 58,476 | 1.1 | — | 13 | 42 | 16 |
| 15 | Argentina | 50,009 | 0.9 | 33 | 22 | 36 | 21 |
| 16 | Ukraine | 48,872 | 0.9 | — | 43 | — | 28 |
| 17 | Austria | 46,739 | 0.8 | 33 | 24 | 46 | 27 |
| 18 | Belgium | 45,230 | 0.8 | 30 | 23 | 48 | 18 |
| 19 | Australia | 43,679 | 0.8 | 28 | 15 | 37 | 16 |
| 20 | Sweden | 43,605 | 0.8 | 28 | 42 | 45 | 18 |

*Source:* Knox and Agnew (1998)

indicate that technological development increases the nations' economical and managerial conditions, which produce a higher standard of life for their people. However, it is argued by many researchers that technological development through globalization may also generate adverse effects on nations' economic and technological conditions. These arguments are analyzed in the following section.

## The Negative Impacts of Technological Development

Technological development generates interdependence among nations. Originators depend partly on the followers' markets for exporting standardized products, capital goods (technology) and importing raw materials and primary products. At the same time, the followers depend on the originators' markets for importing standardized technologies and exporting primary products. However, the originators are less dependent than the followers, since the market structure of the new technologies is relatively more monopolistic than that of primary products. This kind of market structure generates unequal trade conditions, which effects the followers' technological and economic developments adversely, while favoring the originators (Cockcroft, 1972; and Prebish, 1950).

Various suggestions have been made concerning the ways in which technological dependence has adverse effects on followers' technological development. First of all, it has been argued that technological development caused debt problems in developing nations (Batra, 1996). Developing nations borrow capital to support their technological development, but are unable to pay it back. During the 1970s and early 1980s the debts of developing nations, increased very rapidly. By 1985, the developing world owed more than $800 billion to developed nations (World Bank estimates). The interest rates were more than doubled and the followers' debt burden multiplied accordingly. Rising interest rates put developing nations in great difficulty to pay for high import costs and higher interest loans. Debt problems became widespread and led to a worldwide financial crisis (Soros, 1998; Batra, 1996). Poland became technically default on its external debt, and began what would be a twelve-year restructuring process. In 1982, Mexico declared a moratorium on its foreign debt (Lissakers, 1991). By 1987, the falters included Bolivia, Peru, Ecuador, Poland, Costa Rica and other developing nations (Kaufman, 1988). Poland averaged 50 percent from 1985 to 1991 (IMF, 1991). By the mid 1980s capital investment in developing countries had collapsed in their share of foreign direct investment (FDI), decreasing to 13 percent from 25 percent in 1971 (*The Economist*, September 23, 1993). The debt problems stagnated economic growth in many developing nations and caused even negative growth in some countries. The huge debt behaved as a tax on developing countries' investment and growth.

Second, is the infant industry argument (Prebish, 1950). Raul Prebish argued that transferred technologies tended to substitute for technologies that might have been developed by local scientific research and development activities. The followers are continuously ignoring the development of basic research and science, which creates self-perpetuating technological dependence on originators (Cooper, 1972; Steward, 1972–73; Vaitsos, 1972–73). It has also been argued that this dependence leads to an alienation of scientific institutions, because there is no demand for locally developed science and technologies. Thus, science in the follower countries becomes a consumption item, whereas in originators, science is an investment item.

Third, is the inappropriate technology argument. It has been suggested that dependence on originator technologies generates inappropriateness in follower nations, since the foreign technologies are developed for the originators' needs. These technologies generally, are capital intensive, whereas the factor conditions in followers are more appropriate to labor-intensive technologies, (Schumacher, 1999). The transfer of the wrong kind of technology may increase the unemployment and misdistribution of income, as well as the skewed consumption pattern that already exist in follower nations. Many capital intensive technologies, incorporate elements of luxury consumption, like color televisions or electric razors compared with ordinary razors, etc. which usually are consumed by a small group of high income consumers. Thus, transfer of this kind of technology often stimulates the luxury consumption of these groups at the expense of investment projects, which may be more suitable for a large portion of the population.

Fourth, it is also argued that the transfer of technology through direct investment may have negative effect on the followers' economy through losing opportunities of capital accumulation. International corporations, from originator nations, bring their capital gains back to their own countries from their investment in the follower countries. This capital could be reinvested into the follower country to generate further technological and economic development. Thus, international corporations, which do not reinvest their capital gains from their direct-investment into the follower countries, may weaken the follower's economy. Besides, the originators through their international corporations, control some significant portions of the follower countries' domestic investments. This may result in some further economic and political control in the follower countries that may not be favorable for their technological and economic developments.

These and other dependencies of a political and military nature, which exist for developing nations, limit their technological development. The dependents can neither protect their infant technologies by proper trade agreements, nor import technologies without some limitations. The followers' ability to choose technologies as well as their development policy for them will be limited. The dependence increases the originators' growth, while followers can only be developed, as a reflection of this expansion (Cockcraft, Frank and Johnson, 1972). This permits the originators to impose conditions that may be unfavorable to followers and to extract part of the domestically produced surplus, which is essential for the followers' technological development (Santos, 1970).

Fifth, it is also argued that technological development causes corruption and inequality. The governments of many nations are involved in technological development. Some of the government officials and their friends or relatives play crucial roles in selecting the source nations and organizations for technological development. They influence the contractual agreements and other activities required for technology transfer in developing countries. Transparency international, based in Berlin, published a corruption index in 1995, ranking 41 nations in Asia, Europe and America, on a scale of 1 to 10, low score means high corruption. Among the 41 nations, 10 were identified as the most corrupt, with a score close to three or lower (see Table 11.3). Bribing is the major tool of winning the contracts, and getting the related materials through customs. Many government officials in Mexico, India, Indonesia, Turkey, Pakistan and others are accused of these activities by taking bribes (Garten, 1997). Friends and relatives of the political officials in these countries, control the business involved in technology development. These kinds of activities generate income and wealth inequalities among the people.

## *Democratization Through Technological Development*

The U.S.A., Western European nations and Japan, developed most modern technologies. They realize monopolistic returns from each technology that they originated. The technological comparative advantages increased their competitiveness in global market. Technological development also provided opportunities for developing nations to acquire standardized technologies, in a relatively short time, less cost and less risk. Japan was able to develop most of its modem technologies through transferring them. Similarly, cur-

### Table 11.3. Corruption Index of Some Countries

| Country | Corruption Index[1] | External Debt (Billions)[2] 1980 | 1993 |
|---------|---------------------|----------------------------------|------|
| Indonesia | 1.94 | $20.9 | $89.5 |
| China | 2.16 | 4.5 | 83.8 |
| Pakistan | 2.25 | 9.9 | 26.1 |
| Venezuela | 2.66 | 29.3 | 37.5 |
| Brazil | 2.70 | 71.0 | 132.8 |
| Philippines | 2.77 | 17.4 | 35.2 |
| India | 2.78 | 20.6 | 91.8 |
| Thailand | 2.79 | 8.3 | 45.8 |
| Mexico | 3.18 | 57.4 | 118.0 |
| Argentina | 5.24 | 27.2 | 74.5 |

1. A low score means high corruption
2. Excludes private short-term debt

*Source*: Barbara Crossett, "A Global Gauge of Greased Palms," *New York Times*, August 20, 1995. p. E3. World Development Report, World Bank, Washington, DC, 1995, pp. 200 and 201.

rently developing nations, including Big Ten Nations (BTNs) and Newly Industrialized Countries (NICs) have been developing many standardized technologies through transferring them.

The benefits of the developing modern technologies depend mainly, on the relevant technical, economical, political, managerial conditions and the market size of the nations. These conditions are highly developed in the developed nations, which enable them to develop and transfer technologies early. Consequently, they are able to benefit from technologies at the early stages of technological development. On the other hand, developing nations can transfer these technologies after they are standardized. Their benefits begin to increase while the benefits of the originators decrease after they develop these technologies fully. This is because the comparative advantages in these technologies shifts from the originators to followers when a technology is standardized. Thus the originator, benefit from the technologies at the early stages of technology development, and the followers, benefit them at the late stages of technological development, as explained earlier.

The originator and the follower nations maximize the benefits of technological development through globalization. The originators increase their benefits from the technologies by having the access to global market through globalization. At the same time, the followers utilize their resources and benefit from developing standardized technologies, relatively earlier, with a short time, less cost and less risk through globalization. Globalization also increases the nations' competition in the global markets with these technologies and provides better quality and less cost products for all the customers.

The benefits to the nation from technological development, depends mainly on the nature of free and fair trade. Protection hurts a nation's ability to benefit from technological development through globalization (Kraus, 1997; and Cohen, 1998). Protection of the technologies by the originators limits the followers' technological development by not being able to develop these technologies earlier. Eventually, the knowledge of developing these technologies will become like a free good. Therefore, the originator may lose the opportunities to receive larger returns from these technologies. It may be more beneficial for the originators to let followers develop these technologies earlier for a fair return. On the other hand, the followers benefit from the technologies by having access to these technologies rather than waiting for a long time. Thus, free trade benefits both the originators and the followers fairly. If followers protect their markets, this may decrease the originators' benefits by not having access to the followers' markets. The followers' protection may also decrease their benefits by limiting their market potential which could be developed and become a ready market for the future technological development. The protection, also, limits the domestic competition and reduces the quality, and increases the prices of the goods. Thus, free trade is essential for an optimum benefit of both the originators and the followers.

However, in order to generate maximum benefit and eliminate the adverse effects of technological development through trade, free trade should be fair. Otherwise, technological development through free trade alone may generate negative effects on follower nations and favor the originator nations. The comparative advantages of the nations determine the nations' benefit from trade. However, if the globalization is free but not fair, it may always favor the originators' technological development and hurt the followers. Fair trade means fair trade agreements among the nations. However, fair agreements are very difficult to establish when there is a gap of technological, economical and managerial conditions among the nations.

The gap among the nations generates dependency problems. The followers with poor local conditions may not be able to develop standardized technologies but become consumers of the products of these technologies for a long time. The followers' income, derived mainly from the primary goods and raw materials, may not be enough to accumulate necessary capital required for the development of standardized technologies. They may depend on the originators' capital, which may generate debt and dependency problems. Most developing nations suffer from these kinds of problems. As a result, they cannot utilize their labor and other resources at such a level to generate necessary comparative advantages for their technological development. Therefore, they cannot integrate their economy and the originators' economy with equal opportunities. Exclusion of the followers' economy, concerning their markets and resources, may also hurt technological development of the originators. Thus, the fair trade agreements such as GATT, NAFTA and WTO have to be established to provide equal opportunities for the nations with unequal conditions. The recent financial crisis that influenced technological development is partly caused by the unfair trade of the followers.

There is, of course, no standard fair trade agreements that work well for every nation. Both the originators and the followers should establish these agreements to promote their technological development cooperatively fairly, and competitively. They should also be based on not only the short-term benefits, but also long-term benefits. Japanese technological development through trade provides good examples for the followers. They develop the technological and managerial conditions first and finance the technological development of the intermediate technologies internally. They did not borrow capital from outside resources and they established close relations with the originators. Presently, developing nations may use the Japanese experience as a good example for their technological development through trade.

Technological development increases the nation's economic development and provides economic stability. Economic stability encourages political democratization. The government of nations who have high economic growth makes favorable changes toward democratization. Western European nations, United States and Japan have relatively higher economic development mainly because of their high level of technological development. Consequently their economical and political stability provided them conditions to democratize their institutions. On the other hand, the Soviet Union with mostly military technologies could not generated high level of economic growth and political stability.

It is, therefore, imperative for nations to develop appropriate technologies, which provide higher economic growth relative to military technologies.

Appropriate technologies support the economical and political democratization of a nation. Japan hardly has any modern commercial technologies when they started their democratization during the Meiji period. Since then, Japanese governments continuously develop new technologies while democratizes their economical and political activities. Presently, Japan is considered one of the democratize nations among the most advanced countries. Developing appropriate (democratic) technologies played the key role in this success.

The advanced nations including the United States, Western European Nations, and Japan have to democratize their technologies further through developing appropriate technologies. On the other hand developing nations have to transfer appropriate technologies rather than military technologies for their democratization. The Japanese example may provide good lessons for this purpose (Sen, 1982).

# CHAPTER XII

# Utilization of Information Technology for Democratization

*...without communication, there can be no organization,...*
*without organization there can be no progress.*
—Herbert A. Simon

During the last several decades' information technology (IT) has been playing very important role in nations' competitiveness and democ ratization. Information technology increases productivity and democratization through providing crucial competencies of speed, decentralization, centralization, integration and equalization of knowledge, skills, values and resources locally and globally. These competencies enable individuals, organizations and nations to respond quickly to fast changing economical, political and social conditions. This chapter explains how information technology increases competitiveness and the democratization process.

The recent advancements in information technology have played an important role in the nature and application of technology in production and business. During the last two decades, many new corporations and nations entered into the global market and were able to compete successfully, in almost every industry throughout the world. The monopolies in many markets are disappearing. The corporations and nations who wish to produce goods and services are able to do so at any time and anywhere. Consequently, the business world is becoming more competitive and more democratic.

Information technology plays crucial role in developing high total quality and competitiveness. It provides new opportunities and competitive advantages for suppliers, producers and customers everywhere. The suppliers are able to provide a variety of resources for the users any time, any place, and in any quantity demanded. The producers are able to develop a variety of goods and services relatively faster, better quality, and at a lower cost. They can transfer, diffuse, and adopt all the required resources including technology, knowledge, labor, capital, and raw materials required for business. The customers have a variety of choices of goods and services, which are better in quality, lower in cost, and can be purchased any time and at any place (Woodal, Rebuck and Voehl, 1997).

Information technology speeds the production process from suppliers to customers through information, knowledge, and resources. It decentralizes the large and rigid processes to generate flexibility and rapid changeability at every level, for every unit.

Information technology provides opportunities for democratization through open information, communication and close cooperation and teamwork. It helps to divide, connect and integrate small and large, stronger and weaker, through utilizing the best resources and know how. It integrates data, text, voice and image information in its various formats and team-setting structure at the local and global levels. It removes all the barriers between small operations units to large corporations and generates close cooperation and fair competition environment. It brings Just-In-Time (JIT), placeless and boss-less philosophies to reality by connecting everything to everywhere. It makes the local global and the global local, and technologies equalize opportunities and resources. As a result of these changes that information technology provides, the economic, political and business activities are more productive and democratic.

## Evolution and Revolution of Information Technology

Information technology and production have always been applied in economic activities together. As the market conditions have changed through time they have also changed to respond to these changes. Historically and technically, information technology has been complementary to production. Information technology accompanied this movement by progressing from counting on fingers and toes to slide rules, and calculators and to electronic computers.

The first computers were primarily used for scientific purposes and advanced from business to personal use. After World War II, Henry Ford and Alfred Sloan moved automobile manufacturing from craft production to mass production. Parallel to this movement, the first analog computers were introduced in the 1920s along with the digital computers in the 1940s. They were large and consisted of thousands of relays connected by mazes of wire (Woodall, Rebuck and Voehl, 1997). In the late 1950s and the early 1960s transistors replaced vacuum tubes, which allowed for smaller, modular-designed computers. Major corporations, which could afford a computer, started using it for production and for other economic activities. During the late 1960s, miniature integrated circuits replaced transistors, and the computer became smaller and faster. The remote-processing concept was introduced which allowed for a terminal access directly to the computers from various locations.

During the late 1970s and early 1980s, microprocessors replaced integrated circuits and allowed the computer to become smaller, faster, and more powerful. This development made it possible for small businesses to afford and use computers and automation for the production process. During the 1980s, "chips" were developed and customized for each computer's specific needs. The personal computers (PC) were given the power of mainframe computers. The cost was reduced, and computers were used for every aspect of economic activities including design, planning, controlling and distribution, of goods and services (Daniels, 1994).

The fast computing, integrating, linking, and storing capabilities of the computer allowed production processes to become more flexible and fast changing. Consequently, producers could customize a variety of products at a lower cost and increase quality. Information technology works the way people do, it eliminates the boundaries among data, text, voice, and image and provides the basis of team operations. These developments have been characterized as a paradigm shift in economics and in the international business environment (Tapscott and Caston, 1993).

The microprocessor computer on chip is the key element of this new paradigm. Microprocessors are beginning to dominate leading edge computers of every size, which outperform the multi-million dollar mainframes with about a hundred percent less cost. The network-based open systems, which combine many microprocessors into a single large computer, can outperform mainframes in power. It shifts from single to multimedia data, text, voice, and image, which will combine the home computer, television, and telephone into multimedia devices, delivering a vast array of applications. Its power increases geometrically. The number of transistors on a microprocessor chip has grown 150 percent per year and is estimated to rise faster for the future (Tapscott and Caston, 1993).

Software development also moves from craft to factory format; this has been called the industrial revolution in software. Developers use and reuse modules or parts that are standardized and work together interchangeably. Computer-aided software engineering (CASE) is already showing its potential for standardization, interchangeability, and integrateability. These new developments in information technology have a profound impact on the economic activities through production. They help to develop computer-aided design (CAD), computer-aided manufacturing (CAM), integrated manufacturing CAD/CAM, flexible-manufacturing systems (FMS), just-in-time (JIT) productions, and other production activities (Dilworth, 1992). Among these, lean production has made the greatest impact on the production process and has become the most productive and dominant among the automobile producers in the global market (Womack, Jones and Roos, 1990).

## *Information Technology, Total Quality and Competitiveness*

The recent changes in global market conditions concerning quantity, quality, cost, variety, and the dynamism of goods and services generated enormous pressure on producers. Consequently, the new production process has been developed to respond to these changes. One of the most important production developments took place in the automobile industry with a new production process called flexible (lean) productions.

Eiji Toyota and Taichi Ohno at Toyota Motor Company in Japan pioneered the concept of lean production (Womack, Jones and Roos, 1990). Japan has become one of the most productive and competitive automobile producers in the global market, mainly due to this new production process. Flexible production eliminates the problems of both craft and mass production techniques and provides superior core competencies including speed, decentralization, integration and equalization. These competencies enable producers to respond quickly to fast changing market conditions.

Craft production uses highly skilled workers, simple, and flexible tools to make what customers ask for, one item at a time. It cannot produce large quantities to satisfy large demands. Mass production, contrary to craft production, uses mostly semi-skilled professionals to design single-purpose products made by unskilled or semi-skilled workers. Because of the large cost of machinery and rigidity, mass producers add many buffers into the production process such as extra space, suppliers, inventories, and workers to assure smooth production. It is also technologically and economically not feasible to change a new product. The mass producer keeps standard designs in production for as long as possible. The lower cost through large quantities at the expense of variety, flexibility, and dynamism has been the major reason for success in the past and the main cause of its recent failure (Dertouzes, Lester and Solow, 1989).

Flexible production combines the advantages of craft and mass production. It avoids the high cost and small-scale production of craft and rigidity of mass production mainly through information technology. Information technology provides flexibility, agility, and automation in a decentralized and integrated format to produce volumes of products fast and in a large variety. It enables lean production to employ teams of multi-skilled workers in close cooperation and communication at all levels, locally or globally.

Flexible production uses less of everything compared to mass production including capital, labor, raw material, space, inventory and time and uses more of information technology. It reduces defects, waste, and costs and increases the quality of products and productivity and the competitiveness of producers. The Toyota Takaoko assembly plant, which was the originator of lean production, out-performed General Motors Farmington assembly plant in every major production activity including assembly hours, defect, and space per car by 3 to 1. The New United Motor Manufacturing, Inc. (NUMMI) plant at Fremont, California came close to Toyota's productivity by adopting the flexible production process. Japanese and Japanese-American joint producers who used flexible production techniques realized relatively higher productivity compared to American and European automobile producers in 1989. The productivity is comparatively similar for product development and supplying activities (Womack, Jones and Roos, 1990).

As a result of the utilization of information technology Japanese share of world production increased steadily and reached to about 30 percent of the world motor vehicle production in the 1980s by means of exporting. The Japanese share of North American automobile production also increased to about 25 percent by 1990. Partly because of the success of information technology in the United States ten automobile assembly plants were closed, and only one was opened by an American-owned automobile companies during the period of 1987–1990.

# How Does Information Technology
# Increase Total Quality?

Information technology gives life to production, like blood vessels of the human body to human life. Information technology is essential for the existence of the production process. Information technology provides major ingredients for the production activities including product selection, design, development, production planning and control, technology selection, transferring and development. It influences every aspect of the operations management of an organization. It connects every part of the production system at every level, small or large, and provides opportunities for higher productivity and competitiveness at the global market. It does so by speeding, decentralizing, integrating and equalizing the economical, political, technological and social activities. These competencies provide major competitive advantages, which are explained below.

## IT as a Speeder (Changer)

Information technology speeds production by linking all of the relevant parts and teams of the production stream, and by providing necessary information about the quality, quantity, and timeliness of the input and output process for each part. It increases the responsiveness of each part from suppliers, producer to customers, and eliminates waste, reduces inventory, and the risk of running out of resources. It provides existing and new knowledge and other relevant resources quickly and helps their transfer and development. Through its speed, the near and far become one, local becomes global, and global becomes local. The philosophy of Just-In-Time (JIT) and placeless activities become a reality with the help of information technology. It follows and observes the new conditions and informs responsible sources of a quick change and response.

## IT as a Decentralizer and Customizer

IT can provide great flexibility through the decentralization of rigid activities. Smaller units provide greater flexibility that helps to quickly improve and deliver what customers ask for. This is a customization of large activities through flexibility and agility. The objective is to provide a large amount of different products and services in a relatively short time. Information technology links decentralized parts and provides necessary information for rapid changes of the relevant conditions. Any socio-economical and political system which in inter-connected and related through information technology acts as a biological organism, except that it consists of people and electronics to produce certain goods.

The objective of decentralization is not making the parts smaller to achieve the highest flexibility, but to design an appropriate scale that provides the required flexibility and, at the same time, enhances the system to realize the maximum advantages of the holistic result. Information technology simultaneously creates the huge global system while making the parts more flexible and powerful. The success of the whole system depends partly on decentralization and partly on integration through the utilization of information technology. Information technology provides flexibility to experiment and learn quickly in determining the right scale of decentralization and integration.

The system that decentralizes and integrates all of its relevant parts simultaneously is able to generate maximum value for each small part and for the system as a whole. This is what we call mass customization. However, every part of the system is managed by people. Their knowledge, skills, and values are essential for the dynamism of the system concerning competencies including rapid learning, operating, innovating, cooperating, and communicating.

## IT as an Integrator (Uniter)

IT can integrate every part of a socio-economical system and increase partnership among people, teams, and organizations to cooperate and communicate for maximum results. IT also increases competition. None of the people, teams, or organizations does anything alone to produce the best result. However, they can combine the best of each other to produce the best of the best. IT links people, resources, and facilities that are not part of the corporation as though they were participating in the production process. This virtual production process, which is made possible through information technology, provides opportunities to produce everything at any place and at any time. This dynamism of virtualness, called the agile web or agile operations, integrates and shifts competencies to react to fast changing market conditions that demand high quality and a variety of product capabilities (Martin, 1996; Goldman, Nagel and Preiss, 1995). The agile grouping is greater than the sum of the parts. There is no corporation that can have all the competencies. But together, the best of the best can be utilized to replace less competent areas. This provides world-class competition, agility for uncertainty, and response to fast changing market situations.

Many corporations have reorganized themselves to utilize IT in the global market. Ford merged all of its activities, which were distributed among 30 countries into a single operation. Ford merged its seven automotive design centers on four continents and developed its "world car" through IT. AT&T implemented its Global Information Systems Architecture (GISA) to standardize its production systems worldwide. Benetton operates 8,000 shops and 450 factories in over 100 countries. The orders from Spain with an entry computer in France triggers production planning in New York to schedule manufacturing in Dallas which requires chips from Japan to be built into circuit boards in Singapore with the finished production in Dallas and computer-controlled shipment from a warehouse in Milan (Martin, 1996). Boeing produces its 747 and 777 by cooperating with more than 30 countries around the world.

Information technology has shifted the focus to vertical and horizontal integration across organizations globally, which becomes a common phenomenon in the 1990s. Integration through information technology utilizes existing resources optimally, reduces cost and increases quality, making producers more productive and competitive in the global market.

## IT as an Equalizer and Democratizer

IT increases learning and knowledge of the people that are essential for the production and other core activities (Denison, 1985; Drucker 1991 and 1993; Senge, 1993; and Nonaka and Takeuchi, 1995). The production process gains sustainable competitive advantages through quick learning (Arie deGeus, 1997; Garvin, 1993). As information highways turn into super highways, the flow of knowledge becomes a flood and fills the existing knowledge gaps among people, organizations, and nations. This increases the chances of producers competing in the global market with equal competency. Information technology provides opportunities for every producer to compete in the global market, regardless of their size and location. Information technology provides opportunities through pooling and connecting producers to equalize knowledge, skills, techniques, and values necessary for production (Gibson, 1997).

Information technology breaks down the walls and eliminates the layers of pyramidal hierarchy through open and rapid communication. Increasing knowledge and open communication provides each person and team with the major responsibility and control for their work. It will also increase the effectiveness of managerial decision making by shifting authority from top managers to those who perform the work. As decision-making authority, responsibility, and control of each person's work are equalized through information technology and the management process will be democratized. The authoritarian management practices disappear as self-management maximizes each person's productivity and competitiveness in the production and the business system (Snider, 1996; Sen, 1995).

Information technology helped the Japanese to become the most productive and competitive automobile producers in the world. Following the Japanese, North American and European automobile producers have transformed their mass production process into lean production and avoided bankruptcy. However, it took them ten to fifteen years to understand the value of utilizing information technology for production.

Although very important changes have been made to improve the productivity of production systems, there are still many opportunities that IT can provide for the fast-changing global market. Some of the changes that can help increase producers' productivity and competitiveness in the global market are presented next.

## *Utilization of Information Technology for Democratization*

Growth of information technology is relatively much faster than its utilization, especially into the political activities. Because of the slow understanding of the value of information technology, some of our resources are wasted, and under utilized, and many opportunities are lost. This is partly due to our slow understanding of the capacity of information technology, and partly our slow adaptation to change. In order to appreciate the information technology better, we should act quickly and change fast with the information technology. Some ideas are provided here for this purpose.

### Utilize IT Quickly and Appropriately

IT does not mean just using e-mail or the fax. IT has to be utilized for every activity of the organization and nation as a whole system. In order to realize its maximum results, it has to be applied to new techniques rather than using it to improve old techniques. The old techniques were developed to respond to old conditions. Contemporary conditions including technology and resources and the customers' needs are rapidly changing. The political and economical activities have to change quickly to utilize the advantages of information technology and respond to the people's needs. Using information technology for a quick fix or to improve the old techniques marginally will not generate maximum results, but only partial ones. American automobile makers lost a considerable amount of the market share in the global market, and it took them a relatively long time to change their production process. The producers who can utilize information technology quickly for their production processes will be further ahead in productivity and realize high competitiveness in the global market.

## Act Quickly Now by Thinking About the Future

Great productivity and competitiveness can be achieved for the future by shaping it now, not just responding to it. The producers acting with yesterday's mentality and knowledge will not be ready for future conditions. Although the future is uncertain, it should never be left to chance. Information technology provides the fast-moving abilities to adjust to changing conditions generated by uncertainty. Japanese automobile producers acted quickly to develop lean production techniques and to acquire high productivity and competitiveness. It took Detroit automobile makers relatively a long time to change their mental thinking in adopting the lean production process. They were probably still believing in the great success of mass production. The mental and physical changes have to be made quickly and continually by thinking ahead to generate sustainable competitive advantages.

## Learn Fast and Change Fast

Learning as an individual, organization, and nation is the key to knowledge, thinking, and doing things. Information technology accelerates learning through acquiring, storing, transferring, creating, and utilizing the existing knowledge, skills, and social values for production. Contemporary production or operation management practices have given major emphasis to technological knowledge and neglecting value-based (tacit) knowledge (Nonaka and Takeuchi, 1995). Human values which constitute the foundation of tacit knowledge were assumed given and not promoted in the West. Japanese producers have partly utilized human values in their lean production (Ozaki, 1991; Sen, 1992).

Information technology is utilized by the people. In order to realize its maximum impact in production and other activities it has to be integrated with people. Integration of technology and people works best if it is based on good relationships. The maximum productivity and competitiveness can be achieved through quality relationships. Executives, managers, workers, and people should learn, adopt, and utilize universal values for the basis of good relations through utilizing information technology. This way, the lean production system becomes a learning system that integrates both technical and human side of knowledge. This we call "lean and humane" production that can achieve maximum productivity and competitiveness.

## Computerize and Humanize

IT integrates technology and human values into a team, organization, and nation state to achieve the maximum productivity and competitiveness. IT requires new management techniques, which are flexible, fast, dynamic, and humanistic. The contemporary management practices are old and rigid. Just like the mass production technique, they were developed for the conditions of past times, they cannot respond to present conditions. The old pyramidal organizational structure is so rigid that decision-making is monopolized and actions are controlled. It does not have the flexibility, dynamism, and support of most people to generate the real team productivity. It has inherently master-servant relations among its people, rather than an open and close relationship that information technology provides and requires. The contemporary management practices are the obstacles to full integration and utilization of information technology and people. The timeless, placeless, and borderless production conditions demand true democratic management practices to generate maximum productivity and competitiveness.

Many academicians and business experts indicate that democratization of the contemporary management practices is the best preparation for the future (Gibson, 1997). The executives of organizations and governments should think about the future and change management practices accordingly for long-term productivity and competitiveness. It is always safer and better to think and learn to change rather than be forced to change. People often behave unproductively under stress.

## Utilize IT and Democratize

Although some of the economic activities like production have utilized information technology to increase productivity, the political activities are still using hundred year old, rigid and inefficient tools for selecting, electing and decision-making processes. Even the economically most advanced countries like United States have utilized information technology to allow humans to walk on the moon, but politically people are still walking on the slum of the earth. The recent political crisis in many countries throughout the world including the Presidential election crisis in the United States clearly indicate the urgency of utilization of information technology for the democratization. Utilization of information technology in political activities will eliminate many political problems and increase democratization.

Through utilization of information technology and the cable television, news channels our capacity to learn and getting information will be increased. As our knowledge and information increase, our participation in political activities will increase. Currently, people's participation in political activities is limited to voting every four years to elect the candidates to talk and decide for us. Now, utilization of information technology can reverse the process by permitting people to speak back to political figures, elect the representatives directly and even make major decisions by ourselves rather than representatives making the decisions for us. Information technology, made it possible now to reclaim the democracy that Thomas Jefferson would have liked to provide for the people. The logistic problems of direct voting have been overcome by the information technology. Now, people can move in the direction that Jefferson would led toward true (direct) democracy.

Utilization of information technology will eliminate the intermediaries in politics through direct voting, like direct investment, buying, selling, banking and learning. Web sites are springing up giving people ability to vote on important issues. Already, some major news media have utilized information technology to allow people vote and express their ideas, opinions and views on some issues. Similar process can be used to get people's opinion and vote on important issues such as budget surpluses, Social Security, defense spending, national health care, education, gun controls, abortion, and many other important issues.

Currently people are dominated by the biased self-interested news media and isolated from the real sources of information. Utilization of information technology will provide direct and primary source information as original as possible without filtering and manipulation. This way people can make up their own minds, rather than some others controlling their thinking and actions. People will become freer from the media and the intermediaries through utilizing information technology. People will be open to multiple sources of information through the internet. Consequently, it will be impossible for anyone or any organization to control information or shaping people's ideas, opinions, viewpoints and perspectives. People can take as much direct control as possible of the decisions that affect their own lives.

As direct information, learning, selecting, voting and deciding take root, the people become more involved and active in political activities. Consequently, democratization will increase as our thoughts and actions become more efficient, effective and ethical.

# CHAPTER XIII

## Democratization Through Globalization

*Humanity is interdependent. We rise and fall together.*

Globalization is the joint political, economical, technological, social and educational activities among two or more nations and their respective organizations. When these activities take place among international organizations and nations, the democratization process spreads around the globe. The experience gained of one organization or nation becomes a benchmark for the other or others to follow for their democratization. Thus, the globalization demonstrates and provides opportunities for all people, organizations and nations to have access to the best possible knowledge skills and values for their democratization. The people, organizations and nations having access to these resources will be able to learn, follow and transfer the best resources for their democratization. The availability, choice and mobility of these resources will increase the democratization and reduce the relevant time, risk and other costs of democratization.

Globalization will also provide opportunities for local organizations to utilize their resources for technological and economic developments. These developments that are explained in the following sections, interdependently, increase democratization of management practices positively. Centrally controlled and directed economies are shifted to market economies through globalization. This shift accelerates migration from labor-intensive technologies to knowledge-intensive technologies, and from male dominance to emergence of women in management. These activities increased the demand for the knowledge organizations and knowledge employees. In order to supply these demands the nations, organizations and the people seek new knowledge, skills and values throughout the world. This chain reaction, which is generated by globalization, provides further opportunities for democratization.

Globalization provides opportunities to have the best of the knowledge throughout the world. It provides broader, newer, wider, and diversified knowledge that has been proven universally. People equipped with full and global knowledge, skills, and values can think broadly, analyze, and fairly evaluate to make necessary changes toward true democratic management (Sen, 1996).

Globalization promotes competition and cooperation among the organizations and the nations and puts great emphasis on human relations. As globalization increases, people try to equalize their differences, humanize their activities, and harmonize their lives toward democratization. Although this may look ideal for today's conditions, it provides a better and safer vision for the continuous improvement of human development for the future. As the globalization increases democratization will also increase simultaneously through political, economical, technological and social activities. These are explained in the following sections.

## *Globalization Increases Political Democratization*

The United States, Western European countries and Japan have democratized their political institutions first and try to democratize their industrial organizations after that for global competitiveness. Many less democratize nations and others who abolished their authoritarian governments are also trying to democratize their management activities by benchmarking the more democratic nations.

In the last two decades, many governments and organizations throughout the world have been experiencing profound changes in their management practices. Most of these changes involved the widespread trend away from authoritarian management practices toward democratic management (Haggard and Kaufman, 1995; Fukuyama, 1992; and Dankwart, 1990).

Beginning in the late 1970s and early 1980s, many Latin American countries including Argentina, Brazil, Peru, Mexico and Chile started establishing democratic governments. During the 1980s, some Asian countries including South Korea, Taiwan, Thailand, the Philippines, Turkey and Pakistan struggled to establish civilian governments. In the late 1980s, authoritarian governments in Eastern Europe and the Soviet Union collapsed mainly because of their poor economic performance and were replaced by democratic governments. These activities, which Samuel Huntington (1991) called the "third wave," put pressure on many of the authoritarian governments of Africa and the Middle East for democratization. Rustow Dankwart (1990) calls this development "global democratic revolution."

In the early 1990s and presently, many of these countries are still trying to improve their political democratization. Others are abolishing authoritarian management practices and making reforms toward political democratization (Haggard and Webb, 1994).

Parallel to political democratization, there have been even more dramatic changes toward industrial democratization in these countries. They have been privatizing their business organizations, adopting more liberal trade policies, and seeking broader collaborations with other nations for their economic growth. The governments and business organizations seek better management practices to increase their competitiveness through globalization (Carnoy, 1995).

Political factors play an important role in industrial democratization. Top managers of elected governments ordinarily seek opportunities to increase the economic performance of their economy. These elected officials in developing countries who cannot provide economic growth and prosperity for their citizens often fail to win in the next elections, necessitate early elections or military takeovers (Haggart and Kaufman, 1995; Fukuyama, 1992; and Dankwart, 1990). Many developing countries try to democratize their governments by adopting new policies and laws to liberalize their trade activities and privatize their national industries. They establish new policies for joint operation, transfers of new technologies, and knowledge.

Many developed nations including the United States, Western European countries, and Japan have been transferring these resources for their economic and technological developments. Recent developments of the North American Free Trade Agreement (NAFTA), the European Economic Community (EEC), and the Association of South East Asian Nations (ASEAN) were mainly established for these purposes. Democratic governments have historically had to develop institutions and pursue policies, which reflect the democratic vision, and, at the same time, they tried to create a suitable environment for capital accumulation (Bowles and Gintis, 1986). In the information age, democratic governments shape the policies for the domestic business organizations and foreign business enterprises to interact through new policies.

The global activities such as European Unity (EU) and North Atlantic Treaty Organization (NATO) provide opportunities for the participating nations to learn from each other's management practices by working together. For example, the Greek and Turkish people and their governments learn from other EU and NATO countries and try to adjust their political, economical and social laws and activities to the other countries' relative conditions that might be more advanced. It is also desirable to have common or similar management practices among the EU and NATO countries for more productive coordination and communication for the joint operations. Practical real world experiences indicate that the common activities are influenced more by the nations who are relatively more democratized than the others. For example, within the EU and NATO countries, the management practices of Greece and Turkey are influenced by the other partners. When the military leaders took over the governments of Turkey and Greece the United States and other partners urged the military leaders to establish democratic governments in their nations. Similarly, EU countries are urging non-EU countries such as Bulgaria, Poland, and others to democratize their governments and institutions so they can become members of EU and NATO. These kind of global activities provide opportunities and require obligations for nations to democratize their management activities.

These policies often promote democratization for better collaborations and joint operations. Less democratic governments often adopt new policies to adjust themselves with the more democratic countries' policies to increase their trade as well as political conditions toward democratization.

## *Globalization Increases Economical Democratization*

Economic factors including production, consumption, and distribution of goods and services play the key role of satisfying people's needs. Achievement of quality and equality depends, mainly, on the nature of economic activities. Economic success is crucial for the political success and for the success of management. The management of organizations and nations is given high priority to achieve economic success.

Globalization influences nations' democratization through economical activities such as multinational corporations (MNCs) and international agreements such as North Atlantic Free Trade Agreement (NAFTA) and the World Trade Organization (WTO). The MNCs from relatively more democratize countries such as U.S., Germany, and Japan brought their management practices into the less democratic countries such as South

Korea, Singapore, Taiwan, Mexico, Brazil, Turkey and other Newly Industrialized Countries (NICs). The management of host countries try to adopt their management practices to the management practices of the source countries. These activities are often improving the host countries' management practices toward democratization. For example, the management practices of Japan and Germany, which are relatively more democratize than the management practices of the United States did help to democratize management practices of some organizations in the U.S. such as NUMMI, Fuji, Honda, Mitsubishi, BMW and Mercedes. One of the main reasons of the recent mergers and alliances among MNCs is to establish and share the better management practices among many corporations. The governments and local organizations adopt more liberal, diversified and adjustable policies to attract other organizations and nations to establish joint operation and learn from each other (Carnoy, 1995). Less democratic governments often adopt new policies to adjust themselves to more democratic countries' policies to increase their economical as well as political conditions toward democratization. Mexico liberalized management activities to adjust their management practices to the management practices of the United States and Canada through NAFTA. Many other developing nations have been liberalizing and democratizing their economic activities through globalization (Kanter, 1995; Knoke, 1996; Carnoy, 1993; and Hoogvelt, 1997).

The Asia Pacific Economic Cooperation (APEC) was established to increase global economic formation that may increase the democratization of the Pacific Rim countries by adjusting their political activities to the relatively more democratic nations of the United States and Canada. World Trade Organization (WTO) may adopt new rules toward liberalization to handle new activities requiring new globalization. IMF, and WB, helped many governments to liberalize and harmonize their relations for globalization. More economic globalization requires more liberalization that opens doors for more democratization. Relatively more democratized nations influence the less democratized nations through unifying activities and utilizing resources. This way, they become more global and more democratic. Through economic globalization, the prices, rents, wages, interest payments, and dividends become more equal.

Globalization opens the doors for global competition. Organizations seek opportunities to increase their competitiveness through selecting the best and latest effective management practices and managers. This will help organizations to improve their management capabilities. In order to increase the benefits of these processes, the nations and organizations may adopt more liberal and diversified policies to keep up with the most advanced level of management. This process will accelerate the democratization process. The nations that are achieving a high level of growth through globalization also increase their democratization. The most developed nations including the United States, Germany, and Japan have been using globalization to increase their democratization. Developing nations, including the Pacific Rim countries, some Latin America countries (Brazil, Argentina, and Chile), India, Pakistan, and Turkey have all increased their economic growth and democratized their management practices through globalization. (Neher and Marley, 1995; Garten, 1997; and Luckham and White, 1996).

## *Globalization Increases Social Democratization*

Democratization of social values is an integral part of democratization process. Democratization through political, economic, and technological changes requires social changes. The people as individuals in the family, organizations, community and the nation have to change, develop, and adapt their social values for successful democratization. Universal values like love, freedom, care, discipline, respect, justice, peace, ethics, and equality which constitute tacit knowledge (Nonaka and Takeuchi, 1995), play a very important role in democratization. People develop this knowledge by learning and doing and partly by accepting or believing them as part of their culture or religion at home, schools, and in the community and work places. Although, it is difficult to standardize and unify them for a particular group, organization or nation, they can develop, change and adapt for democratization, since democratic principles are universal.

Globalization plays an important role in changing social values for democratization. The transfer of new technologies requires changes in local values to accept and utilize them productively. Globalization helps to spread and accelerate the changes in social values towards democratization (Kidder, 1994; Trompenaars and Turner, 1998; Rosen, 2000; and Knoke, 1996).

Democratization requires value-based understanding, cooperation, and communication. Information technology makes it easier and faster to access these values at any time and any place. Although people ordinarily tend to preserve their own values, globalization provides new opportunities to learn the needs of changing, improving, and developing new values. Utilization of universal values for management practices increases democratization as well as the competitiveness of an organization and nation (Sen, 1992). This is done by using values such as good relations, care, teamwork, generating common goals, and unity among people.

Universal social values are the glue and unifying forces for political, economic, and technological activities. They help to develop appropriate ideologies for economic development and democratization. Many experts in social studies and others have attributed Japanese economic development and its worldwide competitiveness to it value-based management (Ozaki, 1991). Similar developments are taking place in many United States corporations including IBM, Kodak, Hewlett Packard, and Proctor and Gamble (Ouchi, 1981). They use universal social values to generate close human relations and trust. Corporation such as Boeing, United Airlines, Delta Airlines, and 3M have used implicit and informal rules against explicit and formal relations (Tanner and Athos, 1981).

Universal social values are rational, human, and hence transferable to other organizations and nations. They increase cooperation, involvement, participation, and continuous improvement. They upgrade the status of people, recognize the importance of people, and increase trust and unity that are the essential blocks of democratic management. Following Japanese experience, many organizations and nations are utilizing universal values for their management practices (Ozaki, 1991). These activities have to be increased through globalization for democratization.

## *Globalization Increases Technological Democratization*

Globalization plays an important role in technological development as we have seen in Chapter XIII. Technological development through globalization increases a nation's economic development and an organization's competitiveness (Rosenberg and Birdzel, 1986; and Denison, 1985); Japan's economic development and recent global competitiveness are partly the results of its successful technological development through globalization (Sen, 1982).

Japan has been pursuing technological development through globalization since the Meiji restoration. Other nations have also been transferring technologies through globalization to increase their economic growth (Castells, 1995). The transfer of technology requires changes in management practices to accompany new technologies. The recent revolutions in information technologies including microelectronics, and telecommunication have made very significant changes in management practices. It increased the spread of movement and mobility of resources for business operations. It also increased the availability of information, and eliminated the secrecy of knowledge throughout the world. This, in turn, increased joint operations and global collaboration, and democratization.

Production shifts to information processing activities have made it possible for the organizational structure to become more lean and flexible (Womack, Jones and Roos, 1990). These technologies change the vertical integration to horizontal networks, and shift the focus from localization to globalization. The revolution in information technology has combined with organizational changes that developed interdependently at the global level to establish a "new world information economy." With these developments, historically, capital-based technological developments became knowledge-based. South Korea, Taiwan, Hong Kong, and Singapore have made great gains by using knowledge-based technologies (Naisbitt, 1995). These nations, along with Japan, constituted the most dynamic portion of the new global economy. As a result of this development, many of the developing nations became part of the global economy. The authoritarian management of some Communist countries, including the Soviet Union and Eastern European countries that could not adapt to these changes have collapsed. They are trying to democratize their management practices by making political and economic changes through technological development, and globalization.

Recent developments in information technologies make it possible to inform people in broader bases in a shorter time (Tapscott and Caston, 1993). People used to be informed through books, newspapers, radio, and television with a considerable amount of time and effort. Now, the information technology makes it much faster, more global and more effective through the Internet. People can be informed about global issues that are important to them and then they can make better decisions.

The new information technology makes direct voting much easier and more effective. In the absence of new information technology, it was difficult to include many people in voting. It would take a long time and effort for this process. Therefore, people vote only once every four years, and leave the other decisions to the representatives. Now, the new information technology makes it possible for everyone to vote directly on major issues, in a relatively short time, with an affordable cost and unlimited benefits. Technology through globalization makes the true democracy possible (Snider, 1996; and *The Economist*, June 17, 1995).

The advancements in information technology and knowledge have had an enormous impact on contemporary management practices. The organization that can utilize information technology and knowledge in its management practices appropriately is able to provide relatively higher quality products and services at lower prices in the global market. The recent management practices of some automobile organizations in the U.S. and other countries have almost doubled their productivity and have gained competitive advantages in the global market. During 1982-1985, Japanese automobile organizations including Honda, Nissan, Toyota, Mazda, Mitsubishi and Suzuki opened production facilities in the U.S., either on their own or through partnership with one of the American automobile organizations like the New United Motor Manufacturing, Inc. (NUMMI). These organizations quickly became the highest productivity plants in the automobile industry and gained considerable competitive advantages in the global market (Womack, Jones and Roos, 1990). These organizations, with the same workforce that other American automobile plants employed but with relatively more democratic management practices, were outperforming all other plants in the country. Similar results can be seen in other high-tech organizations. Most recently, the productivity of Fuji Film, operating in the U.S., surpassed the productivity of Kodak. The key factor of high productivity of these organizations has been the democratization of their management practices through transferring information technology (Sen, 1997). Transfer of Information technology through globalization makes it easier to utilize social values for democratization, which is explained in the next section.

## *Globalization Increases Educational Democratization*

Education is the foundation of all the managerial activities as we explained in chapter eight. Therefore, democratization of management education is crucial for democratization of management practices. Globalization plays an important role in democratization of education in general.

One of the most important channels of transferring democratic ideas and principles from organizations and nations to other institutions has been through global educational activities. These activities include exchange of students, teachers, scholars, professionals between countries and visitations of people to other countries. All of these activities provide opportunities for the involved people to learn and observe the different practices of democratic ideas and principles. People who have studied, worked and visited other countries also have opportunities to compare these practices with their own and may try to teach, adopt and spread them throughout the world.

# CHAPTER XIV

# What Can Be Done Now for Democratization

*You must be the change you wish to see in the world.*
—Mahatma Gandhi

Democratization starts in the minds of the people, and people change their minds through learning, doing and observing. However, democratization in institutions and nations cannot be achieved by changing a few minds relative to large populations. Democratization can be faster, stable and secure if it starts in every individual's mind. Great individuals such as Jefferson, Lincoln, Gandhi, and other champions of democracy had made very valuable contributions in democratization. It is mainly the people who can understand, utilize and improve the practices of democracy. Therefore, democratization movement should involve its practitioners, the public, managers, parents, and educators. They first democratize themselves to help democratize others through education, learning and observing. This way we may also have more chance to have many great people to expand and move the democratization forward. The following sections include people who must be educated in democracy first for a real, faster stable and secure democratization. It is people whom are educated in democratic values and practice that will be able to spread democratization among the people, institutions and nations.

# Educate Public for Democratization

It is often believed that people, including the youth and adults, have already developed their values and one cannot change their values through education and training. The only effective way to change people values can only be achieved through educating children. However, in order to educate children in values we have to educate the parents, educators and the other managers (leaders) in every institution. Secondly, we must not wait for changes only from parents, educators and managers. Everyone has to make changes themselves as individuals and demand similar changes from others for a real democratization. Individuals at home, work places and other places should think, decide and behave democratically. We have to ask questions without fear of retaliation. Some of your colleagues and the bosses at work may disagree with you or may even penalize you because of your courage and outspokenness. But many others will support your efforts for searching out democratic values. The number of Individuals looking for democratic values may grow and spread thorough establishing democratic teams, communities and organizations. There are already well-established democratic organizations. Join these organizations, do not be afraid, and do not assume that your support will not change anything. These kinds of assumptions are self-defeating. Do not be pessimistic; remember that people are the most important factor of management. If they can get together and generate enough numbers they can win every war. Do not tolerate wrong doings. You get the behavior you tolerate (Dubos, 1968; Friedman, 2000; Sen Amartya, 1999; Kaplan and Robinson, 1998; Schumacher, 1999; Mattson, 1998; and Cohen, 1998) .

# Educate Yourself and Others for Democratization

Read some books about democracy and think what Tocqueville said a long time ago: "Know the good, love the good, and do the good." Try to convince yourself that only the true democratic management will provide opportunities for you and others to live in a good world happily and peacefully. True democratic management will satisfy not only your needs and wants, but also that of others, including your family members, friends, colleagues, citizens and the society as a whole. When that commitment breaks down, and people consider only their own personal well being they can no longer depend on the behaviors that are in the best interests of their institutions. Thus, educating yourself in democratic values will be your best guidance for a good life.

Join a friend, group and association to teach and talk about democracy. Form your own team from your workplace, or community as an employee, consumer or stockholder. Analyze how current management activities affect you and others. You should join and help others to join Business For Social Responsibility, headquarters in Washington D.C. and other groups who work for the democratic management practices.

Support people-owned businesses, community-owned enterprises, small locally owned businesses, governmental and nongovernmental enterprises and nonprofit organizations. Join the Employee Stock Ownership Plans (ESOP) and increase your share. Demand that your institution where you work provide ESOP plans that give you an ownership opportunity and voting right for important issues. Join others to establish small business organizations and invite people to join your organization through issuing stocks.

Get involved with a labor movement that fights for social and economic justice rather than just more money for its members. Think positive and join democratic unions and other worker organizations. Get involved with the activities of workers' union like AFL-CIO and provide your opinion and support for them if you think they act fairly. Join others who are seeking to democratize their institutions through demanding clear and healthy environments, equal opportunity for hiring and opposing layoffs to increase stockholders' profits. Join consumers who are opposing poor quality, and unsafe products. Oppose those corporations who act and promote monopoly in their industry, like the oil and medical industries.

Do not vote for those who engage in big money politics, and support corporate mergers and corporate welfare. Support those who are speaking more directly against corporate power and promoting industrial democracy. Join organizations of consumers groups, such as Alliance of Democracy, Friends of the Earth, Public Citizen and United for a Fair Economy. You can get quick information about these organizations from the World Wide Web. Do not wait for job security from your work place, secure your own job through generating value for the work that you are doing. Increase your value through reeducating, retraining and continuous learning.

Support women and minorities who are discriminated against in the work place. Educate yourself and others about all kinds of prejudices that occur in the work places throughout the world. Strongly demand that institutions and nations respect human rights and democracy over profits.

Stand up for your rights in the family in the workplace, in the community and state. We usually expect others to provide and even determine our rights. The recent contemporary management practices indicate that people who control the managerial decisions and actions are biased. They often think that the rights of people have to be determined and controlled by the top managers who supposed to know the best. In a knowledge society, people should know what are their rights and they should be involved in determining them. They also protect their rights and make sure that these rights are not violated. The people's rights, in contemporary management practices have been violated frequently. The only way to stop these violations is to act together, rather than individually.

You have to join organizations and establish new ones to fight against human violations and undemocratic decisions and behaviors wherever they occur, domestically and globally. Do not think that you or your group is not strong enough to defeat those who control management. Today, your group may not be strong enough to ask for your rights or stop wrong doing; but, if you join the human rights associations and work for their growth you will have enough people to tackle even the strongest undemocratic governments. People have this potential if they can get together and use it; there is no other force to defeat them.

The people who criticize or raise questions about the contemporary management practices in any institution, are considered spoilers, anti-establishment and simply opponents. Consequently, they are being discouraged and often penalized. Therefore, you have to be careful and try to educate people about these issues before taking action. Try and insist on not doing the wrong things even if the conditions force you to do so. If your rights are violated in your home, institution and community, you might be frightened to take action. But your right to vote for economic and political issues is extremely important for your life and others. Therefore, you should become the champion of democratic management. Demand your stakeholder rights to vote in the workplaces through ownership, job security, unionization, participation in major decisions and practicing democratic values. Talk about it among friends, colleagues, and neighbors frequently and seriously enough that others listen and act (McLagan and Nel, 1995; Garfield, 1992; Purser and Cabana, 1998; Renesh, 1992; and Gibson, 1997).

## *Educate Managers for Democratization*

The managers at every level and in every institution including the president, vice president and middle managers have the most effective power that can help to democratize the contemporary management practices. They simply can make the major decisions and take actions to influence others for democratization.

The contemporary management demands too much from the top managers. They often do not have enough time to talk with employees and to read even their own e-mails and other important material. They usually assume that the new knowledge is for the others, and they know what they are doing. Unfortunately, the practical results indicate that the majority of problems and most of the failures that people face today in many institutions and throughout the world are generated by the top managers. Ordinarily the presidents and their vice presidents design the mission, objectives and adopt values and strategies and select the resources for their institutions. They select the other managers who implement the policies of top managers. Therefore, democratization in an organization has to start with the top managers in order to be fast.

Top managers have to take time to understand the value of democratization and the need for it. First, they have to educate themselves by reading relevant materials. They have to realize that their authoritarian management knowledge and practices are old and they are not working presently and will not work in the future. As the Chinese proverb says "if we do not change our direction we are likely to end up where we are going." You may implement the board of trustees' policies that they provide for you at the beginning of your job or you can educate the board of trustees on democratic management practices. However, in order to educate the board of trustees and others, you have to educate yourself about the true democratic management and how your organization get there through democratization (Block, 1994; Martin, 1992; O'Toole, 1995; Band, 1994; Nonaka and Takeuchi, 1995; Albrecht, 1994; Morris, 1997; Yukl, 1994; Minett, 1992; Mills, 1991; Halal, 1996; Ackoff, 1994; Hamal and Prahalad, 1996; and Blair, 1995).

Top mangers' management knowledge is old. In order to renew knowledge one should learn new knowledge that emphasizes democratic behavior and democratic values. After learning the necessary knowledge abut democratic management, top managers must commit themselves to the values and activities of democracy. Top managers can educate key stakeholders and managers about democratic management and create a shared vision, adopt a democratic value and make plans for their implementation. Although there are a variety of steps to follow for this process, learning and understanding the value of true democratic management is the key for the success. The relevant procedure and action plans can be developed through initiating the practices of true democratic management activities, as we discussed in Chapter V.

# Educate Parents for Democratization

Parents are the first and most important source for to teach their children democratic values. Unfortunately, parents teaching values are naturally more authoritarian than democratic. They provide love, care and maximum responsibility for their children, but also teach them the basic right and wrong doings through command and control practices. Simply, parents become the loving bosses of their children for a long time. "The parents know the best," mentality occupies many children's, youths and even the adult minds for their life. Most parents become the most trusted, respected, friendliest and loved teacher for their children.

Although the parents' relations with their children are mostly genuine and protective, most parents are autocratic rather than democratic. This happens unintentionally because the children do not know anything in their early ages. They have to do what the parents want them and tell them to do. They have to listen, and obey the parents. Their minds are not developed enough to act independently. They have to follow the parents' advice as an order. Although the children start thinking, and acting independently as they grew up, their knowledge, values and behaviors are influenced by the authoritarian nature of activities that they learn and developed in the early ages.

Parents' skills and values are mostly authoritarian rather than democratic. It is also difficult and sometimes impossible to teach kids by reasoning and explaining because they cannot understand in their early ages. They are dominated by other people and by their parents. Thus, the parents should do everything to teach their children in a way that reverses authoritarian values. The parents have to teach and act democratically as early as possible. The parents have to teach democratic values more than anything else. Most people carry their values for a long time that they learn at home. The family values provide the foundation for the values knowledge of every individual throughout life. The parents' values and behaviors are the basic model for children as they start developing their own values and model. The parents' values become the seeds for their children, like their genes. Therefore, the parents must learn, teach and practice democracy continuously (Lickona, 1991; Kilpatrick, 1994; and Coles, 1997).

# Educate Educators for Democratization

Teachers teach what they know and what is demanded from them. As we have seen earlier, values knowledge education has been neglected, not only in work places, but also in schools. Therefore, most contemporary teachers are not educated in values knowledge. Every teacher at elementary and secondary schools and at universities and colleges has to prepare his or herself to teach values (Gutmann, 1987; Dewey, 1916; Durkheim, 1961; Kant, 1900; Hunter, 1998; and Ryan and Bohlin, 1999). Every curriculum must have values knowledge courses such as democracy, equality, liberty, peace, human rights and responsibilities. The values knowledge also must be integrated in other courses, especially the management courses. Courses need to teach not just technological aspects of a subject but ethical and environmental aspects as well. The teachers and administrators commit themselves to teaching values through designing new mission and objectives and adopting new strategies and utilizing resources for democratization of curriculum. The school administrators should cooperate with other organizations in the community and with the parents to include their ideas and seek their supports.

Democratization of education should not be stopped after graduation from university and college. It should continue in the work place. Every institution must establish programs to educate their employees in values they adopted in their mission statements. Most of the institutions do not include values in their mission statements. Those institutions that do values statements in their missions, do not utilize them in actual operations. The institutions must have programs, like TQM (and beyond), to train and re-train employees in learning and utilizing values in their activities.

The institutions must also promote values education through adopting values knowledge as a required qualification criteria for employment. Practicing values knowledge must also be an important factor for promotions and rank. The state and government must encourage schools to teach values through requiring and supporting values education financially. The schools must develop curriculums to integrate values knowledge with the technical knowledge as a whole. This can be done through designing programs as whole, rather than individual departments. The faculty can work together to develop programs jointly and teaching them as a team. General knowledge, which include both the technical and values knowledge, must be the foundation for all specialization. The specialized fields like engineering, medicine, finance and others must utilize values in their practices. Integration of values in all other branches of knowledge must be the main objective of teachers and practitioners. Teachers and practitioners must work together for integrating values in our knowledge and practices.

# REFERENCES

## Introduction

Ackoff, Russell L. (1994). *The Democratic Corporation*. New York: Oxford University Press.

Adams, Frank T., and Gary B. Hansen (1992). *Putting Democracy to Work*. San Francisco: Berrett-Koehler Publishers.

Blair, Margaret M. (1995). *Ownership and Control*. Washington, D.C.: The Brookings Institute.

Gates, Jeff (1998). *The Ownership Solution*. Reading, MA: Addison-Wesley.

Halal, William E. (1996). *The New Management: Democracy and Enterprise Are Transforming Organizations*. San Francisco: Berrett-Koehler Publishers.

Lawler III, Edward E. (1992). *The Ultimate Advantage: Creating High Involvement Organization*. San Francisco: Josse-Bass Publishers.

Manz, C.E., and Sims H.P. (1995). *Business Without Bosses*. New York: John Wiley.

March, James G., and Johan, Olsen P. (1995). *Democratized Governance*. New York: The Free Press.

McLagan, Patricia, and Cristo Nel (1995). *The Age of Participation*. San Francisco: Berrett-Koehler Publishers.

Plunket, L.C., and Fournier R. (1991). *Participative Management: Implementing Empowerment*. New York: John Wiley.

Purser, Ronald E., and Cabana Steven (1998). *The Self Managing Organization*. New York: The Free Press.

# Chapter I: "Desirable Total Quality and Competitiveness"

Bernall, J.D. (1954). *Science in History*. London: Watts and Company.

Crosby, P.B. (1979). *Quality is Free: The Art of Making Quality Certain*. New York: New American Library.

Deming, Edwards W. (Spring, 1989). "Out of the Crisis." *Journal of Organizational Behavior Management*.

Dertouzes. L. Michael, Lester, K. Richard, and Solow, M. Robert. (1989). *Made in America: Regaining the Productivity Edge*. Cambridge, MA: The MIT Press.

Drucker, P.F. (1993). *Post Capitalist Society*. New York: Harper Business.

Feigenbaum, A.V. (1991). *Total Quality Control* (4th Edition). New York: McGraw Hill.

Garfield, C. (1992). *Second to None: How Our Smartest Companies Put People First*. Homewood, IL: Business One Irwin.

Garvin, D.A. (1988). *Managing Quality: The Strategic and Competitive Edge*. New York: The Free Press.

Grayson, Jackson, C., Jr. (1988). *A Two-Minute Warning*. New York: The Free Press.

Green, K.C. and Seymour, D.T. (1991). *Who's Going to Run General Motors?* Princeton, NJ: Peterson's Guides.

Gronroos, C. (1983). *Strategic Management and Marketing in the Service Sector*. Cambridge, MA: Marketing Science Institute.

Harbison, F.H. (1973). *Human Resources as the Wealth of Nations*. New York: Oxford University Press.

Hayes, H.R. and Abernathy, J.W. (1980). "Managing Our Way to Economical Decline." *Harvard Business Review*.

Juran, J.M. (1962). *Juran on Quality by Design: The New Steps for Planning Quality into Goods and Services*. New York: The Free Press.

Kennedy, P. (1989). *The Rise and Fall of the Great Powers*. New York: Vintage Books.

Malcolm Baldridge National Quality Award. (1994). Gettysburg, MD: Institute of Standards and Technology.

Parasuraman, A., Zeithaml, V.A. and Berry, I.I. (1985). "A Conceptual Model of Service Quality and its Implications for Future Research." *Journal of Marketing*, pp. 41-50.

Porter, Michael (1990). *The Competitive Advantage of Nations*. New York: The Free Press.

Pursell, Jr. (1981). *Technology in America: A History of Individuals and Ideas*. Cambridge, MA: The MIT Press.

Reich, R.B. (1992). *The Work of Nations*. New York: Vintage Books.

Rosenbluth, Hall F. (1992). *The Customer Comes Second*. New York: William Morrow Company.

Sen, A. (1982). *Science, Technology, and Development: Lessons from Japan*. Ankara: METU Publications.

Tenner, A.R. and DeToro, I.J. (1992). *Total Quality Management: Three Steps to Continuous Improvement.* New York: Addison-Wesley.

Thurow, Lester (1993). *Head to Head: The Coming Battle Among Japan, Europe, and America.* New York: Warner Books.

Walton, M. (1991). *Deming Management at Work.* New York: G.P. Putnam and Sons.

Webster's New World Dictionary. (1994). MA: Merriam-Webster Publishers.

Womack, J.P., Jones, D.T., and Roos, D. (1990). *The Machine That Changed the World.* New York: The Macmillan Company.

## Chapter II: "Understanding Management"

Bernard, Chester I. (1938). *The Functions of the Executive.* Cambridge, MA: Harvard University Press.

Crainer, Stuart (2000). *The Management Century.* San Francisco: Jossey-Bass Publishers.

Drucker, Peter (1954). *The Practice of Management.* New York: Harper and Brothers.
———. (October 5, 1998). "Management's New Paradigms." *Forbes.*

Fayol, Henry (1949). *General and Industrial Management,* translated by Constance Storrs. London: Isaac Pitman and Sons.

Fallett, Parker Mary (1949). *The New State.* New York: Longmans, Green.

Geisler, Murray A. and Wilbur, Streger A. (September–October, 1962). "How To Plan For Management in New Systems." *Harvard Business Review.* pp. 103-110.

Gilbreth, Frank B. and Lillian M. Gilbreth (1917). *Applied Motion Study.* New York: Sturgis and Walton.

Harbison, F.H. (1973). *Human Resources as the Wealth of Nations.* New York: Oxford University Press.

Koontz, Harold (December, 1961). "The Management Theory Jungle." *Journal of the Academy of Management.* Vol. 4, No. 3, pp. 174-188.

Mayo, Elton (1933). *The Human Problems of an Industrial Civilization.* Cambridge, MA: Harvard University Press.

McGregor, Douglas (May, 1960). *The Human Side of Enterprise.* New York: McGraw-Hill.

Mintzberg, Henry (October, 1971). "The Managerial Work: Analysis From Observation." *Management Science* 18, B97-B110.

Richards, Max D. and William A. Nielander (1963). *Readings in Management.* New York: South-Western Publishing Company.

Sen, Asim (1982). *Science, Technology and Development: Lessons From Japan.* Ankara: METU Publications.

Taylor, Frederick W. (1911). *The Principles of Scientific Management.* New York: Harper Brothers.

Ways, Max (July, 1996). "Tomorrow's Management: A More Advantageous Life in a Free Form Corporation." *Fortune.*

Wilson, Charles Z. and Marcus Alexis (August, 1962). "Basic Frameworks For Decisions." *Journal of the Academy of Management.* pp. 150-164.

## Chapter III: "History of Management Development and Total Quality"

Ackoff, Russell L. (May–June 1973). "Science in the System Age: Beyond IE, OR, and MIS." *Operations Research*, 21.

Argyris, Chris (1957). *Personality and Organization: The Conflict Between the Systems and the Individual.* New York: Harper and Row.

Bernard, Chester (1938). *The Functions of the Executive.* Cambridge, MA: Harvard University Press.

Bertalanffey, von Ludwig (December, 1972). "The History and Status of General Systems Theory." *Academy of Management Journal.*

Bullock, J.R. and Lawler, Edward E. (Spring, 1984). "Gainsharing: A Few Questions and Fewer Answers." *Human Resource Management.*

Coleman, Charles J. and Palmer, David D. (December, 1973). "Organizational Applications of System Theory." *Business Horizons.*

Crainer, Stuart (2000). *The Management Century.* San Francisco: Jossey-Bass Publishers.

Crosby, Philip B. (1979). *Quality is Free.* New York: McGraw-Hill.

———. (1988). *The Eternally Successful Organization.* New York: McGraw-Hill.

Davis, Keith (1957). *Human Relations in Business.* New York: McGraw-Hill.

Deming, Edwards W. (1981). *Japanese Methods for Productivity and Quality.* Washington, D.C.: George Washington University.

———. (1982). *Quality, Productivity and Competitive Position.* Cambridge, MA: Center for Advanced Engineering Study. The MIT Press.

———. (1986). *Out of Crisis.* Cambridge, MA: Center for Advanced Engineering Study. The MIT Press.

Dilworth, James B. (1992). *Operations Management.* New York: McGraw-Hill.

Emerson, Harrington (1911). *Efficiency as a Basis For Operations and Wages.* New York: The Engineering Magazine Company.

———. (1913). *The Twelve Principles of Efficiency.* New York: The Engineering Magazine Company.

Fallett, Mary P. (1924). *Creative Experiences.* London: Longmans, Green and Company.

Farmar, R.N. and Richman, B.M. (1965). *Comparative Management and Economic Progress.* Homewood, IL: Irwin.

Fayol, Henry (1949). *General and Industrial Management* (translated), Constance Storrs. London: Isaac Pitman and Sons, Ltd.

Feigenbaum, Armond V. (1983). *Total Quality Control.* New York: McGraw-Hill.

———. (April, 1986). "Total Quality Leadership." *Quality* 25, no. 4.

Gantt, Henry L. (1916). *Industrial Leadership.* New Haven, CT: Yale University Press.

———. (1919). *Organizing for Work.* New York: Harcourt, Brace and Howe.

Garfield, Charles (1992). *Second to None: How Our Smartest Companies Put People First.* Homewood, IL: Business One Irwin.

George, Claude S., Jr. (1972). *The History of Management Thought*. Englewood Cliff, NJ: Prentice-Hall.

Gilberth, Frank and M. Lillian (1917) *Applied Motion Study*. New York: Sturgis and Walton Company.

Guest, Robert H. (July–August, 1979). "Quality of Work Life: Learning From Tarrytown." *Harvard Business Review*, pp. 76-87.

Guzda, Henry P. (May, 1984). "Industrial Democracy: Made in U.S.A." *Monthly Labor Review*, pp. 26-33.

Harbison, Frederick and Myers, C.F. (1959). *Management in the Industrial World*. New York: McGraw-Hill.

Herzberg, Frederick, Mansner, Bernard and Sayderman, B. Barbara (1959). *The Motivation to Work*, 2nd edition. New York: John Wiley.

Hoerr, John (April 15, 1985). "ESOP's: Revolution or Ripoff?" *Business Week*. No. 2890, pp. 94-108.

Ishikawa, Kaoru (1985). *What is Total Quality Control? The Japanese Way*. Englewood Cliffs, NJ: Prentice Hall.

———. (1984). *Quality Control Circles at Work*. Tokyo: JUSE.

———. (September, 1989). "How to Apply Companywide Quality Control in Foreign Countries." *Quality Progress*, 22. no. 9. pp. 70-74.

Juran, Joseph M. (1964). *Managerial Breakthrough*. New York: McGraw-Hill.

———. (1988). *Juran on Planning For Quality*. New York: The Free Press.

Johnson, Richard A., Kast E. Fremont and Rosenzweig, E. James (1973). *The Theory and Management of Systems*. New York: McGraw-Hill.

Kanter, R.M. (1985). *Changes Masters: Innovation for Productivity in the American Workplace*. New York: Simon and Schuster.

———. (1989). "The New Managerial Work." *Harvard Business Review*, 67 (6), pp. 85-92.

Koontz, Harold D. (April, 1980). "The Theory Jungle Revisited." *Academy of Management Review*, pp. 175-187.

Lawler III, Edward E. (1992). *The Ultimate Advantage: Creating High Involvement Organization*. San Francisco: Jossey-Bass Publishers.

Luthans, Fred (1976). *Introduction to Management: A Contingency Approach*. New York: McGraw-Hill.

Maslow, Abraham (1954). *Motivation and Personality*. New York: Harper and Row.

Mayo, Elton (1933). *The Human Problems of an Industrial Civilization*. New York: The Macmillan Company.

———. (1945). *The Social Problems of an Industrial Civilization*. Cambridge, MA: Harvard University Press.

McGregor, Douglas (May, 1954). *On Leadership*. Antioch Notes, pp. 2-3.

———. (1960). *The Human Side of Enterprise*. New York: McGraw-Hill.

Megginson, Leon C. (1967). *Personnel: A Behavioral Approach to Administration*. Homewood, IL: Richard D. Irwin.

Munsterberg, Hugo (1913). *Psychology and Industrial Efficiency*. New York: Houghton-Mifflin Company.

O'Dell, C. (1981). *Gainsharing: Involvement, Incentives, and Productivity*. New
    York: American Management Association.

————. (1987). *People, Performance and Pay*. Houston, TX: American Productivity
    Center.

Ouchi, William (1981). *Theory Z*. Reading, MA: Addison-Wesley.

Rosow, Jerome M. (1980). "Quality of Work-Life Issues For the 1980s." *Work in
    America: The Decade Ahead*. Eds. Clark Kerr and Jerome M. Rosow. New York:
    Van Nostrand, pp. 157-158.

Roethlisberger, Fritz (1977). *The Elusive Phenomena*. Edited by George Lombard.
    Cambridge, MA: Harvard University Press.

Roth, William (1993). *The Evaluation of Management Theory*. Orefield, PA: Roth
    and Associates.

Sashkin, Marshall (Spring, 1994). "Participative Management: Is it an Ethical
    Imperative?" *Organization Dynamics*, 12, pp. 4-22.

Scott, Walter D. (1913). *Increasing Human Efficiency in Business*. New York: The
    Macmillan Company.

Scott, William G. (1967). *Organization Theory: A Behavioral Analysis For
    Management*. Homewood, IL: Richard D. Irwin.

Sheldon, Oliver (1966). *The Philosophy of Management*. New York: Pitman
    Publishing Corporation.

Shetty, K.Y. (1974). "Contingency Management: Current Perspective for Managing
    Organizations." *Management International Review* 14. No. 6.

Smith, Adam (1976). *Wealth of Nations*. New York: Modern Library.

Taguchi, Genichi (1986). *Introduction to Quality Engineering*. Dearborn, MI:
    American Supplier Institute.

Taylor, Frederick W. (1947). *Principles of Scientific Management*. New York: Harper
    and Row.

Tosi, Henry I. Jr. and Slocum, W. John, Jr. (Spring, 1984). "Contingency Theory:
    Some Suggested Directions." *Journal of Management*, 10, pp. 9-26.

Wren, Daniel A. (1972). *The Evolution of Management Thought*. New York: The
    Ronal Press Company.

Zwerdling, Daniel (August, 1978). "Workplace Democracy: A Strategy For Survival."
    *The Progressive*.

# Chapter IV: "Success and Failure of the Contemporary Management Practices"

Ackerman, Susan R. (1999). *Corruption and Government*. New York: Cambridge
    University Press.

Ackoff, R.L. (1994). *The Democratic Corporation*. New York: Oxford University
    Press.

Albert, Michel (1993). *Capitalism Vs. Capitalism* (translated by Paul Havilland).
    New York: Four Walls Eight Windows.

Avishai, B. and Taylor, W. (1989). "Customers Drive a Technology Driven Company." *Harvard Business Review*, Vol. 67, No. 6, pp. 107-114.

Baker, Dean and Mishel Lawrence (1995). Profits Up, Wages Down. Economic Policy Briefing Paper. Washington, D.C.

Batra, Ravi (1996). *The Great American Deception*. New York: Schocker Books.

Beatty, Jack (May, 1994). "Who Speaks for the Middle Class?" *The Atlantic*, p. 73.

Bennis, Warren (November-December, 1966). "The Coming Death of Bureaucracy." *Think* 32, pp. 30-35.

Blair, Margaret M. (Winter, 1994). "CEO Pay: Why Such a Contention Issue?" *The Brookings Review* Washington, DC: The Brookings Institute, p. 23.

———. (1995). *Ownership and Control: Rethinking Corporate Governance for the Twenty-First Century*. Washington, DC: The Brookings Institute.

Braudel, Fernand (1994). *A History of Civilizations*. Translated by Richard Mayne. New York: The Penguin Press.

Brouwer, Steve (1998). *Sharing the Pie*. New York: Henry Holt and Company.

Brown, G.M., Hitchcock, E.E., and Williard, M.L. (1994). *When TQM Fails and What to Do About It*. New York: Irwin.

Chasin, H.B. (1997). *Inequality and Violence in the United States*. NJ: Humanities Press.

Collis, J.W. (1998). *The Seven Fatal Management Sins: Understanding and Avoiding Managerial Malpractice*. Boca Raton, FL: St. Lucie Press.

Danziger, S., and Gottschalk, P. (1995). *American Unequal*. New York: Harvard Business Press.

Davis, Lester A. (1989). *Contribution of Exports to U.S. Employment*. 1980–1989. Washington, D.C.: U.S. Government Printing Office.

Deming, W.E. (1986). *Out of Crisis*. Cambridge, MA: The MIT Press.

Denison, D.R. (1990). *Corporate Culture and Organizational Effectiveness*. New York: John Wiley.

Derber, C. (1998). *Corporation State*. New York: St. Martin's Press.

Dertouzes, L. Michael, Lester, K. Richard, and Solow, M. Robert (1989). *Made in America: Regaining the Productivity Edge*. Cambridge, MA: The MIT Press.

Dicken, P. (1992). *Global Shift*. 2nd edition. London: Harper and Row.

Drucker, P.F. (1993). *Post Capitalist Society*. New York: Harper Business.

*The Economist* (November 4, 1994). "Inequality," p. 19.

*The Economist* (December 10, 1994). "Nice Work," p. 67.

*The Economist* (June 17, 1995). "The Future of Democracy," and "Democracy and Technology," pp. 13, 21.

Estes, R. (1996). *Tyranny of the Bottom Line*. San Francisco: Berrett-Koehler Publishers.

Ernst and Young Quality Improvement Consulting Group (1992). *Total Quality: An Executive's Guide For the 1990s*. Homewood, IL: Richard D. Irwin.

Etzioni, A. (1993). *The Spirit of Community: Rights, Responsibility, and the Communitarian Agenda*. New York: Crown Publishers.

Evan, William M., and R. Edward Freeman (1993). "A Stakeholder Theory of the Modern Corporation: Kantion Capitalism." In *Ethical Theory and Business.* Edited by Tom L. Beauchamp and Norman E. Bowie. NJ: Prentice Hall.

Fallett, Mary P. (1924). *Creative Experience.* London: Logmans, Green and Company.

———. (1984). *Freedom and Coordination.* London: Management Publications Trust.

*Forbes* (July 29, 1997).

Freidman, M. (1970). "The Social Responsibility of Business is to Increase its Profit." In T.L. Beauchamp and N. Bowie (Eds.), *Ethical Theory and Business.* Englewood Cliffs, NJ: Prentice-Hall, pp. 55-65.

Gailbraith, K.J. (1998). *Created Unequal.* The Crisis of American Pay. New York: The Free Press.

Garten, Jeffrey E. (1997). *The Big Ten: The Big Emerging Markets and How They Will Change Our Lives.* New York: Basic Books.

German Information Center (March, 1994). *Unemployment in Germany.*

Gibson, R. (1997). *Rethinking the Future.* London: Nichlas Brealey Publishing.

Gordon, M.D. (1996). *Fat and Mean.* New York: The Free Press.

Green, M. and Berry, J.F. (June 8 and 15, 1985). "Corporate Crime," a Two-Part Report Appearing in the *Nation.*

Halal, W.E. (1996). *The New Management: Democracy and Enterprise Are Transforming Organizations.* San Francisco: Berrett-Koehler Publishers.

Hammer, M. (1997). "Beyond the End of Management." In R. Gibson (edited) *Rethinking the Future.* London: Nichlas Brealey Publishing. pp. 94-105.

Hayes, H.R. and Abernathy, J.W. (1980). "Managing Our Way to Economical Decline." *Harvard Business Review.*

Henderson, Hazel (1996). *Building A Win Win World.* San Francisco: Berrett-Koehler Publishers.

International Finance Corporation (1996). *Emerging Markets Stock Fact Book.* Washington, D.C.: International Finance Corp. pp. 5-6.

Jacobs, M.T. (1991). *Short-Term America: The Causes and Cures of Our Business Myopia.* Harvard Business School Press.

Juran, J.M. (1988). *Juran on Planning for Quality.* New York: The Free Press.

Kennedy, P. (1989). *The Rise and Fall of the Great Powers.* New York: Vintage Books.

Knox, Paul and John Agnew (1998). *The Geography of the World Economy.* New York: John Wiley.

Lawler III, Edward E. (1992). *The Ultimate Advantage: Creating High Involvement Organization.* San Francisco: Jossey-Bass Publishers.

Levin, D.L., and Tyson, L.D. (1990). "Participation, Productivity and the Firm's Environment." In A.S. Blinder (edited), *Paying for Productivity: A Look at the Evidence.* Washington, D.C.: The Brookings Institute.

Lewin, Tamar (May 31, 1995). "Families in Upheaval Worldwide." *International Herald Tribune,* p. 1.

Likert, Rensis (1967). *The Human Organization*. New York: McGraw Hill.

Martin, J. (1996). *Cybercorp: The New Business Revolution*. New York: American Management Association.

Mayo, E. (1933). *The Human Problems of an Industrial Civilization*. New York: The MacMillan Company.

Mazarr, J.M. (1999). *Global Trends 2005*. New York: St. Martin's Press.

McGregor, D. (1960). *The Human Side of Enterprise*. New York: McGraw-Hill.

McNamara, Robert S. (1996). *In Retrospect: The Tragedy and Lessons of Vietnam*. New York: Vintage Books.

Mitchell, J.B., Lewin, D., and Lawler, E.E., (1990). "Alternative Pay System, Firm Performance and Productivity." In A. S. Blinder (edited), *Paying for Productivity: A Look at the Evidence*. Washington, D.C.: The Brookings Institute.

Nonaka, Ikurjiro & Hirotaka Takeuchi (1996). *The Knowledge-Creating Company*. New York: Oxford University Press.

O'Toole, J. (1995). *Leading Change*. San Francisco: Jossey-Bass Publishers.

Ozaki, R.S. (1991). *Human Capitalism: The Japanese Enterprise System as World Model*. New York: Kodansha International.

Pearson, Wallace C. (1994). *Silent Depression*. New York: W.W. Norton Press.

Phillips, Kevin (1993). *Boiling Point: The Decline of Middle Class Prosperity*. New York: Random House.

Quin, J.B. (1992). *Intelligent Enterprise: A Knowledge and Service Based Paradigm for Industry*. New York: The Free Press.

Rawls, John (1971). *A Theory of Justice*. Cambridge: Harvard University Press.

Reich, R.B. (1991). *The Work of Nations*. New York: Vintage Books.

Renesch, J. (1992). *New Traditions in Business: Spirit and Leadership in the 21st Century*. San Francisco: Berrett-Koehler Publishers.

Rosenbluth, Hall F. (1992). *Customer Comes Second*. New York: William Morrow Company.

Senge, P. (1993). *The Fifth Discipline: The Art and Practice of the Learning Organization*. New York: Doubleday.

Simons, Marlise (May 12, 1994). "In French Factory Town, Culprit in Automation." *New York Times*, p. A3.

Slater, P. and Bennis, W.B. (1992). "Democracy On-Line: Tomorrow's Electric Electorate." In E. Cornish (edited), *Exploring Your Future*. Bethesda, MD: World Future Society.

Snider, James H. (1996). "Democracy On Line: Exploring Your Future." Bethesda, MD: World Future Society.

Thurow, Lester C. (1996). *The Future of Capitalism*. New York: William Morrow and Company, Inc.

Toffler, Alvin (1980). *The Third Wave*. New York: Bantam.

Weiss, Alan (1995). *Our Emperors Have No Clothes*. NJ: Career Press.

Will, G. (September 1, 1991). "CEOs Aren't Paid For Performance." *Seattle Times*, p.1

World Bank. (1996). World Bank Publications. WB@www.worldbank.org..

# Chapter V: "True Democratic Management Practices"

Adams, Frank T., and Gary B. Hansen (1992). *Putting Democracy to Work*. San Francisco: Berrett-Koehler Publishers.

Barton, Dorothy L. (Fall, 1992). "The Factory as a Learning Laboratory." *Sloan Management Review*.

Baumol, W.J. (1959). *Business Behavior, Value and Growth*. New York: The Macmillan Company.

Blair, Margaret M. (1995). *Ownership and Control: Rethinking Corporate Governance For The Twenty-First Century*. Washington, D.C.: The Brookings Institute.

Blasi, Joseph R. and Douglas Kruse L. (1991). *The New Owners*. New York: Harper Collins Publishers.

Byrne, John A. (May, 1994). "The Pain of Downsizing." *Business Week*. p. 61.

Carnoy, Martin, et. Al. (1993). *The New Global Economy in the Information Age*. University Park: Pennsylvania State University Press.

Cohen, Carl (1971). *Democracy*. Athens, GA: University of Georgia Press.

Conte, Michael A., and Jan Svejner (1990). "Employee Ownership Plans." In *Paying For Productivity*, edt. by Alan S. Blinder. pp. 143-182. The Brookings Institute.

Davis, Lester A. (1989). *Contribution of Exports to U.S. Employment, 1980–1989*. Washington, D.C.: U.S. Government Printing.

Denison, D.R. (1990). *Corporate Culture and Organizational Effectiveness*. New York: John Wiley.

Derber, C. (1998). *Corporation State*. New York: St. Martin Press.

Dertouzes, Michael L., Lester, Richard K., and Solow, Robert M. (1989). *Made in America: Regaining the Productivity Edge*. Cambridge, MA: The MIT Press.

Drucker, P.F. (1993). *Post Capitalist Society*. New York: Harper Business.

*The Economist*. (June 17, 1995). "The Future Democracy" and "Democracy and Technology," pp. 13, 21.

Estes, R. (1996). *Tyranny of the Bottom Line*. San Francisco: Berrett-Koehler Publishers.

Freeman, R. Edward (1984). *Strategic Management: A Stakeholder Approach*. Boston: Pitman.

Galbraith, K.J. (1998). *Created Unequal: The Crisis of American Pay*. New York: The Free Press.

Garfield, Charles (1992). *Second to None*. Homewood, IL: Business One Irwin.

Halal, W.E. (1996). *The New Management: Democracy and Enterprise Are Transforming Organizations*. San Francisco: Berrett-Koehler Publishers.

Harbison, Frederick H. (1973). *Human Resources as the Wealth of Nations*. New York: Oxford University Press.

Harrison, Bennett (1994). *Lean and Mean*. New York: Basic Books.

Hayes, Robert H., and William J. Abernathy (July–August, 1980). "Managing Our Way to Economic Decline." *Harvard Business Review*. pp. 67-77.

Hoerr, John (April 15, 1985). "ESOP's: Revolution or Ripoff?" *Business Week*. No.: 2890, pp. 94-108.

Kruse, Douglas L. (November, 1993). "Does Profit Sharing Affect Productivity:" Working Paper 4542. Cambridge, MA: National Bureau of Economical Research.

Lawler III, Edward E. (1992). *The Ultimate Advantage: Creating High Involvement Organization*. San Francisco: Jossey-Bass Publishers.

Levin, David I. (1995). *Reinventing the Workplace: How Business and Employees Can Both Win*. Brookings Institute.

Likert, Rensis (1967). *The Human Organization*. New York: McGraw-Hill.

March, James G., and Johan Olsen P. (1995). *Democratize Governance*. New York: The Free Press.

Martin, J. (1996). *Cybercorp: The New Business Revolution*. New York: American Management Association.

Masaaki, I. (1986). *Kaizen: The Key to Japan's Competitive Success*. New York: McGraw-Hill.

Maslow, A.H. (July, 1943). "A Theory of Human Motivation." *Psychological Review*. No. 50, pp. 370-396.

Mills, D.Q. (1991). *Rebirth of the Corporation*. New York: John Wiley.

Mirvis, P.H., and Lawler, E.E. (1977). "Measuring the Financial Impact of Employee Attitudes." *Journal of Applied Psychology*. 62(1), pp. 1-8.

Mitchel, J.B., Lewin, D., and Lawler, E.E. (1990). "Alternative Pay System, Firm Performance and Productivity." In A.S. Blinder (*edt.*), *Paying For Productivity: A Look at the Evidence*. Washington, D.C.: Brookings Institute.

Monks, Robert A.G., and Nell Minow (1995). *Corporate Governance*. Cambridge:Blackwell Business.

Morris, Tom (1998). *If Aristotle Ran General Motors: The New Soul of Business*. New York: Henry Hold.

Nakane, C. (1970). *Japanese Society*. Los Angeles: University of California Press.

Nonaka, I., and Takeuchi H. (1995). *The Knowledge Creating Company*. New York: Oxford University Press.

Ouchi, William (1981). *Theory Z*. Reading, MA: Addison-Wesley.

Ozaki, R.S. (1991). *Human Capitalism: The Japanese Enterprise System as World Model*. New York: Kodansha International.

Peters, T.J. and Waterman, R.H. (1982). *In Search of Excellence*. New York: Harper and Row.

Quin, J.B. (1992). *Intelligent Enterprise*. New York: The Free Press.

Schneider-Lenne, Ellen R. (Autumn, 1992). "Corporate Control in Germany." *Oxford Review of Economic Policy*. pp. 11-33.

Sen, Asim (1982). *Science, Technology and Development: Lessons From Japan*. Ankara: METU Press.

Senge, P. (1993). *The Fifth Discipline: The Art and Practice of the Learning Organization*. London: Century Business.

Slater, Philip and Bennis G. Warren (Sept.–Oct. 1990). "Democracy is Inevitable." *Harvard Business Review*. pp. 167-176.

Snider, J.H. (1996). "Democracy On Line: Exploring Your Future." Bethesda, MD: World Future Society. pp. 105-109.

Stiglitz, Joseph E. (1974). "Incentives and Risk Sharing in Sharecropping." *Review of Economic Studies*. pp. 219-256.

Toffler, A. (1990). *Power Shift: Knowledge, Wealth, and Violence at the Edge of the Twenty-First Century*. New York: Bantam Books.

Will, G. (Sept. 1, 1991). "CEOs Aren't Paid For Performance. *Seattle Times*, p. 1.

Womack, James P., Jones, Daniel T. and Roos, Daniel (1990). *The Machine That Changed the World*. New York: Harper-Collins Publisher.

# Chapter VI: "True Democratic Management Generates Desirable Total Quality"

Arie, deGeus (1997). *The Living Company*. Boston, MA: Harvard Business School Press.

Argyris, Chris (1957). *Personality and Organization: The Conflict Between the System and the Individual*. New York: Harper and Row.

Collis, J.W. (1998). *The Seven Fatal Management Sins: Understanding and Avoiding Managerial Malpractice*. Boca Raton, FL: St. Lucie Press.

Dumaine, Brian (May 7, 1990). "Who Needs Boss?" *Fortune*. pp. 52-60.

Garfield, C. (1992). *Second to None*. Homewood, IL: Business One Irwin.

Hackman, J.R. (1984). "The Design of Work Teams." in J.W. Lorsch (edited). *Handbook of Organizational Behavior*. Englewood Cliffs. NJ: Prentice-Hall.

Hassett, George (November, 1981). "But That Would Be Wrong." *Psychology Today*.

Horr, John (July 10, 1989). "The Payoff from Teamwork." *Business Week*. pp. 56-62.

Kanter, R.M. (1985). *Change Masters: Innovation for Productivity in the American Work Place*. New York: Simon and Schuster.

Katzenbach, J.R. (1998). *Teams at the Top*. Boston: Harvard Business School Press.

Kayser, T.A. (1990). *Mining Group Gold: How to Cash in on the Collaborative Brain Power of a Group*. Elsegundo: Serif.

Lickona, Thomas (1991). *Education for Character*. New York: Bantam Books.

Likert, R. (1967). *The Human Organization*. New York: McGraw-Hill.

London, Perry (May, 1987). "Character Education and Clinical Intervention: A Paradigm Shift for U.S. Schools." *Phi Delta Kappa*.

Manz, C. E., and Sims H. P. (1980). "Self Management as a Substitute of Leadership: A Social Learning Theory Perspective." *Academy of Management Review*.

———. (1995). *Business Without Bosses*. New York: John Wiley.

Masaaki, Imai (1986). *Kaizen: The Key to Japan's Competitive Success*. New York: McGraw-Hill.

McGregor, D. (1960). *The Human Side of Enterprise*. New York: McGraw-Hill.

Nakane, C. (1970). *Japanese Society*. Los Angeles: University of California Press.

Nirenberg, John (1993). *The Living Organization: Transforming Teams Into Workplace Communities*. New York: Irwin Professional Publishing.

Ouchi, William (1981). *Theory Z*. Reading, MA: Addison-Wesley.

O'Toole, J. (1985). *Leading Change*. San Francisco: Jossey-Bass Publishers.

Ozkanli, Ozlem (2002). "The Relationship Between Human Resources Management Practices and Performance." Global Awareness Society International. Conference Proceedings. Vancouver, Canada.

Peters, J.T. and Waterman Jr. H.B. (1982). In *Search for Excellence: Lessons from America's Best-Run Companies*. New York: Harper and Row Publishers.

Porter, Michael (1990). *The Competitive Advantage of Nations*. New York: The Free Press.

Purser, Ronald E. and Cabana Steven (1998). *The Self Managing Organization*. New York: The Free Press.

Rosenberg, Nathan, and Bridzel, E.L. (1996). *How the West Grew Rich: The Economic Transformation of the Industrial World*. New York: Basic Books.

Sen, Asim (1982). *Science, Technology and Development: Lessons From Japan*. Ankara: METU Press.

Shonk, J.H. (1992). *Team-Based Organizations*. Irwin, IL: Business One Irwin.

Tichy, N.M. and Devanna M.A. (1990). *The Transformational Leader*. New York: John Wiley.

Wallerstein, Judith S. (1989). *Second Chances: Men, Women and Children a Decade After Divorce*. New York: Ticknor and Fields.

Womack, J.P., Jones, D.T., and Roos, D. (1990). *The Machine That Changed the World*. New York: The Macmillan Company.

## Chapter VII: "Democratization of Management"

Ackoff, R.L. (1994). *The Democratic Corporation*. New York: Oxford University Press.

Conner, Daryl R. (1992). *Managing at the Speed of Change*. New York: Villard Books.

Dalziel, Murray M. and Stephen C. Schoonover (1988). *Changing Ways*. New York: AMACOM.

Deal, Terrence E. and Allan A. Kennedy (1982). *Corporate Cultures*. Reading, MA: Addison-Wesley.

Deming, Edwards W. (1986). *Out of Crisis*. Cambridge, MA: MIT Center for Advanced Engineering Study.

Diamond, Larry, Juan, Ling J., and Seymour, Lipset M. (1994). *Democracy in Developing Countries*. 4 Vols. Boulder, CO: Lynne Rienner Publishers.

Drucker, P. F. (1994). "The Age of Social Transformation." *Atlantic Monthly*. p. 53.

Gibson, Rowan (1996). *Rethinking the Future*. London: Nicholas Brealey Publishing.

Harrison, Lawrence E. and Samual Huntington (editors) (2000). *Culture Matters: How Values Shape Human Progress*. New York: Basic Books.

Halal, William E. (1996). *The New Management. Democracy and Enterprise Are Transforming Organizations*. San Francisco: Berrett-Koehler Publisher.

Held, David (1996). *Models of Democracy*. Stanford, CA: Stanford University Press.

Kennedy, P.M. (1993). *Preparing for the Twenty First Century*. New York: Random House.

———. (1987). *The Rise and Fall of the Great Powers*. New York: Vintage Books.

Kidder, Rushworth M. (1994). *Shared Values for a Troubled World*. San Fransisco: Jossey-Bass Publishers.

Kinkead, Eugene (1959). *In Every War But One*. New York: W. W. Norton.

La Marsh, Jeanenna (1995). *Changing the Way We Change*. Reading, MA: Addison-Wesley.

Lebow, Rob and William L. Simon (1997). *Lasting Change*. New York: Van Nostrand Reinhold.

Luckham, Robin and Gordon White (1996). *Democratization in the South*. New York: Manchester University Press.

Makridakis, Spyros G. (1990). *Forecasting, Planning and Strategy for the 21st Century*. New York: The Free Press.

March, James G. and Johan, Olsen P. (1995). *Democratized Governance*. New York: The Free Press.

Marshall, Edward M. (1995). *Transforming The Way We Work*. New York: AMACOM.

Martin, James (1996). *Cybercorp, The New Business Revolution*. New York: AMACOM.

Mazarr, Michael (1999). *Global Trends 2005*. New York: St. Martin's Press.

Minkin, Barry H. (1995). *Future in Sight*. New York: Simon and Schuster.

Neher, Clark D. and Ross Marlay (1995). *The Wind of Change. Democracy and Development in South Asia*. Boulder, CO: West View Press.

O'Toole, James (1995). *Leading Change*. San Francisco: Jossey-Bass Publishers.

———. (1987). *Vangaurd Management*. New York: Berkley Books.

Peters, Tom (1992). *Liberation Management*. New York: Alfred A. Knoef.

Sen, Amartya (1999). "Democracy as a Universal Value." *Journal of Democracy*. pp. 3-17.

Sen, Asim (May, 1996). "Democratization of Management Through Globalization." Global Awareness Society International. Conference Proceedings. San Francisco, CA.

Senge, Peter (1993). *The Fifth Discipline. The Art and Practice of Learning Organization*. New York: Doubleday.

Slater, Philip and Bennis G. Warren (Sept.-Oct., 1990). "Democracy is Inevitable." *Harvard Business Review*. pp. 167-176.

Smith, Henderick (1995). *Rethinking America*. New York: Random House.

Thurow, Lester C. (1996). *The Future of Capitalism*. New York: William Morrow and Company, Inc.

Trompenaars, Fons and Charles Hampden-Turner (1998). *Riding the Waves of Culture*. New York: McGraw-Hill.

# Chapter VIII: "Democratization of Management Education"

AACSB, *Newsline*, Fall 1997, Vol. 28, No. 1.

Argyris, Chris (1957). *Personality and Organization: The Conflict Between the System and the Individual*. New York: Harper and Row.

Arie deGeus (March–April, 1997). *The Living Company*. Boston, MA: Harvard Business School Press.

Blanchard, Kenneth and Michael O'Connor. (1995). *Managing By Values*. Escondido, CAP: Blanchard Training and Development, Inc.

Collis, J.W. (1998). *The Seven Fatal Management Sins: Understanding and Avoiding Managerial Malpractice*. Boca Raton, FL: St. Lucie Press.

Crainer, Stuart (2000). *The Management Century*. San Francisco: Jossey-Bass Publishers.

Davis, S. and Botkin, J. (Sept.–Oct. 1994). "The Coming of Knowledge Based Business." *Harvard Business Review*.

Deal, Terrence, and Kennedy, Allan A. (1982). *Corporate Cultures*. Reading, MA: Addison-Wesley.

Drucker, P.F. (1993). *Post Capitalist Society*. New York: Harper Business.

———. (November, 1994). "The Age of Social Transformation." *Atlantic Monthly*. p. 53.

Estes, R. (1996). *Tyranny of the Bottom Line*. San Francisco: Berrett-Koehler Publishers.

Etzioni, A. (1993). *The Spirit of Community: Right, Responsibility, and the Communitarian Agenda*. New York: Crown Publishers.

Fallett, Parker M. (1994). *Freedom and Coordination*. London: Management Publications Trust.

Freeman, Edward R. (1984). *Strategic Management: A Stakeholder Approach*. Boston: Pitman.

*Fortune* (January 12, 1997).

Gates, Bill (1995). *The Road Ahead*. New York: Viking.

George, Claude S., Jr. (1972). *The History of Management Thought*. Englewood Cliff, NJ: Prentice-Hall, Inc.

Halal, William E. (1996). *The New Management*. San Francisco: Berrett-Koehler Publisher.

Hayes, H.R. and Abernathy, J.W. (1980). "Managing Our Way to Economical Decline." *Harvard Business Review*.

Herzberg, Frederick (February, 1968). "One More Time: How Do You Motivate Employees?" *Harvard Business Review*.

Kilpatrick, William (1992). *Why Johnny Can't Tell Right From Wrong*. New York: Simon and Schuster.

Lebow, R. and W.L. Simon (1997). *Lasting Change: The Shared Values Process that Makes Companies Great*. New York: Bantam Books.

Lickona, Thomas (1992). *Education For Character*. New York: Bantam Books.

Likert, Rensis (1967). *The Human Organization.* New York: McGraw-Hill.

Maslow, Abraham (July, 1943). "A Theory of Human Motivation." *Psychological Review*, 50, pp. 370-396.

Mayo, Elton (1933). *The Human Problems of an Industrial Civilization.* New York: The Macmillan Company.

McGregor, D. (1960). *The Human Side of Enterprise.* New York: McGraw-Hill.

Morris, Tom (1997). *If Aristotle Ran General Motors: The New Soul of Business.* New York: Henry Holt and Company.

Newman, John H. (1992). *The Idea of University.* Notre Dame, IL: University of Notre Dame Press.

Nonaka, I. and H. Takeuchi (1995). *The Knowledge Creating Company.* New York: Oxford University Press.

Peyrefitte, Alain. (1992). *The Immobile Empire.* New York: Knopf.

Peters, Thomas J. and Robert H. Waterman. (1984). *In Search of Excellence*, New York: Warner Books. p. 279.

Polanyi, M. (1996). *The Tacit Dimension.* London: Rootledge and Kegan Paul.

Porter, W. Lyman and Lawrence E. McKibbin (1998). *Management Education and Development: Drift or Thrust into the 21st Century?* New York: McGraw-Hill.

Prahalad, C.K. and G. Hamel (May–June,1990). "The Core Competence of the Corporation." *Harvard Business Review*, pp. 79-91.

Quin, J.B. (1992). *Intelligent Enterprise: A Knowledge and Service Based Paradigm for Industry.* New York: The Free Press.

Reavis, Charles A. and Griffith, Harry (1992). *Restructuring Schools: Theory and Practice.* Lancaster, PA: Technomic Publication.

Reich, R.B. (1992). *The Work of Nations.* New York: Vintage Books.

Rifkin, Jeromy (1993). *The End of Work.* New York: G.P. Putnam's Sons.

Rose, Colin and Malcolm J. Nicholl (1997). *Accelerated Learning for the 21st Century.* New York: Delacorte Press.

Roth, William (1993). *The Evolution of Management Theory.* Orefield, PA: Roth and Associates.

Rushworth, Kidder M. (1994). (edited) *Shared Values for a Troubled World.* San Francisco. Jossey-Bass Publishers.

Schumacher, E.F. (1999). *Small Is Beautiful: Economics As If People Mattered.* New York: Hartley and Marks.

Sen, Asim (1992). "Utilization of Social Values for Effective Management of Technology: The Case of Japan." *Management of Technology.* (edited) by Halil M. Tarek and Bulent Bayraktar. Georgia: Industrial Engineering and Management Press. pp. 1020-1029.

———. (2001). "Democratization of Management Education." Global Business and Technology Association Proceedings. Istanbul, Turkey.

Senge, Peter (1993). *The Fifth Discipline: The Age and Practice of the Learning Organization.* New York: Doubleday.

Slater, Philip and Bennis G. Warren (Sept.–Oct. 1990). "Democracy is Inevitable." *Harvard Business Review*, pp. 167-176.

Stalk, G., P. Evans, and L.E. Shulman (March–April, 1992). "Competing on Capabilities: The New Rules of Corporate Strategy." *Harvard Business Review*. pp. 57-69.

Stewart, Thomas A. (1997). *Intellectual Capital: The New Wealth of Organizations*. New York: Doubleday.

Taylor, F.W. (1911). *The Principles of Scientific Management*. New York: Harper and Brothers.

Teece, D.J., G. Pisano, and A. Shuen (1991). *Dynamic Capabilities and Strategic Management*. Center for Research in Management. University of California, Berkeley.

Terpstra, Vern (1978). *The Cultural Environment of International Business*. Cincinnati: South Western Publishing Co.

Toffler, Alvin (1980). *The Third Wave*. New York: Bantam.

Trompenaars, Fons and Charles Hampden-Turner (1998). *Riding the Waves of Culture*. New York: McGraw-Hill.

Womack, James P., Jones, Daniel T., and Roos, Daniel (1990). *The Machine That Changed the World*. New York: Harper Perennial.

Wren, Daniel A. (1972). *The Evolution of Management Thought*. New York: The Ronal Press Company.

# Chapter IX: "Political Democratization"

Batra, Ravi (1996). *The Great American Deception*. New York: John Wiley.

Bowles, Samuel and Herbert Gintis (1986). *Capitalization and Democracy*. New York: The Basic Books.

Budge, I. (1996). *The New Challenge of Direct Democracy*. Cambridge, MA: Polity Press.

Carnoy, Martin, et al. (1995). *The New Global Economy in the Information Age: Reflections on Our Changing World*. University Park, PA: The Pennsylvania State University Press.

Crossette, Barbara (August 20, 1995). "A Global Gauge of Greased Palms." *New York Times*. p. E.3.

Dahl, R.A. (1989). *A Preface to Economic Democracy*. Cambridge, MA: Polity Press.

Dankwart, Rustow A. (Fall 1990). "Democracy: A Global Revolution." *Foreign Affairs*, 69, No. 4, pp. 75-90.

Denison, Edward (1985). *Trends in American Economic Growth, 1929–1982*. Washington, DC: The Brookings Institutes.

Derber, C. (1998). *Corporation State*. New York: St. Martin's Press.

Fukuyama, Francis (1992). *The End of History and the Last Man*. New York: Avon Books.

Galbraith, James K. (1998). *Created Unequal: The Crisis in American Pay*. New York: The Free Press.

Haggard, Stephen and Kaufman, Robert R. (1995). *The Political Economy of Democratic Transitions*. Princeton, NJ: Princeton University Press.

Haggard, Stephen and Webb, Steven B. (1994). *Voting for Reform: Democracy, Political Liberalization, and Economic Adjustment.* New York: Oxford University Press.

Huntington, Samuel P. (1991). *Democratization in the Late Twentieth Century.* Norman, OK: University of Oklahoma Press.

Kennedy, P. (1987). *The Rise and Fall of the Great Powers.* New York: Vintage Books.

Luckham, Robin and Gordon White (1996). *Democratization in the South.* New York: Manchester University Press.

Makin, John H. and Ornstein, Norman J. (1994). *Debt and Taxes.* New York: Random House.

Neher, Clark D. and Ross, Marlay (1995). *Democracy and Development in Southeast Asia: The Winds of Change.* Boulder, CO: Westview Press.

Veblen, Thorstein (1934). *The Theory of Leisure Class.* New York: Modern Library.

## Chapter X: "Economical Democratization"

Baily, Martin N., Gary, Burtless, and Robert E. Litan (1993). *Growth with Equity: Economic Policy-Making for the Next Century.* Washington, DC: The Brookings, Institute.

Baker, Dean and Mishel Lawrence (1995). "Profits Up, Wages Down." Economic Policy Briefing Paper. Washington, D.C.

Beatty, Jack (May, 1994). "Who Speaks for the Middle Class?" *The Atlantic*, p. 73.

Becker, Gary (1957). *The Economics of Discrimination.* Chicago: University of Chicago Press.

Blair, Margaret M. (Winter, 1994). "CEO Pay: Why Such a Contention Issue?" *The Brookings Review*, p. 23.

Bloom, David E. and Freeman, Richard B. (May, 1992). "The Fall of Private Pension Coverage in the United States." *American Economic Review*, p. 539.

*The Economist* (November 4, 1994). "Inequality," p. 19.

*The Economist* (July 24, 1994). "Rich Man and Poor Man," p. 71.

Feenberg, Daniel R. and James M. Poterba (December, 1992). "Income Inequality and the Income of Very High Income Tax Payers." NBER Working Paper No. 4229.

Garten, Jeffrey E. (1997). *The Big Ten: The Big Emerging Markets and How They Will Change Our Lives.* New York: Basic Books.

German Information Center (March, 1994). *Unemployment in Germany.*

Henderson, Hazel (1996). *Building A Win Win World.* San Francisco: Berrett-Koehler Publishers.

Inoue, Shinichi (1997). *Putting Buddhism To Work.* New York: Kodansha International. (translated by Duncan Ryoker Williams).

Jensen, Arthur (1981). *Straight Talk About Mental Tests.* New York: The Free Press.

Knox, Paul and John Agnew (1998). *The Geography of the World Economy.* New York: John Wiley.

Leontief, Wassily (1951). *The Structure of the American Economy.* New York: Oxford University Press.

Lewin, Tamar (May 31, 1995). "Families in Upheaval Worldwide." *International Herald Tribune*, p. 1.

Marx, Karl (1887). *Capital: A Critical Analysis of Capitalist Production.* Vol. I. Sonneuschen, London: republished by Allen and Unwin, 1938.

Ozaki, R.S. (1991). *Human Capitalism: The Japanese Enterprise System as World Model.* New York: Kodansha International.

Phillips, Kevin (1993). *Boiling Point: The Decline of Middle Class Prosperity.* New York: Random House.

Ricardo, David (1981). *Principles of Political Economy, and Taxation.* Cambridge: Cambridge University Press.

Robinson, Joan (1993). *The Economics of Imperfect Competition.* London: The Macmillan Company.

Rose, Nancy I. (Winter, 1994–95). Executives Compensation. NBER Reporter.

Simons, Marlise (May 12, 1994). "In French Factory Town, Culprit in Automation." *New York Times*, p. A3.

Smith, Adam (1994). *An Inquiry into the Nature and Causes of The Wealth of Nations.* Edited by Edwin Cannon. Modern Library Edition. New York: Random House.

Thurow, Lester C. (1996). *The Future of Capitalism.* New York: William Morrow and Company, Inc.

# Chapter XI: "Democratization Through Technological Development"

Akamatsu, Kaname (Sept.–Dec. 1962). "A Historical Pattern of Economic Growth in Developing Countries." *Developing Economies.*

Alexander, Robert J. (December, 1967). "The Import-Substitution Strategy of Economic Development." *Journal of Economic Issues.*

Ayres, Clarence E. (1944). *The Theory of Economic Progress.* New York: Schocker Books.

Batra, Ravi (1996). *The Great American Deception.* New York: John Wiley.

Cockcroft, James D., Frank, Gunder, A., and Johnson, Dale L. (1972). *Dependence and Underdevelopment: Latin America's Political Economy.* Garden City, NY: Doubleday.

Cohen, Daniel (1998). *The Wealth of the World and The Poverty of Nations.* Cambridge, MA: The MIT Press.

Crosette, Barbara (August 20, 1995). "A Global Gauge of Greased Palms." *New York Times*, p. E.3.

Cooper, Charles (October, 1972). "Science, Technology and Production in the Underdeveloped Countries: An Introduction." *Journal of Development Studies.*

Denison, Edward F. (1969). *The Sources of Economic Growth in the United States.* Supplementary Paper No. 13. New York: Committee for Economic Development.

*The Economist* (September 25, 1993). "More Money, Survey of Third World Finance."

Fabricant, Solomon (1954). "Economic Progress and Economic Change." 34th Annual Report of the National Bureau of Economic Research. New York.

Garten, Jeffrey E. (1997). *The Big Ten: The Big Emerging Markets and How They Will Change Our Lives.* New York: Basic Books.

Hirschman, Albert O. (1970). *The Strategy of Economic Development.* New Haven: Yale University Press.

International Finance Corporation (1996). *Emerging Markets Stock Factbook.* Washington, DC: International Finance Corp., pp. 5-6.

International Monetary Fund. (1991). *International Financial Statistics Yearbook.* Washington, DC: IFC.

Jorgenson, D.W., and Griliches, F. (May, 1969). "The Explanation of Productivity Change:" *The Survey of Business Survey.*

Kaufman, R. Robert (1988). *The Politics of Debt in Argentina, Brazil and Mexico.* Berkeley: Institute of International Studies.

Knox, Paul and John Agnew (1998). *The Geography of World Economy.* New York: John Wiley.

Krauss, Melvin (1997). *How Nations Grow Rich: The Case for Free Trade.* New York: Oxford University Press.

Kuznets, Simon (1953). *Economic Change.* New York: W.W. Norton Company.

———. (June, 1973). "Modern Economic Growth: Finding and Reflections." *American Economic Review.*

Lissakers, Karin (1991). *Banks, Borrowers, and the Establishment: A Revisionist Account of the International Debt Crisis.* New York: Basic Books.

Mansfield, Edwin (1968). *Industrial Research and Technological Innovation, an Econometric Analysis.* New York: W.W. Norton.

Marber, Peter (1998). *From Third World to World Class: The Future of Emerging Markets in the Global Economy.* Reading, MA: Perseus Books.

OECD (1967). Review of National Science: Paris.

Oldham, C.D.G., Freeman, G. and Turkcan, E. (November 10, 1967). Transfer of Technology to Developing Countries. United Nations Conference on Trade and Development, Second Session, TD/28/Supp. 1.

Pearson, Lester B. (1969). *Partners in Development. Report of the Commission on International Development.* New York: Frederick A. Praeger.

Porter, Michael (March-April 1990). "The Competitive Advantage of Nations." *Harvard Business Review.*

Prebisch, Raul (1950). *The Economic Development of Latin America and Its Principal Problems.* New York: United Nations.

Rostow, W.W. (1969). *The Stages of Economic Growth.* Cambridge: Cambridge University Press.

Santos Dos Theotonia (May, 1970). "The Structure of Dependence." *American Economic Review.*

Schumacher, E.F. (1999). *Small is Beautiful: Economics As If People Mattered.* New York: Hartley and Marks.

Sen, Asim (1982). *Science, Technology and Development: Lessons From Japan.* Ankara: METU Press.

Solow, Robert (August, 1957). "Technical Change and the Aggregate Production Function." *The Review of Economics and Statistics.* p. 39.

Soros, George (1998). *The Crisis of Global Capitalism.* New York: Public Affairs.

Steward, Frances (October, July, 1972–1973). "Choices of Technique in Developing Countries." *Journal of Development Studies.*

Vaitsos, Constantine (October, 1972–1973). "Patents Revisited: Their Function in Developing Countries." *Journal of Development Studies.*

Veblen, T.B. (1919). *The Place of Science in Modern Civilization.* New York.

Vernon, Raymond (May, 1966). "International Investment and International Trade in the Product Life Cycle." *Quarterly Journal of Economics.*

World Bank (1995). "Workers in an Integrating World." *World Development Report.* Washington, DC: World Bank. *WB@www.worldbank.org*

# Chapter XII: "Utilization of Information Technology For Democratization"

Arie deGues (1997). *The Living Company.* Boston, MA: Harvard Business School Press.

Daniels, Caroline N. (1994). *Information Technology: The Management Challenge.* Workingham, England: Addison-Wesley.

Denison, Edward (1985). *Trends in America Economic Growth, 1929–1982.* Washington, DC: The Brookings Institute.

Dertouzes, Michael L., Richard K. Lester and Robert M. Solow (1989). *Made in America: Regaining the Productivity Edge.* Cambridge, MA: The MIT Press.

Dilworth, James B. (1992). *Operation Management, Design, Planning and Control for Manufacturing and Services.* New York: McGraw-Hill. pp. 212-239.

Drucker, Peter F. (November–December, 1991). "The New Productivity Challenge." *Harvard Business Review.*

———. (1993). *Post Capitalist Society.* New York: Harper Business.

Garvin, David A. (July–August, 1993). "Building a Learning Organization." *Harvard Business Review.*

Gibson, R. (1997). *Rethinking the Future.* London: Nichlas Brealey Publishing.

Goldman, Steve L. , Roger N. Nagel and Kenneth Preiss (1995). *Agile Competitors and Virtual Organizations.* New York: Van Norstrand Reinhold. pp. 3-43.

Martin, J. (1996). *Cybercorp: The New Business Revolution.* New York: AMACOM, pp. 1-33.

Nonaka, Ikurjiro & Hirotaka Takeuchi (1995). *The Knowledge-Creating Company.* New York: Kodansha International.

Ozaki, R.S. (1991). *Human Capitalism: The Japanese Enterprise System as World Model.* New York: Kodansha International.

Sen, Asim (1997). "The Impact of Information Technology on the Production

Process." Global Awareness Society International Proceedings. Montreal, Canada.

———— (1995). "Global Competitiveness Through Democratic Management." IMDA. Middletown, PA: Pennsylvania State University Press, pp. 530-535.

———— (1982). "Utilization of Social Values for Effective Management of Technology: The Case of Japan." *Management of Technology III*, edited by Halil M. Tarek and Bulent A. Bayraktar. Georgia: Industrial Engineering and Management Press, pp. 1020-1029.

Senge, P. (1993). *The Fifth Discipline: The Art and Practice of the Learning Organization*. New York: Doubleday.

Snider, James H. (1993). "Democracy On Line: Exploring Your Future." Bethesda, MD: World Future Society, pp. 105-109.

Tapscott, Don and Art Caston (1993). *Paradigm Shift: The New Promise of Information Technology*. New York: McGraw-Hill.

Womack, James P., Jones, Daniel T., and Roos, Daniel (1990). *The Machine That Changed the World*. New York: Harper-Collins Publisher.

Woodall, Jack, Deborah K, Rebuck and Frank Voehl (1997). *Total Quality in Information Systems and Technology*. Delray Beach, Florida: St. Lucie Press.

## Chapter XIII: "Democratization Through Globalization"

Bowles, Samuel and Herbert Gintis. (1986). *Capitalization and Democracy*. New York: Basic Books.

Carnoy, Martin, et al. (1995). *The New Global Economy in the Information Age: Reflections on Our Changing World*. University Park, PA: The Pennsylvania State University Press.

Castells, Manuel (1995). "The Informational Economy and the International Division of Labor." in Carnoy Martin, *The New Global Economy in the Information Age*.

Dankwart, Rustow, A. (Fall 1990). "Democracy: A Global Revolution." *Foreign Affairs*, 69, No. 4. pp. 75-90.

*The Economist* (June 17, 1995). "The Future of Democracy," and "Democracy and Technology."

Fukuyama, Francis (1992). *The End of History and The Last Man*. New York: Avon Books.

Garten, Jeffrey E. (1997). *The Big Ten*. New York: Basic Books.

Haggard, Stephen and Kaufman, R. Robert (1995). *The Political Economy of Democratic Transitions*. Princeton, NJ: Princeton University Press.

Haggard, Stephen and Webb, B. Steven (1994). *Voting for Reform: Democracy, Political Liberalization, and Economic Adjustment*. New York: Oxford University Press.

Hoogvelt, Ankie (1997). *Globalization and Post Colonial World*. Balitmore, MD: The John Hopkins University Press.

Huntington, Samuel P. (1991). *Democratization in the Late Twentieth Century.* Norman, OK: University of Oklahoma Press.

Kanter, Rosabeth M. (1995). *World Class.* New York: Simon and Schuster.

Kidder, Rushworth M. (1994). *Shared Values for a Troubled World.* San Francisco: Jossey-Bass Publishers.

Knoke, William (1996). *Bold New World.* New York: Kodansha International.

Luckham, Robin and Gordon White (1996). *Democratization in the South.* New York: Manchester University Press.

Naisbitt, John (1995). *Megatrends Asia.* New York: Simon and Schuster.

Neher, Clark D. and Ross, Marlay (1995). *Democracy and Development in Southeast Asia: The Winds of Change.* Boulder, CO: Westview Press.

Nonaka, Ikurjiro and Hirotaka Takeuchi (1995). *The Knowledge Creating Company.* New York: Oxford Universtity Press.

Ouchi, William (1993). *Theory Z.* Reading, MA: Addison-Wesley.

Ozaki, R.S. (1991). *Human Capitalism: The Japanese Enterprise System as a World Model.* New York: Kodansha International.

Rosen, Robert (2000) *Global Literacies: Lessons on Business Leadership and National Cultures.* New York: Simon and Schuster.

Rosenberg, Nathan and Birdzel, E.L. (1996). *How the West Grew Rich: The Economic Transformation of the Industrial World.* New York: Basic Books.

Sen, Asim (1982). *Science, Technology and Development. Lessons From Japan.* Ankara: METU Press.

———. (1992). "Utilization of Social Value for Effective Management of Technology: The Case of Japan." In *Management of Technology III.* edited by Halil M. Tarek and Bayraktar A. Miami, Florida.

———. (1996). "Democratization of Management Through Globalization." Global Awareness Society International Proceedings. San Francisco, CA.

Snider, James H. (1996). "Democracy on Line: Exploring Your Future." Bethesda, MD: World Future Society.

Tanner, Richard P. and Anthony G. Atos (1981). *The Art of Japanese Management.* New York: Simon and Schuster.

Tapscott, Don and Art Caston (1993). *Paradigm Shift: The Promise of Information Technology.* New York: McGraw-Hill..

Trompenaars, Fons and Charles Hampden-Turner (1998). *Riding the Waves of Culture.* New York: McGraw-Hill.

Womack, J. P., Jones, D.T. and Roos D. (1990). *The Machine That Changed the World.* New York: The Macmillan Company.

## Chapter XIV: "What Can Be Done Now For Democratization"

Ackoff, Russell L. (1994). *The Democratic Corporation.* New York: Oxford University Press.

Albrecht, Karl (1994). *The Northbound Train: Finding the Purpose, Setting the Direction, Shaping the Destiny of Your Organization.* New York: AMACOM.

Band, William A. (1994). *Touchstones: Ten New Ideas Revolutionizing Business.* New York: John Wiley.

Blair, Margaret (1995). *Ownership and Control.* Washington, D. C.: The Brookings Institute.

Block, Peter (1994). *Stewardship: Choosing Service Over Self-Interest.* San Francisco: Berrett-Koehler Publishers.

Cohen, Daniel (1998). *The Wealth of the World and Poverty of Nations.* trans. by Jacqueline Lindenfeld. Cambridge, MA: The MIT Press.

Coles, R. (1997). *The Moral Intelligence of Children: How To Raise a Moral Child.* New York: The Free Press.

Dewey, John (1916). *Democracy and Education.* New York: The Free Press.

Dubos, Rene (1968). *So Human an Animal.* New York: Charles Scribner's Sons.

Durkheim, Emile (1961). *Moral Education.* New York: The Free Press.

Garfield, Charles (1992). *Second to None.* Homewood, IL.: Business One Irwin.

Gibson, Rowan (1997). (edited). *Rethinking the Future.* London: Nicholas Brealey Publishing.

Gutmann, Amy (1987). *Democratic Education.* Princeton, NJ: Princeton University Press.

Friedman, Thomas (2000). *The Lexus and the Olive Tree.* New York: Anchor Books.

Halal, William E. (1996). *The New Management.* San Francisco: Berrett-Koehler Publishers.

Hamal, Gary and C. K. Prahalad (1996). *Competing For the Future.* Boston, MA: Harvard Business School Press.

Hunter, James C. (1998). *The Servant. Rocklin*, CA: Prima Publishing.

Kaplan, Richard A. and Marcus S. Robinson (1998). *A Time for C.A.R.I.N.G.* Rochester, N.Y.: Magna Publications.

Kant, Immanual (1900). *Kant on Education.* Trans. by Annette Churton. Boston: MA. Health and Co.

Kilpatrick, William (1994). *Books That Build Character.* New York: Touchstone Books.

Lickona, Thomas (1992). *Education For Character.* New York: Bantam Books.

Martin, R. (Nov.–Dec., 1993). "Changing the Mind of the Corporation." *Harvard Business Review.* pp. 81-94.

Mattson, Kevin (1998). *Creating a Democratic Public.* University Park, PA: The Pennsylvania State University Press.

McLagan, Patricia and Cristo Nel (1995). *The Age of Participation.* San Francisco: Berrett-Koehler Publishers.

Mills, D.Q. (1991). *Rebirth of the Corporation.* New York: John Wiley.

Minnett, Steve (1992). *Power, Politics and Participation in the Firm.* Aldershot, Hants, England: Aveburg, Ashgate Publishing Limited.

Morris, Tom (1997). *If Aristotle Ran General Motors: The New Soul of Business.* New York: Henry Holt and Company.

Nonaka, I., and H. Takeuchi (1995). *The Knowledge Creating Company.* New York: Oxford University Press.

O'Toole, J. (1995). *Leading Change*. San Francisco: Jossey-Bass Publishers.

Purser, Ronald E. and Steven Cabana (1998). *The Self Managing Organization*. New York: The Free Press.

Renesh, John (1992). *New Traditions in Business*. San Francisco: Berrett-Koehler Publishers.

Ryan, Kevin and Karen E. Bohlin (1999). *Building Character in Schools*. San Francisco: Jossey-Bass Publishers.

Schumacher, E. F. (1999). *Small is Beautiful: Economics As If People Mattered*. Vancouver, BC: Hartley and Marks Publishers.

Sen, Amartya (1999). *Development As Freedom*. New York: Alfred A. Knoof.

Yukl, Gary (1994). *Leadership in Organizations*. Englewood Cliffs, NJ: Prentice Hall.

# ABOUT THE AUTHOR

Asim Sen is a Professor of Management. He was born in Turkey, where he completed the early stages of his education, and advanced stages in the United States. He received a variety of scholarships to complete his education. His education in Turkey includes Kuleli High School (Kuleli Lisesi) in Istanbul and at the Air Force Academy (Hava Harp Okulu) in Izmir. At these schools he learned the basic principles of command and control management. He also learned and observed the importance of values such as friendship, trust, respect, discipline, love of duty, responsibility, honesty, integrity, and other social values for successful management practices. After his education, he practiced command and control management while working at the Turkish Air Force as an Officer. He also experienced and observed the positive impacts of working with equal opportunities for the common objectives of the military teams.

He received a variety of scholarships for his advanced studies in the U.S. He studied Aerospace Engineering and received a B.S. degree from University of Michigan, and completed his graduate studies at the Polytechnic University of New York with an M.S. degree in Applied Mechanics. After his graduation, he worked as a Senior Research Engineer and Manager at Boeing Corporation located in Seattle, Washington; Grumman Corporation at Long Island, New York; and Aeronautical Research Associates of Princeton, New Jersey. He has consulted for the United Nations, the National Aeronautics and Space Administration and many other public and private organizations. He observed many aspects of the authoritarian management practices and their impacts on total quality in these organizations.

His keen interest in management and total quality led him to increase his knowledge about the economical, political, and social aspects of management through post-graduate studies. He obtained scholarships from Rutgers University in New Brunswick, New Jersey where he completed his M.A. and Ph.D. degrees in Economics and Industrial Organizations. During his doctoral studies, he conducted research about the why and how aspects of total quality and economic development. He studied the sources of Japanese success in total quality and discovered that the Japanese Management practices have played the crucial role for achieving the high total quality. His research about the Japanese success was published as a book titled *Science, Technology and Economic Development: Lessons From Japan.*

After his doctorate, he decided to teach and do research in the academic institutions. He has been teaching Operations Management, Strategic Management, and other management and economics courses in a variety of Universities. These Universities include: Rutgers University, Bosphorus University, Middle East Technical University, and the Military Academy (Kara Harp Okulu), and currently St. John Fisher College. During his teaching, he practiced participative management as a Chair and Director of Management Programs at St. John Fisher College. He also experienced and observed participative management practices in many other academic institutions.

He has been researching in the areas of total quality, productivity, and democratic management. He has published more than fifty articles and given over one hundred presentations at international conferences about these topics. He has organized and chaired many international conferences. He served in many professional organizations as president, vice president and board member. He is presently President of the Global Awareness Society International (GASI), regional Vice President of the Assembly of Turkish American Associates (ATAA), and board member of Global Business and Technology Association (GBATA).

His experiences in the military, industry, and academic institutions in diverse cultures and different nations provided him enormous opportunities to learn, observe, and understand the impacts of different management practices on total quality. His multi-disciplinary knowledge, wide experience about management, and his deep concern about the present problems caused by contemporary management practices inspired him to write this book.

# INDEX

**A**

AACSB, Newsline, 110, 115, 211
Abernathy, J.W., 20, 114, 198, 204, 206, 211
Ackerman, S.R., 54, 81, 202
Ackoff, R.L., 41, 59, 63, 98, 193, 197, 200, 202, 209, 219
Adams, F.T., xix, 78, 197, 206
Advanced technology, 147
Aeronautical Research Associates of Princeton, xiii, 224
AFL-CIO, 191
Africa, 124, 126, 181
Agnew, J., 52, 54, 135, 151, 155, 157, 204, 214, 216
Air Force Academy (see Hava Harp Okulu), xiii, 224
Akamatsu, K., 151, 215
Albert, M., 57, 62, 202
Albrecht, K., 193, 219
Alexander, R.J., 151, 215
Alexis, M., 21
American Automobile Organizations, 20, 187
ANSI, 5
Appropriate technology, 164
Argentina, 123, 126, 157, 161, 180, 184
Argyris, C., 39, 86, 110, 200, 208, 211

Arie, deGues, 83, 109, 172, 208, 217
Aristotle, 119
Arthur D. Little's School of Management, 110
Asia Pacific Economic Cooperation (APEC), 183
ASQC, 5
Assembly of Turkish American Associates (ATAA), 224
Association of South East Asian Nations (ASEAN), 125, 181
AT&T, 64, 77, 172
Athos, G.A., 185, 219
Authoritarian (Command and Control), Management Practices, xi, xviii, xix, 25, 56, 57, 62
Authoritarian Political Practices, 126
Avishai, B., 60, 203
Ayres, C.E., 148, 215

**B**

Bailey, M. N., 140, 218
Baker, D., 55, 136, 203, 214
Band, W.A., 193, 220
Batra, R., 55, 56, 128, 129, 158, 203, 215
Baumol, W.J., 171, 206
Becker, G, 139, 214
Behavioral Management (see Organizational Behavior), 36

Benetton, 172
Bennis, W., 63, 70, 98, 111, 205, 207, 210, 212
Berlin, 56, 160
Bernall, J.D., 14, 198
Bernard, C.I., 22, 41, 199
Berry, I.I., 41, 198
Bertalanffey, V.L., 41, 200
Big Ten Nations (BTNs), 135, 152, 161
Birdzel, E.L., 86, 185, 219
Bismark, 140
Blair, M.M., xix, 54, 62, 64, 78, 136, 193, 197, 203, 206, 214, 220
Blanchard, K., 111, 211
Blasi, J.R., 78, 79, 206
Block, P., 193, 220
Bloom, D.E., 54, 136, 214
BMW, 183
Boeing Company, xiii, 172, 185
Bohlin, K.E., 195, 221
Bosphorus University, xiii, xvi, 224
Botkin, J., 116, 211
Bowles, S., 125, 181, 213, 218
Braudal, F., 57, 203
Brazil, 18, 123, 126, 135, 152, 155, 157, 164, 183
Britain, 51, 54, 111, 119, 136, 157
Brouwer, S., 55, 203
Brown, G.M., 58, 60, 203
Buddha, 95, 119
Buddhist Economy, 144
Budge, I., 125, 213
Bulgaria, 125, 182
Bullock, J.R., 43, 200
Burtless, G, 140, 218
Bush, George, 130
Byrne, J.A., 75, 80, 206

**C**
Cabana, S., xix, 86, 192, 198, 209, 220
Canada, 52, 55, 122, 157, 183
Carnoy, Martin, 125, 181, 183, 206, 218
Castells, Manuel, 185, 218

Caston, A., 67-168, 186, 218
CEO's of Fortune 500, 54, 136
Chaparrel Steel, 64, 84
Characteristics of the Real Team, 86
Chasin, H.B., 56, 203
Chief of Knowledge Officer (CKO), 110
Chief of Learning Officer (CLO), 110
Chile, 123, 126, 180, 184
China, 18, 129, 157, 161
Churchill, 140
Cohen, Carl, 70, 206
Cohen, Daniel, 162, 190, 215, 220
Coleman, Charles, 41, 200
Coles, R., 197, 220
Collis, J.W., 60, 62, 81, 114, 203, 208, 211
Comparison of Management Practices, 49, 50
Competitiveness, 19, 20
Computer Aided Design (CAD), 168
Computer Aided Manufacturing (CAM), 168
Concept of Technology, 147
Conceptualization of Democratization Process, 100
Confucius, 119
Conner, Daryl R., 98, 209
Conte, M.A., 78, 206
Contemporary Economical Activities, 136
Contemporary Management Practices, xix, 42-48
Contemporary Political Activities, 121-129
Cooper, Charles, 159-215
Core Factors of Management, 101
Corruption index of some countries, 161
Craftsmen, 30
Crainer, Stuart, 33, 108, 111, 199, 200, 211
Critical Path Method (CPM), 34
Crosby, P.B., 4, 46, 198, 200
Crossette, Barbara, 161, 213

**D**

Dahl, 128, 213

Dalziel, Murray M., 98, 209

Daniels, C.N., 167, 217

Dankwart, Rustow A., 123-125, 181, 213, 218

Danziger, S., 54, 61, 203

Davis, Keith, 38, 200

Davis, Lester A., 53, 75, 203, 206

Davis, S., 116, 211

DDI (telephone company), 144

Deal, Terrence, 103, 111, 209, 211

Decentralizer and Customizer, 170

Decision Making, 79-82

Delta Airlines, 185

Deming, Edwards W., xviii, 20, 45, 51, 60, 99, 198, 200, 203, 209

Democracy and Enterprise, 63, 197, 204, 206, 209

Democratic Management, 11, 49, 50, 67, 69-84

Democratic Party, 130

Democratic Revolution, 124

Democratization of Economic Activities, 141-144

Democratization of Management and Its Core Factors, 97-99

Democratization of Management Education, 105-112

Democratization Process, xiii, 98-104

Democratization Through Globalization, 179-187

Democratization Through Technological Development, 145-160

Denison, D.R., 60, 74, 145, 172, 185, 203, 206, 213, 215, 217

Derber, C., 54, 56, 71, 131, 203, 206, 213

Dertouzes, L. Michael, 19, 169, 198, 203, 206, 217

Desirable Total Quality and Competitiveness, xvii, 3, 8-9, 12-13, 67, 85

Determinants of Knowledge Management, 118

Determinants of Management Success, 25-27

DeToro, I.J., 5, 199

Developing and Utilizing Values Knowledge, 115-120

Dewey, John, 119, 195, 220

Dicken, P., 53, 203

Dilworth, James B., 36, 168, 200, 217

Drucker, P.F., 14, 21, 22, 62, 63, 81, 98, 109, 119, 172, 198, 199, 203, 206, 209, 211, 217

Dubos, Rene, 190, 220

Dumaine, Brian, 86, 208

Durkheim, Emile, 195, 220

**E**

East Asia, 52, 125, 155, 181

Eastern Europe, 123, 125, 137, 181, 186

Eastern European Nations, xviii

Eckhard, H., 185

Economic Development Approach, 40

Economical Democratization, 135-144

Educate Educators, 194, 195

Educate Managers, 192, 193

Educate Parents, 194

Educate Public, 190

Educate Yourself, 190-192

Education, 27, 105-112

Educational Democratization, 187

Effectiveness, 7

Efficiency, 7

Egypt, 129

Elite groups, 130, 131

Elite organizations, 130, 131

Emorson, Harrington, 33, 200

Employee Ownership, 77-79

Employee Stock Ownership Plan (ESOP), 43, 78, 191

Employment, 82-84

England (see Britain), 18, 32, 82

Environmental Approach, 40

Equality, xi, xii, xiii, xvii, 3, 9-13
Equal Opportunities (see Equality), 3
Equalizing and Shifting Comparative
     Advantages, 152
Equalizer and Democratizer, 172
Erhard, L., 142
Ernst, 58, 59, 203
Estes, R., 56, 71, 114, 203, 206, 211
Etzioni, A., 56, 60, 61, 114, 203, 211
Europe, 31, 55, 129, 136, 160, 199
European democracy, 133
European Economic Community (EEC),
     125, 181
European Political Democracies, 133
European Union (EU), 86, 125, 182
Evans, William M., 109, 213
Evolution and Revolution of
     Information Technology, 166
Explicit Knowledge, 106
Export-Processing Zone (EPZ), 52, 156

**F**
Fabricant, Solomon, 145, 148, 216
Fallett, Parker Mary, 22, 36, 62, 110, 199,
     200, 204, 211
Farmer, R. N., 40, 200
Fayol, Henry, 22, 34, 199, 200
Feenberg, Daniel R., 54, 136, 214
Feigenbaum, A.V., 45, 198
Flexible Manufacturing Systems
     (FMS), 168
Followers, 151, 152
Forbes, 53, 204
Ford Motor Company, 143, 172
Ford, H., 143, 167
Fortune, 110, 136, 211
Fournier, R., xix, 197
France, 19, 34, 53, 78, 122, 136, 156
Free Market, 137-139
Free Market Economics
(see Free Market), 137-139
Freedom (see Liberty), xi, xii, 3, 9-13
Freeman, R. Edward, 54, 70, 136, 150,
     206, 211

Freidman, M., 61, 204
Friedman, Thomas, 190, 220
Frontier technologies, 147
Frontiers of TQM Movement, 45, 46
Fuji Film, 20, 183
Fukuyama, Francis, 123, 181, 213, 218
Fuller, B., 3

**G**
Galbraith, K.J., 55, 204
Galileo, 31
Gandhi, M., 189
Gantt, H. L., 33, 200
Garfield, C., 14, 44, 86, 192, 198, 208, 220
Garten, Jeffrey E., 56, 135, 153, 160, 184,
     203, 214, 216, 218
Garvin, D.A., 5, 172, 198, 217
Gates, Bill, 109, 211
Gates, Jeff, xix, 197
GATT, 163
Geisler, Murray A., 22, 199
General Electric, 64, 77
General Motor (GM), 64, 82, 116, 169
George, Claude S.Jr., 31, 33, 108, 111,
     201, 211
Georgetown University, xv
German Information Center, 55, 136,
     204, 214
Germany, xiii, xx, 19, 53, 55, 58, 61, 64,
     74, 81, 83, 122, 136, 142-144, 156
Gibson, R., 62, 98, 192, 204, 217, 220
Gilbreth, Frank B., 33, 199
Gintis, H., 125, 181, 213, 218
Global Awareness Society
     International (GASI), 224
Global Business and Technology
     Association (GBATA), 224
Global Information Systems
     Architecture (GISA), 172
Globalization, 180-187
God, 30, 31
Goldman, Steve L., 171, 217
Gore, Al, 130

Gottschalk, P., 54, 61, 203
Grayson, Jackson C., Jr., 18, 19, 198
Great Britain (see Britain), 122, 150
Greece, 122, 182
Green, K.C., 17, 198
Green, M., 61, 204
Griliches, F., 148, 216
Gronross, C., 4, 198
Group decision-making, 79-82
Growth of Worldwide Democratization, 124
Grumman Corporation, xiii, 223
Guest, Robert H., 43, 201
Gutmann, Amy, 195, 220
Guzda, Henry P., 43, 201

**H**

Hackman, J.R., 86, 208
Haggard, Stephen, 121-126, 180, 181, 213, 218
Halal, William E., xix, 63, 98, 114, 197, 204, 206, 220
Hamal, Gary, 109, 193, 212, 220
Hammer, M., 62, 63, 204
Hansen, G.B., xix, 78, 197
Harbison, F.H., 14, 40, 82, 198, 199, 201, 206
Harrison, Bennett, 80, 206
Harrison, Lawrence, 103, 209
Hassett , George, 89, 208
Hava Harp Okulu (see Air Force Academy), xiii, 224
Hayes, R.H., 20, 61, 81, 114, 198, 204, 206, 211
Held, David, 78, 98, 209
Henderson, Hazel, 55, 139, 204, 214
Herzberg, Frederick, 39, 110, 201, 211
Hewlett Packard, 64, 74, 185
Hicks, J., 138
Hirschman, Albert O., 149, 216
History of Management Development, 29
Hitchcock, E.E., 58-60, 203

Hoerr, John, 43, 78, 201, 207
Honda, 20, 183, 187
Hong Kong, 53, 155, 156, 186
Hoogvelt, Ankie, 183, 218
Horizontal Circular Network Organizational Structure, 49, 74-77
Horr, J., 86, 208
Hugo, V., 121
Human Relations, xii, 36-40, 74-77, 86-93
Hunter, James C., 195, 220
Huntington, Samuel P., 121, 123, 181, 209, 214, 219
Huxley, A., 29

**I**

IBM, 64, 74, 84, 185
Imamori, K., 144
Impacts of Technological Development, 154
Inappropriate technology, 158-160
India, 18, 129, 161, 184
Indonesia, 56, 160
Industrialized Countries (ICs), xviii
Inequality, 56-57
Infant technologies, 160
Information economy, 186
Information Technology (IT), xii, 165, 168, 170-173, 175
Inoue, Shinichi, 139, 143, 214
Integrative Management Approach, 40-42
Integrator (Uniter), 171
International Finance Corporation, 53, 156, 204, 216
International Monetary Fund (IMF), 158, 183, 216
Ishikawa, K., 46, 201
ISO-9000, 5
Italy, 53, 156, 157

**J**

Jacobs, M.T., 61, 204
Japan, xiii, xviii, xx, 18, 25, 52, 53, 55, 61,
        74, 79, 84, 97, 111, 125, 142, 143,
        154, 156, 164, 168, 172, 180, 184,
        185
Jensen, Arthur, 140, 214
Johnson, Richard A., 41, 160, 201
Jones, D.T., 20, 82, 86, 111, 168, 169,
        186, 199, 208, 209, 213, 218, 219
Jorgenson, D.W., 148, 216
Juran, J.M., 45, 198, 201
Just-in-Time (JIT), 35, 166, 168, 170

**K**

Kant, Immannual, 119, 195, 220
Kanter, R.M., 44, 86, 183, 201, 208, 219
Kaplan, Richard A., 190, 220
Kara Harp Okulu (see Military
        Academy), xiii, 224
Kast, E.F., 41, 160, 201
Katzenbach, J.R., 86, 208
Kaufman, Robert R., 121, 123, 126, 128,
        180, 181, 216, 218
Kayser, T.A., 86, 208
Kennedy, P.M., 18, 57, 62, 64, 99, 103,
        111, 129, 198, 204, 210, 214
Keppler, 31
Keynes, 138
Kidder, Rushworth M., 103, 184, 210,
        219
Kilpatrick, William, 119, 194, 211, 220
Kinkead, Eugene, 103, 210
Knoke, William, 183, 184, 219
Knowledge Management, 26, 108-120
Knox, Paul, 52, 54, 135, 151, 155, 157,
        204, 214, 216
Kodak, 20, 77, 185, 187
Koontz, Harold, 21, 201
Krauss, Melvin, 162, 216
Kruse, Douglas L., 78, 79, 207
Kuleli Lisesi (Kuleli High School), xv,
        223

Kuznets, Simon, 148, 216
Kyocera Corporation, 144

**L**

LaMarsh, Jeanenna, 98, 210
Laotzu, 119
Late Followers, 151-154
Lawler III, Edward E., xix, 43, 60, 74, 78,
        197, 201, 204, 207
Lean and Humane, 175-177
Lean production, xii, 168, 169
Lebow, Rob, 98, 108, 111, 210, 211
Lenne, S., 81, 207
Leontief, Wassily, 138, 215
Less Developed Countries (LDCs), 154
Lester, R. K., 19, 169, 198, 203, 206, 217
Levin, D.I., 60, 204, 207
Lewin, Tamar, 60, 78, 136, 204, 215
Liberia, 154
Liberty (see Freedom), xi, xii, 3, 9-13
Lickona, Thomas, 89, 119, 208, 211, 220
Lifelong Mission, xvii
Light technologies, 147
Likert, Rensis, 74, 86, 114, 205, 207, 212
Lincoln, Abraham, 127, 189
Lissakers, Karin, 158, 216
Litan, E.R., 140, 214
London, Perry, 89, 208
Long-term employment, xii, 82-84
Lopke, 143
Luckham, Robin, 126, 184, 210, 219
Luthans, Fred, 42, 201

**M**

Major Practices of True Democratic
        Management, 72-82
Makin, John H., 129, 214
Makridakis, Spyros G., 98, 210
Malcolm Baldridge National
        Quality Award, 4, 198
Management Activities
        (see Management Practices), 69
Management Concepts, 21, 22

Management Education, 27, 28
Management Knowledge, 105, 108
Management Science (see Scientific Management), 32
Mansfield, Edward, 147, 216
Manufacturing, 155
Manz, C.E., xix, 86, 197, 208
Marber, Peter, 145, 216
March, James G., xix, 70, 98, 197, 207, 210
Marley, S., 126, 184, 210, 214, 219
Marshall, Edward M., 98, 210
Martin, J., 64, 77, 83, 98, 115, 171, 172, 193, 205, 207, 210, 217, 220
Marx, Karl, 138, 215
Masaaki, I., 72, 74, 86, 207-208
Maslow, Abraham, 38, 83, 110, 201, 207, 212
Mattson, K., 190, 220
Mayo, Elton, 22, 36-38, 62, 110, 199, 201, 205, 212
Mazarr, J.M., 55, 98, 205, 210
Mazda, 20, 187
McCain, John, 132
McGregor, Douglas, 39, 62, 186, 201, 205, 208, 212
McKibbin, L.E., 116, 212
McLagan, Patricia, xix, 192, 197, 220
McNamara, Robert S., 65, 205
McRobie, G., 145
Megginson, Leon C., 38, 201
Mercedes, 183
Mexico, 18, 123, 126, 135, 152, 155, 157
Middle East, 124, 181
Middle East Technical University, xv, 224
Military Academy (see Kara Harp Okulu), xiii, 224
Mills, D.Q., 75, 193, 207, 220
Ministry of International Trade and Industry (MITI), 86
Minkin, Barry H., 98, 210
Minnett, Steve, 193, 220

Minow N., 78, 207
Mintzberg, Henry, 22, 199
Mirvis, P.H., 80, 207
Mishel, L., 55, 136, 203, 214
Mitchell, J.B., 60, 78, 205
Mitsubishi, 20, 183, 187
Monks, Robert A.G., 78, 207
Morris, Tom, 71, 115, 193, 207, 212, 220
Mother Teresa, 103
Motorola, 77, 84
Multiple Dimension Qualities, 4, 5
Munsterberg, Hugo, 33, 201

**N**
Nader, Ralph, 132
NAFTA, 125, 163, 181, 182
Nagel, R.N., 171, 217
Naisbitt, John, 29, 186, 219
Nakane, C., 74, 80, 81, 89, 207, 208
NATO, xiii, 182
Negative Impacts of Technological Development, 158
Neher, Clark D., 126, 184, 210, 214, 219
Nel, C., xix, 192, 197, 220
Netherlands, 122, 157
New Management, 63
New United Motor Manufacturing, Inc. (NUMMI), 20, 82, 111, 119, 169, 183, 187
New Zealand, 123, 128
Newly Industrialized Countries (NICs), xviii, xx, 19, 52, 53, 56, 154, 155, 183
Newman, John H., 116, 212
Newton, 31
Nicholl, M.J., 110, 212
Nielander, W.A., 22, 199
Nirenberg, John, 86, 208
Nissan, 20, 111, 187
Nonaka, Ikurjiro, 63, 81, 106, 109, 111, 172, 174, 184, 193, 205, 207, 217, 220, 335

## O

OECD, 54, 136, 150, 216
Ohno, T., 168
Oldham, C.D.G., 150, 216
Olsen, J., xix, 70, 98, 197, 207, 210
Open System Approach, 40
Operations Research, 35
Organizational Behavior
   (Behavioral Management), 36
Organizational structure, 74, 76
Originators' Technological
   Development, 149
Ornstein, N.J., 129, 214
Ouchi, William, 43, 86, 185, 202, 207, 219
Ozaki, R.S., 64, 72, 143, 174, 185, 205, 207, 217, 219
Ozkanli, O., 86, 209

## P

Pacific Rim Countries, 53, 156, 183
Pakistan, 123, 126, 160, 161, 180
Palmer, D.D., 41, 200
Parasuraman, A., 41, 198
Participative Management, 42
Pearson, Lester B., 151, 216
Pearson, Wallace C., 55, 205
Peru, 123, 126, 158, 180
Peters, T.J., 72, 86, 98, 111, 209, 210, 212
Peyrefitte, Alain, 113, 212
Philippines, 52, 123, 126, 156, 161, 180
Phillips, Kevin, 55, 136, 205, 215
Pisano, G., 109, 213
Plato, 119
Plunket, L.C., xix, 197
Poland, 122, 158
Polanyi, M., 106, 212
Politechnic University of New York, xiii
Political Democratization, 121
Porter, Michael, 19, 145, 209, 212
Porter, W. Lyman, 116, 212
Portugal, 122, 155
Positive Impacts of Technological
   Development, 154

Poterba, J.M., 54, 136, 214
Prahalad, C.K., 109, 193, 212, 220
Prebisch, Raul, 158, 159, 216
Preiss, K., 171, 217
Pre-Scientific Management, 30
Preston Corporation, 74
Process of Technological
   Development, 148
Product Life Cycle (PLC), 149
Productivity as a Quality, 7
Project Evaluation Review Technique
   (PERT), 34
Pursell, Jr., 14, 198
Purser, Ronald E., xix, 86, 192, 198, 209, 220

## Q

Quality, 3-20
Quality Characteristics, 9-11
Quality Circles (QC), 46
Quality of Work Life (QWL), 43
Quin, J.B., 62, 81, 108, 205, 207, 212

## R

Rawls, John, 63, 205
Real Team Relations, 86
Reavis, Charles A., 119, 212
Rebuck, D.K., 166, 218
Recent Democratization Activities, 121
Reich, R.B., 14, 62, 108, 198, 212
Renaissance, 31
Renesch, J., 62, 205
Representative Democratic
   Management, 127
Ricardo, David, 138, 215
Richards, Max D., 22, 199
Richman, B.M., 40, 200
Rifkin, Jeromy, 109, 212
Robinson, Joan, 139, 190, 215
Roethlisberger, Fritz, 37, 202
Role of Government in Economics, 139
Role of Values in Management, 112
Romania, 125

Roos, D., 20, 82, 86, 111, 168, 169, 186, 199, 208, 209, 213, 218, 219
Roosevelt, 140
Rose, Colin, 110, 212
Rose, Nancy I., 136, 215
Rosen, Robert, 184, 219
Rosenberg, Nathan, 86, 185, 219
Rosenbluth, Hall F., 4, 59, 198, 205
Rosenzweig, E.J., 41, 160, 201
Rosow, Jerome M., 43, 202
Roth, William, 30, 31, 108, 111, 202, 212
Rushworth, Kidder M., 106, 212
Russia, 146, 157
Rutgers University, xiii, 224
Ryan, Kevin, 195, 221

**S**
Samuelson, P., 139
Santos Dos Theotonia, 160, 216
Schumacher, E.F., 105, 159, 190, 212, 216, 221
Scientific Management (see Management Science), 32
Scott, W.D., 33, 202
Scott, W.G., 38, 202
Semco, 64, 74, 84
Sen, Amartya, 190, 221
Sen, Asim, 17, 26, 74, 80, 89, 98, 111, 145, 148, 151, 164, 173, 174, 180, 187, 198, 199, 207, 209, 210, 212, 217, 219
Senge, P., 63, 81, 98, 109, 172, 205, 207, 210, 212, 218
Sheldon, O., 38, 202
Shetty, K.Y., 42, 202
Shonk, J.H., 86, 209
Shuen, A., 109, 213
Simon, A. Herbert, 165
Simon, W.L., 98, 108, 111, 210, 211
Simons, Marlise, 55, 136, 205, 215
Sims, H.P., xix, 86, 197, 208
Singapore, 53, 155, 156, 172, 183, 186
Slater, Philip, 63, 70, 98, 111, 205, 207, 210

Slocum, W.J., 42, 202
Smith, Adam, 31, 77, 98, 137, 202, 210, 215
Snider, James H.Jr., 64, 73, 81, 173, 186, 205, 208, 218, 219
Social Democratization, 184
Solow, Robert, 19, 169, 198, 203, 206, 217
Soros, George, 158, 217
Source of Values, 117
South Korea, 52, 53, 123, 126, 135, 152, 155, 156, 180, 186
Soviet Union (see Russia), xviii, 146
Spain, 122, 157
Speeder (Changer), 170
Stakeholders' Authority, 73
Stalk, G, 213
Streger, W.A., 22, 199
Steward, Frances, 159, 217
Stewart, Thomas A., 109, 213
Stiglitz, Joesph E., 79, 208
St. John Fisher College, xiii, 224
Styles of Management, 24
Suzuki, 20, 187
Svejner, J., 78, 206
Sweden, 122, 157

**T**
Taiwan, 52, 53, 123, 126, 155, 156, 180, 183, 186
Takeuchi, G, 6, 63, 81, 106, 109, 111, 172, 174, 184-193, 202, 205, 207, 217, 220
Tanner, Richard P., 185, 219
Tapscott, Don, 167, 168, 186, 218, 219
Taylor, F.W., 22, 32, 33, 35, 37, 41, 60, 106, 199, 202, 213
Technological Development, 145, 148, 154, 160
Technological Life Cycle (TLC), 148
Teece, D.J., 109, 213
Tenner, A.R., 5, 199
Terpstra, Vern, 111, 113, 213

Thailand, 123, 126, 161, 180
The Concept of Technology, 147
The Contingency Approach, 42
The Economist, 54, 64, 73, 81, 136, 158, 186, 203, 206, 214, 216, 218
Theory of Moral Sentiments, 138
Third Wave, 123, 181, 205, 213
Three Steps to Quality, 45
Thurow, Lester C., 19, 54, 55, 62, 63, 98, 136, 199, 205, 210, 215
Tichy, N.M., 86, 209
Toffler, Alvin, 62, 81, 108, 205, 208, 213
Tosi, Henry I. Jr., 42, 202
Total Equality (see Equality), xii, xiii, xvii, 24, 71
Total Liberty (see Liberty), xi, xiii, xvii, 15, 71, 23
Total Productivity, 7
Total Quality, xvii, 3, 8, 13, 19
Total Quality Management, (TQM), xii, 44-50
Toyota, 20, 82, 168, 169, 187
Toyota Motor Company, 168
Toyota, E., 168
Traditional Management, 43, 44, 49, 50, 58, 59, 62
Transparency International, 56, 160
Trompenaars, Fons, 103, 111, 184, 210, 213, 219
True democracy (see Direct democracy), 28, 49, 50, 64, 65, 67, 70, 110, 129, 133, 186, 197,
True Democratic Management, xii, xiii, xviii, 67, 69, 70, 72, 85, 90
Turkcan, E., 150, 216
Turkey, 18, 56, 123, 125, 126, 135, 152, 160, 180, 182-184, 212, 224
Turkish Air Force, xiii
Turner, C.H., 103, 111, 113, 184, 210, 213, 219
Tyson, L.D., 60, 204

**U**

Ukraine, 157
Undemocratic, 133, 192
Understanding the Management Practices (see Management Activities), 1, 21
Unions, 32, 191
United Airlines, 185
United Kingdom, 53, 156
United Nations (UN), xiii, 86
United States of America (USA), xiii, xviii, xx, 18-20, 28, 34, 43, 51, 53, 56, 58, 61, 63, 64, 73, 77-81, 86, 89, 122, 127, 135, 137, 143, 145, 150, 156, 157, 160, 163, 164, 181, 187
Universal Values, 107, 111, 119, 175, 184, 185
University of Michigan, xiii, xv
Utilization of Information Technology for Democratization, 166

**V**

Vaitsos, C., 159, 217
Value Based Management, 26
Values Knowledge, 26, 112, 115, 118
Veblen, Thorstein, 129, 138, 148, 152, 214, 217
Venezuela, 123, 161
Vernon, Raymond, 149, 217
Voehl, F., 166, 218

**W**

Wallerstein, Judith S., 89, 209
Walton, M., 4, 199
Waterman, R.H., 72, 86, 98, 111, 209, 210, 212
Webb, S.B., 121, 124, 126, 128, 181, 214, 218
Weiss, Alan, 60, 115, 205
Western European Nations, xviii
White, G, 55, 60, 61, 80, 205, 208
Will, G, 55, 160, 161, 180, 205, 208
Willard, M.L., 58-60, 203

Wilson, Charles Z., 21, 199
Womack, J.P., 20, 82, 86, 168, 169, 186,
    187, 199, 208, 209, 213, 218, 219
Woodall, Jack, 167, 218
Work Place Democracy, 43
World Bank (WB), 52, 155, 158, 183,
    205, 217
World Car, 172
World Trade Organization (WTO), 182,
    183
World War II, 35, 57
World's Manufacturing Output, 157
Wren, Daniel, 31, 33, 37, 108, 111, 202,
    213

**X**
Xerox, 64, 77

**Y**
Yeditepe University, xiii
Young, 36, 58, 59, 203
Yukl, Gary, 193, 221

**Z**
Zeithaml, V.A., 4, 198
Zero defects, 66
Zwerdling, Daniel, 43, 44, 202